Making
People
Productive

What Really Works
in Raising Managerial
and Employee Performance

Michael Nash

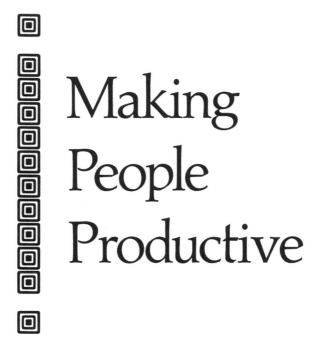

Making
People
Productive

Jossey-Bass Publishers

San Francisco • London • 1985

MAKING PEOPLE PRODUCTIVE
What Really Works in Raising Managerial and Employee Performance
by Michael Nash

Copyright © 1985 by: Jossey-Bass Inc., Publishers
433 California Street
San Francisco, California 94104
&
Jossey-Bass Limited
28 Banner Street
London EC1Y 8QE

Library of Congress Cataloging-in-Publication Data

Nash, Michael N.
    Making people productive.

    Bibliography: p. 219
    Includes index.
    1. Employee motivation. I. Title.
HF5549.5.M63N37   1985   658.3'14   85-45292
ISBN 0-87589-670-7

Manufactured in the United States of America

The paper in this book meets the guidelines for
permanence and durability of the Committee on
Production Guidelines for Book Longevity of the
Council on Library Resources.

JACKET DESIGN BY WILLI BAUM

FIRST EDITION

Code 8546

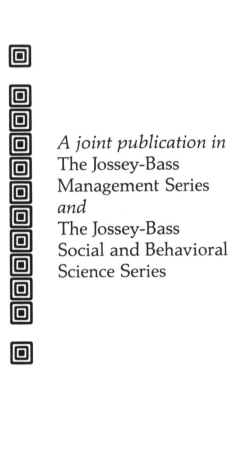

A joint publication in
The Jossey-Bass
Management Series
and
The Jossey-Bass
Social and Behavioral
Science Series

For Kelly and Alyssa.
My Blood, My Bones.

Preface

There's always an easy solution to every human problem—neat, plausible, and wrong.
                                        —*H. L. Mencken*

The purpose of this book is to provide managers with practical, proven guidelines for making employees productive throughout the employment cycle. The guidelines are based on a review of research in organizational and industrial psychology, filtered through my experience as a management consultant. The content of this book is research and its implications.

My focus is on how to achieve greater productivity through informed use of an organization's human resources. There are other methods to improve productivity—investment capital, national economic policy, improved technology—but this book will not cover them. Here, the focus is on people— employees and managers—and on what research in industrial and organizational psychology tells us about how to make them more effective.

My goal is to give thinking managers reliable information that psychologists have learned about effectiveness, competence, and productivity in the workplace. I have written this book for practitioners who want to apply research findings from the behavioral sciences to their work. The plan of the book is to tell you, using the employment cycle as a framework, about what is known about effective employees and effective managers.

This book is organized into fourteen chapters. The first two chapters introduce the concept of productivity. Chapters Three through Seven are about individual productivity—how to make people productive through better selection, matching of people with jobs, and training. Chapters Eight through Eleven describe the effective manager, general managerial techniques for improving productivity, and specific important techniques of goal setting and compensation. Chapters Twelve through Fourteen cover turnover, satisfaction, and a summary of conclusions and practical guidelines.

I have organized my material in this fashion to show the many different ways companies can make people more effective. Of the three major paths to organizational effectiveness—training, motivation, and selection—most companies rely on only one. Few companies integrate the three approaches, and even fewer look at productivity and effectiveness from the standpoint of the employment cycle.

Another goal of this book is to be an antidote both to the quick-fix artists and to the human potential advocates who dominate management psychology. It is my belief that I will serve managers better by providing them with facts that are based on research in psychology and that bear on the challenge of making people productive. I am unconvinced that humanistic concepts can give managers much help: "Concepts are extremely useful to the human mind . . . but concepts change and change very fast. What remains are the facts, the experimental facts" ("Nobel Establishment," 1967).

In integrating research findings for the reader, I have filtered the data through my consulting experiences with over 300 organizations. My goal has been to separate what is useful from what is not. Thus, the service I hope to provide managers is to make some sense of the abundant research that exists.

The field of management psychology suffers from a deluge of research publications and little progress has been made in tying research findings into any kind of coherent whole. This mountain of unorganized data makes single-variable prescriptions for productivity seductive. Research over the past fifty years has shown us that manipulation of just one variable produces only modest gains in employee productivity and that those gains are short-lived. Even the most powerful single variables—for example, goal setting—produce average gains of only about 17 percent in productivity. Maximum gains in productivity are achieved only when a large number of relevant variables have been correctly aligned. To make people productive, managers need to do things right throughout the employment cycle.

I wrote this book after an extensive hand-search of the psychological literature on making people productive. I read *Psychological Abstracts* back to 1975. My review is not exhaustive, but it is representative. I scanned thousands of entries in the Applied Psychology section of *Psychological Abstracts* and summarized hundreds of research abstracts in words I thought would be understandable by and useful to the average manager.

The need for this book seems clear because American organizations share two common problems. The first is a productivity problem. The second is an information problem. We need more productivity. We need less and more useful information (Garvey and Griffith, 1971).

We are drowning in information, and that influences how we try to improve productivity. Because of the information glut and the need for improved productivity, managers are attracted to books and people that offer simple solutions to a complex problem. A different approach is the use of multiple-variable solutions based on integrated research information. Such an integrated approach is valuable not only to managers but also to the industrial and organizational psychologists who advise them (Cooper, 1983). Because such integrated approaches are more difficult to construct, as well as more difficult to read and use, they appear less frequently and are less popular. Nevertheless, it is this more difficult approach which this book will take.

The information problem facing managers and their advisors is that we have too much data, it's unorganized, and we don't know how to use it. As Dipboye (1983) points out, "Industrial psychologists frequently have been admonished to close their mindless accumulation of validity studies and to orient their research towards developing a theory of human capability in the workplace" (p. 749). I will not offer any new theory of productivity; we also have enough theories. Instead, I'll tell you which theories work. I believe you'll find this more useful.

Translating research findings into concrete recommendations is not a matter of mere convenience; the success of an organization is partially dependent on the ability of behavioral scientists and practitioners to do it (Hackman, Lawler, and Porter, 1983). It is the job of psychologists to explain the complex behavior of people at work and to help practicing managers by giving them specific prescriptions for the best ways to manage employees for optimized productivity (Stanton, 1983).

This book explores horizontally, through the entire employment cycle, the theme of productivity, providing summaries of the most important tools that can be used to improve organizational effectiveness. It shows how to apply the findings of research to the practice of management. I take a positivistic approach, using the word as Webster defines it, "recognizing only matters of fact and experience."

It is customary in a preface to acknowledge your helpers. My first thank you has to go to the more than 500 people whose research I cite. Without them I too would have nothing to write about except my own opinions. Next, I need to thank my clients, who are my laboratory. They provided me with the anecdotes that I have used to embellish the research. Finally, I would like to thank my wife, Amerina Nash, who prepared the bibliographical references, and my typist, Flo Kress, who transcribed the original dictation of the manuscript and its several revisions.

Palos Verdes, California
September 1985

Michael Nash

$$
\begin{array}{|l|}
\hline
^3 \qquad \Delta \\
\text{Li} \\
6.939 \\
\hline
\end{array}
$$

Contents

The Author

Michael Nash is president of Nash and Company, Inc., a Palos Verdes, California, management consulting firm specializing in compensation and organization development. In consulting with hundreds of organizations, Nash has worked with all the techniques described in this book.

Nash received his B.S. degree in chemistry from the University of Michigan (1964) and his Ph.D. in clinical psychology from the University of Chicago (1969). He was partner and general manager of the Hay Group (1969–1982) before starting his own company.

Nash is a member of the American Psychological Association, the American Society of Personnel Administrators, and the American Compensation Association. Listed in Who's Who in the West, he was elected to Sigma XI, the national honorary research society. He is the author of a dozen articles and three books, including *Managing Organizational Performance* (1983).

Making People Productive

What Really Works in Raising Managerial and Employee Performance

1

Managing for Productivity

While there is consensus that American organizations are suffering from a loss of productivity, there is disagreement about the reasons. This chapter outlines some of the more common explanations of the problem and reviews typical solutions offered to improve productivity.

A number of reasons have been given for America's drop in productivity. These include inadequate capital outlay, reduced investment in research and development, increased government regulations, the shift from a manufacturing economy to a service economy, increased taxation, a changing work force that includes more women and older employees, alienated workers who are no longer motivated to produce, lower overall quality of labor, more powerful labor unions, and fewer and lower-quality natural resources.

Six of these reasons involve the human resources of an organization, rather than its financial and physical resources. Considerable opportunity for productivity improvement can come from better deployment, utilization, and management of human resources.

1

Of course, poor human resource utilization of one kind or another is not the only reason for our malaise. Few problems have single causes, and low productivity comes about from an organization's failure to apply human, financial, and technical resources in the most effective manner. Still, much of the productivity problem is a people problem, the result of poor initial selection, inadequate training, and a lack of worker motivation, all problems that plague the modern corporation (Bowles, Gordon, and Weisskopf, 1983).

The Role of the Blue-Collar Worker

It has become a cliché in some quarters that the increase in the service sector since 1960 is partly to blame for the drop in productivity in the United States. Accompanying the shift from a manufacturing economy to a service economy is a drop in the number of blue-collar workers and a rise in the number of pink-collar and white-collar workers—people who hold clerical and technical, professional, and management positions. There are fewer blue-collar workers, and the quality of their work is said to be dropping, but the Bureau of Labor Statistics takes issue with blaming the service economy for lower productivity. According to the Bureau of Labor Statistics, lower productivity "is not primarily or even importantly the result of shifts in employment to service-producing industries" (Koretz, 1983).

If the decrease in blue-collar workers is not one of the causes of lower productivity, what about the quality of their work? Historically, the quality (cost) of labor has been accounted for by four major variables: sex, age, education, and industry. We can measure the quality of an hour of labor by its price, which in turn is determined by the worker's knowledge, skills, abilities, strengths, energies, and persistence.

Between 1889 and 1960, increases in the average quality of labor grew slowly: 0.4 to 0.9 percent per year. Since 1960, government legislation in employment and labor law has forced employers to treat sex, age, and even education as equal variables. These historically have been part of the discriminant calculation for quality of labor. The evidence for declines in productivity attributable to blue-collar workers is suggestive, at best. Minimally, we can conclude that the quality of blue-collar labor is not improving; it may be eroding.

The Role of the White-Collar Worker

As of 1980, there were two and a half times as many white-collar workers as blue-collar workers. The white-collar and service work force now constitutes about 72 percent of the nation's workers. The principal concentration of these service employees is in the financial and medical fields.

White-collar productivity depends primarily on the efficient utilization of time. The average American white-collar worker produces only four hours of work in an eight-hour day (Olson, 1983). To improve white-collar productivity, the white-collar worker force needs to work more consistently and efficiently, not necessarily harder or faster. When you couple Olson's opinion with Peter Drucker's observation that most organizations probably have 20 to 30 percent more managers than they really need, making gains in productivity through streamlining the white-collar work force looks promising.

The Role of Technology

In addition to believing that gains in productivity can come from streamlining the white-collar work force, Drucker (1984) believes that sustained growth in the U.S. economy will come from the entrepreneur, although not necessarily from high technology. According to Drucker (1984), over the last ten years the U.S. economy has been shifting to an entrepreneurial economy, accounting for about half of the total growth in the U.S. economy since 1965.

Others, of course, disagree. Lehrer (1983) believes that technology is the most important variable in seeking improved productivity. Certainly, technology is important. Estimates of the variance in productivity attributable to technology range as high as 72 percent. The introduction of computers, robots, and other new technologies into the workplace has led some ob-

servers of the work scene to believe that "America is on the
verge of a second industrial revolution" (O'Toole, 1981, p. 12).
According to these futurists, scientific changes will radically re-
structure the workplace and the nature of work in the United
States. Workers who will do best will have the special skills and
professional training that will allow them to compete in this
more technically advanced environment (Treadwell and Redburn, 1983).

Technology is a sword with two edges. Technology has
been advanced both as a cause of declining U.S. productivity
and as a solution. The argument for technology as a cause of
poor productivity is that the United States is not investing
enough capital in research and development, and that the capital it does invest is overweighted on the side of defense spending. The argument for technology as a solution is that advances
in technology are our best chance for rapid gains in improved
productivity.

Macro Factors Related to Productivity

At the macro level, there are two categories of factors
thought to be related to improved productivity. The first category is lists of things thought to improve productivity. The second category is single, specific things. Let us look first at the
lists.

Dennison (1979, p. 2) lists five different major contrib-
utors to productivity and the percentage of their impact: technology (38.1 percent), capital (25.4 percent), labor quality
(14.3 percent), economies of scale (12.7 percent), and resource
allocation (9.5 percent). In this extreme reckoning, people do
not matter much, with labor quality accounting for less than 15
percent of productivity. Capital investment and improved technology account for two thirds of the variance in improved productivity. Ross (1977) offers another extreme list of factors
related to productivity, all of which are worker-oriented. He includes satisfying work, participation in decisions, compensation
on the basis of performance, clear communications and authority, competent supervision, recognition of achievement, and opportunity for self-development.

Managers should use such "shopping lists" cautiously. Ruch and Hershauer (1974) studied companies reputed to be highly productive. They concluded that what works in one company does not necessarily work in another, and that there is a great deal of diversity in what really works. The only commonality they found among the companies they studied was a belief in the importance of productivity. Productive companies are characterized by an attitude that low productivity is unacceptable and unnecessary. Productive companies expect to be productive. Earlier, industrial and organizational psychologists sought universal patterns of work values, attitudes, and motivations common to productive companies (O'Toole, 1982). More recently, researchers have come to believe that organizational productivity is a company-by-company affair.

Programs to Improve Productivity

The actual practices of companies show that they are using a wide variety of techniques and programs to enhance productivity. A survey of 49,000 companies, with at least 100 employees each, revealed that 14 percent had some special productivity program ("Senior Managers Speak Out," 1982). Training was the most popular type of program, with 76 percent of the companies using this technique. Close behind was performance appraisal, mentioned by 72 percent of the companies. Next were goal setting, at 64 percent, and quality circles, at 44 percent.

The most popular program among employees was flex time (44 percent). Goal setting was the next most popular choice (40 percent of employees), and training was picked by 37 percent. Two approaches—setting goals and training—were popular with employers and employees alike. Quality circles (28 percent) and performance appraisal (28 percent) were the programs least popular with employees.

Although the purpose of the programs varied from company to company, approximately half the companies indicated that they used the programs to cut costs and improve morale. Only about a third indicated that the primary purpose of the programs was to improve productivity. Less than a quarter of the respondents hoped to improve quality or reduce turnover through their programs. Most companies reported that the programs brought them some success. Two thirds indicated they thought morale had improved as a result of the programs, and half reported lower costs, better quality, or improved overall productivity.

Individual authors have their favorite productivity prescriptions. Reich (1983) favors training and calls for massive vocational retraining of Americans to create a highly skilled and flexible labor force. Bowles, Gordon, and Weisskopf (1983) claim that in three years they could eliminate 50 percent of the waste in American organizations by using lateral plant capacity, employing the unemployed, getting workers to be more effective, creating smaller companies, limiting defense spending, paying a higher minimum wage, eliminating the corporate tax, taxing progressively beginning at $50,000, nationalizing the banks, and paying wages for childrearing.

The Work in America Institute (1984) report recommends three work innovation programs: gainsharing, self-management teams, and consultative groups. The institute supports the idea that the key to a successful productivity program is to start small, to have a top executive initiate the program and continually support it, to involve everyone, and to provide feedback about results.

Any successful productivity program requires that the organization develop a positive attitude toward productivity. The program should emphasize increased output, not decreased expense. It is easier to motivate employees to produce more than it is to get them to cut expenses. Since people rarely work at full capacity, the idea is to incite them to call on their reserves, to produce more in less time. Part of the success of a productivity management program is derived from the changes in expectations and attitudes about how people are willing to work.

America's Future Productivity

The successful organizations of the future will be those that are productive. Increasingly, companies will have to involve all employees in productivity improvement processes, even if it means some temporary sharing of power (Toffler, 1980). Management, while primarily responsible for improvements in productivity, will need to impress employees with the importance of improved productivity and make them accept improved productivity as part of the price of employment benefits. Employees will have to share responsibility for thinking through and setting their own goals and for managing themselves by objectives and self-control (Drucker, 1980). For the revitalization of America to be real, it must be born both of machines and of people. It must be mental as well as mechanical (Popper, 1984).

The Role of Industrial and Organizational Psychology

Industrial and organizational psychology can help managers improve productivity. Psychological research has the potential to improve productivity at both the macro (national) and the micro (individual) levels (Alluisi and Meigs, 1983). Traditionally, managers have not looked first to psychologists for assistance in managing human resources, but they should. Performance of people at work has engaged the attention of psychologists for almost a century (Katzell and Guzzo, 1983). The earliest research was on workers' performance. Later, attention shifted to adjustment and job satisfaction. Even today, these dual concerns prevail, under the labels *productivity* and *quality of work life* (Katzell and Guzzo, 1983).

There is a difference between industrial psychology and organizational psychology that the reader should understand but need not worry about. Contributions of industrial psychology include measurement, personnel selection, training, and work design. Industrial psychology is much older than organizational psychology. Industrial psychology goes back to shortly after the turn of the century (Darley, 1969). Traditional issues have included psychological testing, leadership development, performance appraisal, and personnel. Organizational psychology is a new specialty area within psychology. Its roots are in the human relations movement of the late 1950s and early 1960s. It looks at the behavior of people in organizations. Among its techniques are sensitivity training, process consulting, surveys and feedback, and encounter groups.

In the minds of some practitioners, the two fields have tended to merge (Stagner, 1982). The broad divisions of a combined industrial and organizational psychology include selection, training, job performance, satisfaction, mental health, and social influences on work. The most recent research in the field has focused on perceptions and attributional errors, job commitment, and job involvement as parts of worker attitude, motivation, need for power, and leadership (Mitchell, 1982).

There is an abundance of research in industrial and organizational psychology. Much of it is considered poor, redundant, and without refinement or validation (Kahn, 1974). The research literature of organizational psychology especially is scientifically undefined, anecdotal, and autobiographical. While industrial psychology research is more precise, it is often insignificant as well as dull (Campbell, Daft, and Hulin, 1982).

Given these criticisms, can industrial and organizational psychology help managers make people productive? Probably so. Katzell and Guzzo (1983) reviewed 207 industrial and organizational psychology experiments published in the decade from 1971 to 1981. All used one or more of eleven psychological approaches to improving employee productivity. The results are encouraging. In 87 percent of the experiments, there was improvement in at least one concrete measure of productivity. The programs that worked best were training, goal setting, compensation, participatory supervision, and sociotechnical systems design. Their results are shown in Table 1.

Summary

Poor productivity has been blamed on everything and everyone. A favorite scapegoat is the blue-collar worker, but the facts fail to support the accusation. We can say that the number of blue-collar workers has declined, and so has the quality of their labor. Still, we cannot hold them primarily to blame for the decline in productivity.

The United States has shifted from a manufacturing to a service economy, increasing the number of white-collar jobs. White-collar workers work at only half speed, and there may be

Table 1. Frequency of Experiments Showing Effects by Type of Productivity Program and Outcome Measure.

Program	Output		Outcome Measure[a] Withdrawal		Disruption		Attitudes	
	n	%	n	%	n	%	n	%
Recruitment and selection	0/0		3/6	50	0/0		1/1	100
Training and instruction	46/50	92	12/17	71	4/5	80	7/9	78
Appraisal and feedback	26/28	93	6/10	60	4/5	80	4/6	67
Goal setting	21/22	95	6/9	67	4/5	80	7/10	70
Financial compensation	18/20	90	7/9	78	0/0		3/4	75
Work redesign	22/25	88	8/10	80	3/3	100	7/10	70
Supervisory methods	23/25	92	11/12	92	1/1	100	7/7	100
Organizational structure	6/6	100	1/1	100	1/1	100	0/0	100
Decision-making techniques	4/4	100	0/0		0/0		0/2	0
Work schedules	11/18	61	8/11	73	1/1	100	7/9	78
Sociotechnical systems redesign	18/19	95	7/10	70	5/6	83	9/9	100

[a]Total experiments equal 207. Denominators show the number of experiments studying effects on type of outcome measure. Numerators show number of those experiments reporting at least one positive effect. In some experiments, more than one type of program and more than one type of outcome measure were studied.

Source: Katzell and Guzzo, 1983. Reprinted by permission of the authors.

too many managers over them. While improvement in productivity will come through better management of the white-collar work force, that alone is also not the answer. Advances in technology definitely will help. Robotics, computers, and related technology can and will improve productivity, but the manager's best chance for direct and immediate productivity improvement still lies in better management of human resources.

Many people have offered suggestions for improving productivity. Companies have tried most of them. Each company is different, and no single program is likely to cure everyone's ills. Industrial and organizational psychology can help companies improve productivity. Up to 87 percent of the interventions by industrial and organizational psychologists have resulted in improvements in at least one concrete measure of productivity. The programs that work best are compensation, goal setting, training, and sociotechnical systems design.

2

Theories
of What Makes
People Productive

In this chapter we look at psychological theories that attempt to explain and predict productive behavior. What kinds of people will be most successful in which jobs? Can people be trained to be more effective? Are there motivators that can be applied to improve productivity? Are certain types of leadership more effective than others in achieving productivity goals? A number of psychologists have developed theories that address these questions. Reviewing these theories here will provide a useful background for later chapters, which address specific phases of the employment cycle.

Theory X and Theory Y

Among the best-known of all management theories is McGregor's (1967) Theory X and Theory Y. No doubt every reader of this book is familiar with the theory, but not with experimental tests of its results. McGregor said that most managers subscribe to a particular theory about people in organizations. He called this Theory X. Theory X managers hold common beliefs. These beliefs include the following:

1. Managers are responsible for organizing and directing the activities of the organization and its employees.
2. Unless managers actively manage people, employees are passive or even resist achieving the objectives of the organization.
3. The average employee is indolent, gullible, unambitious, stupid, and resistant to change.
4. Employees care primarily about themselves, next about other employees, and lastly about the organization.

This managerial viewpoint of the employee, argued McGregor, causes friction between management and workers and results in poor productivity. McGregor proposed a new theory of management, Theory Y. Theory Y managers believe the following:

1. People are not naturally passive or resistant; organizations make them that way.
2. People bring to the work environment a natural motivation, potential for development, and capacity for responsibility. Management does not need to create these characteristics. It needs to elicit them.
3. The primary task of management is to structure work to create harmony and overlap between the goals of individuals and the goals of the organization.
4. Work is not inherently onerous to people. It is as natural and as enjoyable as play or rest. Employees will exercise self-direction and self-control in pursuing organizational goals to which they feel personally committed.
5. Employee commitment to organizational goals is a function of the degree to which rewards are associated with the achievement of those goals. The most significant type of reward is not money but rather satisfaction, self-esteem, and self-actualization.
6. Under the proper conditions, the average employee will not merely accept responsibility but will actively seek it.
7. Imagination and creativity are widely distributed among employees. Managers simply fail to elicit these qualities.

8. Most employees have far more intelligence than their jobs require.

McGregor's ideas have been field tested. The best-known study was done at Non-Linear Space Systems, a small electronics firm in southern California. The research began about 1960 under the sponsorship of the president, who was an advocate of McGregor's ideas. Two years after Theory Y techniques were introduced into Non-Linear Systems, McGregor spent several months there and wrote a book, reporting favorably about techniques based on his ideas and their results (McGregor, 1967). The techniques included changing the supervisor's role to that of a helper, technical advisor, teacher, and troubleshooter. The supervisor did not control or discipline workers or set standards of performance. Other techniques included teaching and training, rather than directing and controlling; small production teams; and participatory decision making. Finally, employees were paid salaries substantially higher than those in the surrounding community.

McGregor wrote that two years after the introduction of Theory Y techniques, productivity improved 30 percent and customer complaints decreased 7 percent. Another researcher, who was there at the time, disagrees. Malone (1975) countered that there was no increase in productivity at any time and no improvement in quality; job satisfaction increased for production workers but decreased for managers; productivity actually declined over the five years and the company nearly went bankrupt before it reverted to a more traditional type of management. Kay (1973), supporting Malone, writes that the president, who was responsible for introducing Theory Y techniques into his company, later attributed the company's financial problems to those very techniques.

McGregor's name and theories remain popular among managers who mistakenly believe that his ideas work, but his theories are no longer of interest to academicians because research into McGregor's hypotheses has failed to support his views. The positive findings about Theory Y have involved job satisfaction, not productivity. Workers are not necessarily motivated to higher levels of performance under Theory Y conditions. Managers should be cautious about trying to manage according to Theory Y. There is some possibility that productivity can actually decline when these concepts are used.

Motivation-Hygiene Theory

After McGregor, probably the next most widely known theory of psychology in the workplace is that of Herzberg (1966). It was Herzberg who first suggested to managers that workers are motivated by two types of factors. One set of motivators is called *satisfiers*. Satisfiers are such things as achievement, recognition, the work itself, responsibility, and advancement. The second set of motivators involves hygiene-type factors, potential *dissatisfiers*. These include supervision, interpersonal relations (especially with supervisors), working conditions, job security, benefits, and salary. By removing dissatisfaction, hygiene factors can improve performance, up to a stasis point. They cannot generate genuinely positive feelings or motivate really high levels of performance. Only intrinsic factors can do that.

Early research on Herzberg's theory found that recognition, achievement, responsibility, and the work itself were associated with job satisfaction, but the same research also found that some factors could serve equally well as either satisfiers or dissatisfiers. These factors were opportunity for growth, salary, status, and feelings of esteem. Other research found the same dual nature in need for recognition, achievement, and advancement. At least 10 percent of the time, these can operate as either satisfiers or dissatisfiers.

Ultimately, researchers found that none of Herzberg's motivators fall neatly into the classes of satisfiers or dissatisfiers. They all work both ways. More important, researchers found that Herzberg's motivators influence job satisfaction, but not performance. Here was another irony: The second most widely known theory of work psychology was also not relevant to productivity. Little empirical support has been found for its theoretical assumptions. Self-actualization has been found to be neither a satisfier nor a dissatisfier. Salary, interpersonal relations, status, and security (which Herzberg argues can only dissatisfy, not motivate) have been found to be satisfiers. A sense of achievement and the intrinsic nature of the work itself (which Herzberg argues can only be satisfiers) can be dissatisfying.

Still, Herzberg's ideas appeal to managers. Why? Miner (1980) believes that in an unreligious age, Herzberg's theory has become a substitute for the Protestant ethic. Managers want to believe that money (salary, fringe benefits, and working conditions) cannot buy satisfaction.

Herzberg's theory has not and will not make people productive, although it may improve the quality of their work life. Managers looking for proven theories to help them get more out of their employees must look beyond the humanists.

Equity Theory

A more helpful psychology of work theory for managers is equity theory, a body of concepts and hypotheses dealing with the perception of fairness. The major motivating force in equity theory is a striving for perceived fairness or equality. Equity theory tries to understand exchanges among individuals and groups and the effects of perceived imbalance on these exchanges.

When evaluating perceived fairness or unfairness between themselves and someone else, individuals perform a mental arithmetic. They compare the sum total of their input and the consequent output with the sum of the input and output of other people. In the fairness equation, inputs include education, intelligence, experience, training, skill, seniority, age, effort, and risk taking. Outputs are rewards. They include pay, nature of the work, quality of supervision, benefits, status, power, and respect.

The person is motivated toward equity. Equity satisfies, while inequity does not. In a fair world, equality of input should result in equality of outcome. Inequity is defined as a state in which an individual's perceived ratio of inputs to outcomes is out of balance, as compared to the ratios of other individuals. For example, a person perceives himself as working harder than someone else but earning less. Perceptions vary, because inputs and outputs are not valued equally by everyone. For some, education is the primary input that should be rewarded; for others, it is seniority; for still others, it is hard work, or taking a chance. Similarly, the outputs of money or fame are not equally important to everyone.

Perceived inequity results in a sense of dissatisfaction. If the inequity sensed is one of under-reward, then the dissatisfaction usually takes the form of anger. More rarely, if the inequity sensed is over-reward, then the subsequent emotion is guilt. (In 300 consulting assignments, only one group of managers has told me about feeling over-rewarded. It was in an oil company.) Feelings of inequity create a state of tension proportional to the amount of the perceived inequity. According to the theory, this tension becomes a motivating force directed toward removing the inequity. It is a spur to action.

Most of the experimental work done on equity theory has involved how people are paid. A number of experimental hypotheses can be derived from equity theory. One hypothesis is that groups will reward individual members who treat others equitably and will punish those who do not. Another hypothesis is that when people perceive inequity, they feel either angry or guilty. Still another hypothesis is that individuals who perceive inequity will act to restore equity by modifying either their own inputs and outcomes or the inputs and outcomes of others. This process has direct implications for productivity.

Equity theory predicts that individuals who perceive themselves as underpaid will reduce the quality of their output and increase the quantity. Individuals who feel overpaid will raise the quality of their output while leaving quantity unchanged or lowering it. The impact on productivity is now clear:

Perceived Inequity	Impact on Productivity
Underpaid	Increased quantity
Overpaid	Increased quality

Perceptions of inequity and their consequences on behavior are time-limited. Gergen, Morse, and Bode (1974) warn employers that they should not expect long-term increase in productivity as a result of increasing wages. Employees eventually rationalize the relationship between their work and their pay and conclude that they are receiving their just rewards.

It is more dangerous to over-reward employees than to under-reward them, and not just because over-rewarding is more expensive. Consistently over-rewarding people may create a backlog of dissatisfaction (Miner, 1980). When in doubt, it may be better to underpay. How people are paid has major consequences for productivity. (Compensation will be the subject of a later chapter.)

When workers are paid by the piece, under-rewarded individuals increase the quantity of their work in an attempt to increase their total reward (Garland, 1973), but when underpaid workers are paid a straight hourly rate and thus cannot affect the outcome side of the equation, they achieve equity by reducing the quantity of their work.

Perceptions of being under-rewarded lead to increased absenteeism and turnover. People steal time to compensate for low wages. When pay inequities are generally known in the organization, the results are cynicism, anger, disruptive behavior, and even litigation (Hinton, 1972).

A hypothesis of equity theory is that employee groups encourage equity and discourage inequity. How strong a motivator is fair and equitable treatment by managers? Research (Lawler, 1981) indicates that people are indeed motivated to behave fairly or equitably, although the strength of the need to achieve equity varies by individual and according to the circumstances. For managers to behave equitably, two conditions must be present. First, there must be a clear understanding of inputs, such as effort, performance level, and qualifications. Second, the manager must be able to ascertain how the individual is doing on these measures, relative to some reference.

Equity theory is supported by empirical evidence. Productivity, in terms of both quantity and quality, is influenced by people's perceptions of whether they are being treated fairly, and managers generally are motivated to behave equitably toward their employees (Lawler, 1981). Still, equity theory has had little impact on existing management practices. It is mainly compensation specialists who concern themselves with equity, arguing that the best compensation systems are those perceived to be fair.

The potential for anger (and litigation) over perceived inequities, especially among women, is currently getting the most attention. Individual differences exist in need or motive for equity (Adams, 1976). In my own consulting work, I find women have a stronger need for equity than men do. When comparing themselves to others, women appear more likely to perceive parity, while men are more likely to perceive differences. One of my clients is a company where two women vice-presidents think that all the company's vice-presidents should be paid the same and that the title should be the primary criterion for pay. The three male vice-presidents perceive differences in job content, experience, and skill and think all five vice-presidents should be paid differently.

Equity is hard to achieve because of disagreement on the relative importance of job inputs and outputs. Belcher and Atchison (1976) found sizable differences in the ranking of inputs and outputs between clerical and production workers. The data from their study at a large public utility are shown in Table 2. Equity is an important part of organizational life, but we have much to learn about how it can be applied practically to improve productivity.

Expectancy Theory

Among researchers on the psychology of productivity, Herzberg's motivation-hygiene theory is being replaced by expectancy theory in popularity. Among managers and practitioners, however, it is still relatively unknown and little used (Pinder, 1977). The origins of expectancy theory are not clear. Positive thinking, as a populist psychology, is similar to expectancy theory, as is work on the placebo effect (Nash and Zimring, 1969) and the literature on self-fulfilling prophecy (Jones,

Table 2. Importance of Various Inputs and Outcomes For Clerical and Production Workers.

Inputs	Ranking Clerical Workers	Ranking Production Workers	Outputs	Ranking Clerical Workers	Ranking Production Workers
Quality of work performed	1	13	Job security	1	4.5
Reliability	2.5	2	Pay	2.5	1
Acceptance of responsibility	2.5	8	Competent supervisor	2.5	4.5
Job knowledge	4	13	Possibility of growth	4.5	2.5
Cooperation with others	5.5	10.5	Fair supervisor	4.5	6.5
Self-improvement	5.5	17.5	Recognition	7	8
Attitude	8	8	Adequate working conditions	7	11
Quantity of work performed	8	4.5	Interpersonal relations (supervisor)	7	11
Initiative	8	13	Achievement	10	9
Adaptability-Versatility	11	6	Interpersonal relations (peer)	10	13.5
Judgment	11	16	Adequate planning and management	10	6.5
Intelligence	11	2	Adequate personnel policies	12	15.5
Experience	13	4.5	Amount of work	13	13.5
Personal appearance	14.5	15	Responsibility	14.5	11
Oral communication skill	14.5	17.5	Advancement	14.5	2.5
Education	16.5	10.5	Routine work	16	19
Written communication skill	16.5	8	Status	17	15.5
Personal involvement with task accomplishment	18	2	Difficult work	18	18
			Personal life	19	17

Source: Adapted from Belcher and Atchison, 1976.

1980). While the origins are unclear, the concept itself is simple enough.

The basic hypothesis of expectancy theory is that a worker does what she expects to lead her to a desired end result. If the worker sees high productivity as the path leading to the attainment of her goals, she will be a high producer. Conversely, if she believes low productivity is the pathway to the achievement of goals, she will be a low producer (Georgopoulos, Mahoney, and Jones, 1957). Put simply, you do what you expect will get you what you want. You perceive a path to your goal and have expectancies or estimated probabilities that your desired payoff will occur as a consequence of job behavior. This schema closely follows the popular psychology of the positive thinkers, who advise picking out a goal, visualizing yourself already enjoying the rewards of that goal, and following a conscious plan and your subconscious intuition in the direction of your goal.

Vroom (1964) gets much of the credit for applying expectancy theory to employee motivation and productivity. Expectancy theory works best in contexts conducive to it (Graen, 1969). According to Graen, there must be a clearly established contingency relationship between the person's behavior and the desirable outcome. If the person does not perceive that relationship, the expectancy theory will not work. Thus, for expectancy theory to exert its motivational pull, employers need to reward performance, reward performance proportionately, and promote the better people. Managers who want to make people productive should establish the expectancy that more production earns more rewards.

Deci (1975) says that this is all wrong and that pay for performance lowers motivation. Deci argues that the introduction of an extrinsic reward, such as money, for behavior that in the past was intrinsically rewarding will decrease the overall level of motivation. He says that intrinsic motivation also decreases when a person receives negative feedback about performance on an intrinsically motivated activity. Conversely, intrinsic motivation increases when a person is given positive feedback and interpersonal support. Deci advises paying people average wages for being present, not for performing, so that pay will be perceived as noncontingent and its effect on intrinsic motivation will be minimal.

Staw (1977) believes this "Deci effect" is real but of little practical value for companies. For the Deci effect to occur, the work itself must be interesting, there should be no preexisting precedent for receiving payment, and the size of the reward must be significant. So, although the Deci effect says that paying for work lowers motivation, this phenomenon is unlikely to occur, because most jobs are not inherently satisfying and there always exists a precedent for receiving payment.

Does expectancy theory have any practical implications for companies seeking to improve productivity? Yes. Four useful and practical recommendations can be gleaned from the research. Managers should:

1. collect systematic information regarding the rewards employees want from their jobs as well as their perceptions of the probability of obtaining those rewards on the basis of their efforts.
2. make sure employees understand their responsibilities, so that their efforts are focused on what is important.
3. tie reward to performance, establishing a contingency between behavior and reward to increase expectations and avoid making across-the-board wage and salary increases.
4. monitor employees' attitudes and shape compensation programs to fit those attitudes.

Not everyone interprets expectancy theory as supportive of pay-for-performance notions (Meyer, 1975; Pinder, 1977). Applications of expectancy theory in the workplace are premature, they argue, because the theory itself has not been fully validated. Incentive pay, they say, is undignified and demeaning. Others caution against extrapolating from expectancy theory to an open pay policy (Miner and Miner, 1977), urging companies not to follow an open pay system and to stop short of fully communicating their pay policies.

What, then, is the current status of expectancy theory?

Of what use is the theory to managers trying to improve productivity in their organizations?

Unfortunately, expectancy theory remains of more interest to the theoretician than to the practitioner. Expectancy theory has wide support among management psychologists. It fits with older theories and common-sense experiences. These professional and amateur psychologists now agree: Stay positive; you get what you expect; you become what you think about, so expect the best; and expect what you want.

Expectancy theory has the potential to become a popular view of people in the workplace. Why? First, it is a hedonistic theory. It suggests that people tend to act in their own best interests. Second, it has the advantage of being substantiated by common sense and everyday experience (amazing, but you really do seem to get what you expect). Third, expectancy theory says that people can affect their environments by rational, conscious ideas and control their careers by controlling their thoughts. This is a more pleasant and manageable view of human behavior than one that says we are controlled by unconscious motivation. Expectancy theory does not deny the existence of the unconscious. It says that you can deliberately program your subconscious by feeding it positive expectations. Expectancy theory yields correlations with outcome measures consistently at the .50 level (Miner, 1980). Imagine that! Isn't that fantastic? Half the explanation of any outcome is what you expect to happen. The rest is skill, luck, the environment, and numerous other factors, but fully half is deciding what you want and expecting to get it. That is a truly wonderful finding: Productivity can be improved by expecting improved productivity.

The Goal-Setting Theory of Productivity

Goal-setting theory overlaps with expectancy theory. Goals are the targeted work behaviors we strive to achieve to get the rewards we expect. I have covered goal setting at some length in another book (Nash, 1983). Here, I shall describe goal-setting theory in simpler terms and show its relationship to productivity. The basic hypothesis of goal setting theory is simply this: *When an individual has specific goals or standards of performance, performance will be greater than when specific goals or standards are lacking.*

Goal-setting theory per se is generally attributed to Locke (1967) who says his views are not a theory of motivation but more of a motivational technique. Regardless of whether or not the formulations have the attributes of a rigorous theory of behavior, they still have much practical value for executives. One of Locke's most valuable adages is that managers interested in increasing productivity should set specific hard goals. Specific hard goals result in higher levels of performance and less boredom than vague or easy goals do. Of course, goals should not be set too high, because there is a level of difficulty beyond which goal acceptance will not occur. Locke argues that one reason monetary incentives work is that they facilitate the acceptance of and commitment to hard goals. Similarly, participation in goal setting improves performance, not because of participation but because the goals set are communicated.

Under goal-setting theory, what is most important is the existence of the goal. Incentives are inciting and participation is useful, but what ranks first and foremost in importance is setting the goal.

In his research, Locke has found that performance is consistently higher when harder goals are set. Unless an individual is highly motivated, it may be up to management to set and stretch goals. When subjects are permitted to set their own goals, they may choose fairly easy ones, with consequent lower levels of performance. In at least half a dozen experimental studies, Locke has shown that goal setting energizes employees and focuses their energies. Specific hard goals significantly improve the performance of even initially nonmotivated personnel.

Locke has also researched the effect of feedback, or knowledge of results, on performance. Again, establishment of the goal was more important than feedback regarding results. He says there is no additional improvement effect from knowledge of results over and above the effect that can be attributed to the differential setting of goals. (My personal experience leads me to disagree: Knowing how you are doing, and keeping score, helps.) Locke also examined the effect of monetary incentives on performance (Locke, Bryan, and Kendall, 1968), in a total of five studies. The subjects were all students, not employees, but the results are still of practical significance. On the basis of his research, Locke concludes that increased performance can be entirely attributed to assigning hard goals, not to paying incentives. Thus, management behaviors are not important in improving productivity. Paying incentives is not important. Allowing people to participate in setting goals is not important. The message is loud, and the message is simple. If you want to improve performance:

"SET SPECIFIC HARD GOALS."

Locke and his colleagues reached other conclusions worth noting. Your satisfaction with your job is a function of the degree to which you have achieved your targeted goal. The closer the fit between targeted performance and actual performance, the greater the satisfaction. For employers concerned with employee morale and with quality of work life, this conclusion has important implications. Goals should not be set so high that large discrepancies between actual and targeted performance are inevitable. Such experiences are bound to result in dissatisfaction with the job or with the terms of employment.

For goal setting to work, work must contain some intrinsic satisfaction. If the work is too routine, repetitive, or prescribed, then even setting hard specific goals may not help much. Here is another precaution: Goal setting may hinder teamwork. When goals are set and pursued, there is a reduction in the need to communicate with others. Employees focus on the goal, not on teamwork. If teamwork is important, group goals need to be mixed with individual goals. In establishing a management bonus program, I usually recommend that the incentive payment be split between individual goals and group goals.

Locke believes that the degree of difficulty of the goals set is crucial to the achievement of a high level of performance.

He reports a linear correlation of .78 between goal difficulty and performance, on the basis of twelve studies he conducted (1967). Additionally, Locke argues that, if his theory is to work, goals must be accepted. Goals should not be set so high that people expect that they cannot achieve them. On the basis of my consulting experience, I believe that, for people to believe in a goal, they must feel that they have at least one chance in ten of achieving it.

Some important exceptions exist to Locke's views on the value of incentives. Pritchard and Curts (1973) and Terborg (1976) think Locke was wrong in saying that incentives do not matter; Locke erred because the incentives he used were too small. They obtained significant results showing that incentives do affect performance, provided that the incentives are sufficiently large. Latham, Mitchell, and Dossett (1978) found that monetary incentives need not be very large for there to be an incremental effect of adding incentives to the goal-setting process. A bonus of as small as 3.5 percent of salary yielded performance effects above and beyond those attributable to goal setting alone.

Probably the best solution to the goal setting-versus-incentive controversy is to use both. The best results are achieved when hard specific goals are set and appropriately large monetary incentives are tied to them. Also, in my experience, it is important to keep score at least on a monthly basis with respect to how well you are doing as compared to your goal for performance.

Although most of Locke's work was done in a laboratory setting, goal-setting theory has been validated in field research as well. Here are two examples. Ronen (1978) found that productivity among loggers was highest when specific production goals were established and when the supervisor worked hard to ensure that the goals were accepted by the workers. In a public agency, workers assigned specific quotas for coding performed at a higher level than workers who were not assigned quotas (Umstot, Bell, and Mitchell, 1976). Individual differences are important and should be considered in establishing goals to improve productivity. Workers who are better educated and more highly motivated generally respond better to more demanding goals. Locke's views to the contrary, there is evidence that the goal-setting process is improved when it is coupled with knowledge of results and supervisory praise for achievement (Kim and Hamner, 1976).

Participation in the goal-setting process may make less difference in productivity than once thought (Nash, 1983). Participation is more related to job satisfaction than to productivity. This satisfaction can disappear completely after as little as six months (Ivancevich, 1972). Performance improvements attributable to goal setting can also dissipate quickly. In two studies reported by Ivancevich (1976, 1977), improvements in performance and productivity after the installation of a management-by-objectives process evaporated in twelve months. In these studies, participation was no more effective in improving performance than merely being assigned goals, and in some cases being told what to do was better. For example, technicians unfamiliar with participatory techniques did better when they were assigned goals by their superiors.

What can we conclude about goal setting and its applicability for practicing managers? From the research (Miner, 1980), we can conclude that individual differences must be considered in thinking about goal specificity, goal difficulty, and participation in goal setting. Setting specific goals is associated with higher-level performance among people with high achievement motivation. Setting difficult goals yields higher performance from people who have high needs to achieve and are high in confidence and self-assurance. Tough goals also produce better results among whites as compared to blacks and among the better educated. All this suggests that goal setting, while useful, is most effective with those who are probably least likely to need a nudge in setting goals.

Participation in goal setting is not as uniformly useful a process as it was once thought to be. Participation in goal setting can result in the setting of easier goals, with resultant lower performance. But participation in goal setting does generate more difficult goals and better performance among the less well educated, among blacks, and among individuals who have relatively weak needs to achieve. These groups are the least helped by goal setting. Yet they do best when they participate in setting goals. The participatory process serves to focus and energize, communicate, and get commitment.

The message from goal-setting theory for managers is that by getting employees to set and strive for specific hard goals, managers can improve overall performance and productivity. The ideal approach is to train individual supervisors in the techniques of goal setting and to help them understand the impact that individual differences have on the end results (Miner, 1980). The focus of expectancy theory is inside the employee, while the focus of goal setting is outside. In the next theory we consider, the focus stays outside and shifts to the behavior of managers.

Leadership Theory: Consideration and Structure

This theory of leadership was popularized by Blake and Mouton (1964). Stated simply, it says that leader behaviors that correlate with productive enterprises include initiating structure and showing consideration. The ideal leader is a motivator high in both structure and consideration.

Showing consideration includes trusting, respecting, showing warmth, expressing concern for personal needs, engaging in two-way communication, and involving subordinates in decision making. *Initiating structure* includes setting goals, organizing and defining work, delineating roles for subordinates, assigning tasks, planning work, and enforcing standards for performance.

Moderator variables affect the leadership variables of initiating structure and showing consideration. One moderator variable is the leader's power. Another and related variable is the amount of the leader's role conflict with subordinates. Still another moderator is whether the subordinate internalizes or externalizes the locus of control—that is, whether subordinates attribute success and failure to their own efforts or to forces outside themselves.

Early formulations of the leadership theory were simple

(Fleishman, 1973). Showing consideration and initiating structure were independent and equally important variables for leadership success. The most effective leaders were above average in both consideration and structure. It was this basic form of leadership theory that Blake and Mouton (1964) popularized under the title of *Managerial Grid* with a nine-point scale for each variable.

Recent research has complicated the theory by interjecting a host of moderators said to affect the relationship between leadership behavior and job performance. Initially, the ideal leader was thought to be someone high in both structure and consideration, yet there is little experimental proof that leaders who are high on both consideration and structure are the most effective managers (Larson, Hunt, and Osborn, 1976; Nystrom, 1978). Apparently it is sufficient to be high either on one construct or on the other: To be an effective manager, you do not have to be both an angel in dealing with people and a demon in setting goals. Moreover, it has been found that managers do not have nearly so much control over the performance of subordinates as was initially thought. Employees bring to their jobs a predisposition to perform. Subordinates' performance affects leaders' behavior, and vice versa.

The structure-and-consideration theory of management showed promise in the early stages, but with maturity it has yielded few practical applications for managers, beyond those developed by Blake and Mouton. There is enough research evidence to warrant advising managers that they should organize work, set goals, and try to be nice. Still, training programs to produce managers high on both constructs, while well intentioned, may be unnecessary. The words *structure* and *consideration* now have a permanent place in the manager's lexicon, but the theory is not a magic formula for ensuring productivity. Certainly, managers will positively affect productivity if they communicate clearly what they expect from employees and if they are tidy about structuring the work. It certainly helps labor relations when managers show consideration for workers. The ideal manager may indeed be a 9,9—high on both structure and consideration. But most of us are much less.

Behavior Modification in the Workplace

One of the most scientific of psychological theories is behavior modification. Under behavior modification theory, productivity is improved as the manager learns to manipulate reinforcers to induce desired employee behavior. The major hypotheses of the theory are concerned with what happens when reinforcers are manipulated in various ways. The theory is scientific because it has its roots in learning theory and steers clear of fuzzy concepts like thoughts and feelings. The behaviorist is concerned with outside behavior and how to shape it.

To increase the output of desired behavior, managers learn to manipulate positive reinforcement. To weaken or reduce undesired behavior, managers learn to extinguish and punish behavior. In a work environment, the major reinforcers a manager can use are money, praise, recognition, and career advancement. The effectiveness of reinforcers differs from person to person, on the basis of personal history.

One of the most comprehensive reviews of the application of behavior modification techniques to the workplace is that of Hamner (1974). He describes nine steps to reinforce desired worker behavior:

1. Select rewards that are stable and powerful for the individual.
2. Make the occurrence of the reward dependent on the occurrence of the desired behavior.
3. Develop strategies for approximating behavior, so that the ultimate desired behavior can be elicited. Reinforce separate aspects and approximations of the ultimate desired behavior until the entire repertoire is elicited.
4. Offer different rewards to different individuals on the basis of performance standards.
5. Tell the employee what behavior you will reinforce.
6. Tell an employee what he or she is doing wrong.
7. Do not punish behavior in front of others.
8. Do not over- or under-reward. Make the consequences equal to the behavior.

9. Remember that your failure to respond as a manager also has reinforcing consequences.

Behavior modification has practical implications for incentive compensation. Behavior can be rewarded differently, with the differences represented by schedules. In rewarding behavior, four reinforcement schedules are possible:

1. *Fixed interval:* Reinforcement or reward is given after a set period of time has passed.
2. *Variable interval:* Reinforcement is delivered according to a random sequence of time intervals, usually lying within prearranged arbitrary values.
3. *Fixed ratio:* Reward is given after a fixed number of desired behaviors has occurred.
4. *Variable ratio:* A reward is given after the occurrence of a desired number of responses, and the number changes from one reinforcement to the next, varying around an average.

Expectancy theory, discussed previously, favors the continuous reinforcement of the desired behavior, while behavior modification theory itself favors partial reinforcement, especially variable intervals. Yukl, Latham, and Pursell (1976) found that continuous reinforcement is better than variable reinforcement for inducing productivity in inexperienced agricultural workers. The highest rate of productivity was achieved not on straight wage rate or on a variable wage rate but under conditions of continuous incentive reinforcement. Latham, Mitchell, and Dossett (1978), however, found that a variable-ratio incentive schedule produced the highest rate of productivity when workers were experienced. These workers were rat trappers. A variable-ratio incentive plan dropped the cost of catching a rat from $12.86 per rat on straight pay to $6.75 per rat under incentive pay conditions.

Incentive pay as a behavior modification technique can influence the quantity (but not necessarily the quality) of output. Incentive pay makes people more productive. Besides the direct manipulation of reinforcers through techniques like incentive pay, behavior modification offers interested managers other useful techniques. Hamner and Hamner (1976) surveyed ten organizations that implemented behavior modification techniques. Nine of them considered the procedures successful. Applications were quite broad. Behavior modification has been used in reducing absenteeism, improving sales, and improving customer service. The most common reinforcers were positive feedback and praise from the supervisor. Used too often, however, praise loses its effect as a reinforcer and actually becomes an irritant. Managers should mix praise with incentives, using both in moderation. Behavior modification has also been used to reduce (extinguish) employee complaints by ignoring them. This is a generalizable finding. The behavior modification literature says it is better to ignore undesired behavior than to punish it.

Despite its effectiveness, behavior modification has few friends and many enemies. Some critics argue that it is old wine in new bottles—turn-of-the-century Frederick Taylor scientific management principles. Others say the theory ignores cognitive variables and is therefore impotent to explain behavior as complex as that of people at work in organizations, and that the predictive power of behavior modification is less than that of either expectancy theory or goal-setting theory, both of which are more humanistic and less cold-blooded. Finally, still others say that there is no real effect from the manipulation of reinforcers. The improvements are temporary Hawthorne effects, attributable merely to increased managerial attention and not to a specific technique.

The harshest critics of behavior modification theory are those concerned with what they think are its ethical implications. They see in behavior modification the potential for totalitarian management, masked as scientific efficiency, a Big Brother (or Sister) in the workplace. Opposition to behavior modification is sufficiently strong so that there have been court decisions regulating its use in the treatment of the mentally ill. Such regulation could be extended to the world of work.

Despite all these reservations, behavior modification theory has resulted in practical guidelines for managers attempting to improve productivity in their organizations. Behavior modification requires the manager to identify and quantify desirable behaviors. It encourages the manager to establish base rates to determine the possible extent of improvements in productivity. It requires the manager to understand employees well enough to determine the rewards that, for them, will reinforce desired behaviors. It requires the manager to estimate the size and frequency of the reinforcement needed to bring about increases in a desired behavior. Behavior modification makes management think. The quantitative analyses of both employee behavior and management behavior are the unique and difficult part of behavior modification. Critics need not worry. Behavior modification at work will never catch on, because it is too much work.

Sometimes it is possible to skirt the laborious quantification process by using modeling techniques. In this procedure, the behaviors of a good boss or employee are exemplified in a role model. The task is then to emulate, mirror, or imitate these desired behaviors. Videotapes, role playing, and visual imagery are all useful in learning the desired behavior. Visual imagery— mental modeling in a person's mind—seems to produce results that are as good as formal training: You think and imagine your way to success. Because mental rehearsal is less embarrassing than actual role playing and less threatening than the manipulation of reinforcers, it has considerable potential. This is another example of psychologists rediscovering an old secret: You can become what you think about.

Behavior modification resembles goal setting in that long-term application of the technique results in dissipation and diminution of its effects. To counteract this, managers should switch back and forth between goal setting and behavior modification techniques. For example, elicit behavior first by using praise, and then shift to using money. Because the effects diminish, start with smaller rewards and gradually increase their size as the effect of the rewards diminish. Finally, since variety itself is a reward, the thoughtful manager will periodically introduce new elements into the reward matrix so as to keep the interest of the employee.

Summary

We have reviewed psychological theories concerned with prediction of performance. We looked at a number of encompassing theories: Herzberg's motivation-hygiene theory, McGregor's Theory X and Theory Y, expectancy theory, equity theory, leadership theory, and behavior modification.

The biggest disappointments were motivation-hygiene theory, Theory X and Theory Y, and leadership theory. There has been very little research confirmation of their hypotheses. More useful are goal-setting theory, equity theory, and expectancy theory.

The data regarding equity theory and performance is convincing. The effects of both under-reward and over-reward on behavior are fairly clear. Under-rewarding increases quantity of output. Over-rewarding may increase quality of output.

Goal-setting theory also is credible. Goal specificity, goal difficulty, and, in some circumstances, participation in goal setting are positively related to performance, at least for some employee populations. This is one simple rule all managers should write in large letters on the wall above their desks: "SET SPECIFIC HARD GOALS." Managers need to be careful not to focus exclusively on individual goals at the expense of teamwork and corporate goals. They need to remember that the effects of goal setting dissipate over time. They may wish to avoid the unnecessary intricacies of a management-by-objectives approach.

Expectancy theory also is an aid to the practicing managers. People behave in ways consistent with their expectations. If desirable outcomes are made available to employees, and if they can believe that their behavior will lead to the acquiring of those outcomes, then performance will improve. People get what they expect. There is real magic in positive thinking and visual imagery. In the workplace, as in other aspects of life, we are the beneficiaries or the victims of our own self-fulfilling prophecies. Managers can improve productivity, modifying the behavior of their employees, through manipulating rewards that increase output. Continuous reinforcement works best with inexperienced workers. Variable-ratio reinforcement is more effective for experienced employees.

Expectancy theory may be the most useful in the highly competent work context of professionals and managers. Behavior modification may be best in the more highly structured and controllable context of production and clerical workers. Neither theory offers much help in improving quality. Both theories are useful in establishing work contexts to improve quantity.

Miner (1980) sums up nicely the utility of psychological theories and performance: "Overall, we can be confident that certain motivational theories—achievement motivation, equity, goal setting, and expectancy, in particular—can prove useful in predicting performance . . . . It is equally evident that these predictions are severely restricted by the domain of the theory and apply to certain individuals under certain circumstances. There is no such thing as a general theory of performance at present; there is little reason to believe one will emerge in the near future" (p. 405).

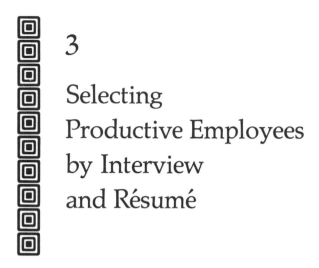

3

Selecting
Productive Employees
by Interview
and Résumé

In the employment cycle, selection is the initial managerial task that managers must perform competently to maximize productivity in their organizations. The first chance the organization has to have productive employees is while people are still candidates for employment, and it is one of the most critical. Selecting the right employee may be the single best thing a manager can do in the entire employment cycle to ensure productivity. Despite the importance of selection, few companies are selection-oriented.

"Blessed is he who has found his work, let him ask no other blessedness" (Thomas Carlyle, *Past and Present*, 1843). Properly selected employees are immediately more productive because they initially fit better with their jobs. Properly selected employees require less training and respond better to training because they are fit better with their jobs. Properly selected employees are also easier to manage because they have greater intrinsic interest in their positions and are more readily reached by various management techniques. Management has much to gain and nothing to lose by emphasizing proper selection techniques. Despite the obvious advantages of correct selection, the hiring practices of most organizations are casual, unscientific, and naive.

There are three major devices for selecting people: personal histories, interviews, and psychological tests (Grant, 1980). The first two procedures are far more popular than the third. This chapter is about the two most common methods of selecting people, the interview and the résumé. (Chapter Four covers psychological assessment in sufficient depth for managers to understand its advantages and potential pitfalls in making people productive.)

Of late, industrial psychologists are focusing more on the importance of the fit between the person and the job (Brousseau, 1983). All other efforts to improve productivity are impeded if the worker lacks the necessary aptitude to perform the work or is not much interested in it (Dipboye, 1983). Valid selection procedures produce increases in work force productivity (Schmidt and Hunter, 1983) that have a real dollar impact on the organization (Schmidt, Hunter, and Pearlman, 1982). While selection is popularly thought of as a procedure that takes place at the time of initial employment, selection also takes place each time an individual is promoted, transferred, or reassigned (Taylor and Nevis, 1961).

Government Intervention in the Selection Process

As it has in so many other areas of employee relations, the government has intervened in the selection process. In 1978, the government published its *Uniform Guidelines on Employee Selection Procedures,* involved concepts of what constitutes the selection procedure, employment decisions, applicants, and adverse impact. The impact of the government on selection now has its own literature (Stanton, 1980; Quaintance, 1980).

The government does not like psychological tests, a reason why the use of psychological testing has declined and the use of interviews and résumés has increased. Tenopyr (1981) concludes that although the government does not like tests, at present no better alternative to tests is available, and that a government-mandated search for alternatives to testing is a waste of time and resources. After reviewing the literature on the validity of selection by interview and résumé, I feel inclined to agree with Tenopyr.

The Literature on Selection

The literature cited here are but a few snowflakes in a blizzard of articles on the subject. Over 300 articles on the subject of personnel selection and classification appeared in journals of psychology just from 1978 to 1980 (Tenopyr and Oeltjen, 1982). This total does not include the literature on selection that has appeared in general periodicals.

The early selection literature concerned itself with studies on the background of highly visible business leaders. It began with a search for sweeping generalities about the traits of successful executives, and for decades it consisted of biographical surveys of those who had made it to the top of the management pyramid (Newcomber, 1955; Kirkland, 1956; Quinn, Taber, and Gordon, 1968). Biographical data continue to be successful predictors of job behavior. Studies show that biographical data can be related to profits and that the technique has remained valid over a number of years (Tenopyr and Oeltjen, 1982). The predictive capacity of data holds across industries and across majority and minority groups.

Research on the interview has focused on what happens during the interview rather than on what should happen (Tenopyr and Oeltjen, 1982). There have been numerous studies of how selection decisions are made during the interview process. Many of these studies are concerned with subjective aspects of the process and with the liability of discrimination. What should the interviewer look for? The list of variables going into selection by interview is long. One of the most useful variables to focus on in an interview and in résumés is the person's interests.

A fitting occupation predicts individual productivity. How do the interests of an individual predict occupational entry? Very well. The most effective predictor of occupational entry is a person's inventory of interests (Crowley, 1983). The least effective predictors are the ambitions that other people hold for those entering jobs. Interests form early, and initial vocational goals tend to remain constant and are a good predictor of later occupational success.

One of the best predictors of occupational choice is interest. While psychologists using tests can identify interests, it is not possible to correctly identify interests by asking people what they are interested in, nor is it always possible to identify or interpret your own interests (Attarian, 1978). Interests, while important, are tricky to assess.

Interest patterns emerge early, stabilize by the age of eighteen, and remain constant in most individuals ten or twenty years later. A study by Zoittowski (1974) found that interests in over 125 students counseled at Iowa State University had stayed stable even after twenty-five years. As adults, 53 percent were engaged in occupations consistent with their high-interest scores, although a surprising 32 percent were engaged in occupations consistent with their lower scores. Those working in occupations consistent with their interests reported that they were more satisfied with their jobs but did not necessarily feel they were any more competent at them.

Are there critical variables that predict proficiency in an occupational specialty? According to Flanagan (1954), proficiency in an occupational specialty can be attributed to six subvariables: possessing the fundamental training required for that specialty, keeping informed in one's specialty, being able to apply the training and information obtained in one's specialty, ingenuity in the specialty, striving to improve effectiveness in the specialty, and handling related assignments.

Why do people choose particular careers? Reasons include genetic influences, environmental conditions, learning conditions, intellectual abilities, emotional preferences, and promotional skills. We are also influenced by the perceptions others hold of occupations. Different jobs generate different stereotypes. Occupations have different images, and we see people working in them as more or less assertive, intelligent, likable, emotional, and responsible (More and Suchner, 1976). The social prestige of a career can be an important factor in why people choose one job or one job family over another. The social prestige of a career, in turn, is partly determined by the amount of education the career requires (the more education, the higher the prestige), as well as by the independence of the job (Rezke, 1978). This explains why the entrepreneur, the self-employed businessperson, commands more status and respect than does the hired manager. While people also vary considerably in their interest in money, few people choose careers solely for the financial renumeration.

Thus, the selection of a career is predicated on the congruence between one's interests and the nature of the work. As much as any factor can, this congruence ensures productivity because the individual is intrinsically motivated to do the work. People move toward desired activities and perform them better, and away from disliked activities and perform them less well.

The first task of management is to review a prospective employee's interests and work history to be sure that they are congruent with the job. Less important, but still important, is the congruence between the interests and values of the candidate and the interests and values of other people in the organization. It is best to have compatibility not only between the person and the job but also between the person and other persons in the company (Kuder, 1977). More than any other factor, vocational interest is the most likely predictor of occupational productivity.

Aptitudes and Abilities

In addition to the interests of candidates, the manager striving to make people productive through an improved selection process needs to know their abilities. Interest and ability are different. Ability is made up of intellectual ability and personality ability. In the long run, a sustained interest in a functional area is eventually more important for success than the initial ability brought to the function.

It would be simple for managers if they could just ask candidates to describe their interests and rate their own abilities and managers could take them at their word. It would eliminate the need for selection skill, both on the part of the manager and on the part of people like myself, who help managers select. Unfortunately, the correlation between self-assessment of abilities and actual tested abilities is so small as to have no practical significance (DeNisi and Shaw, 1977). Managers should ask candidates what they are good at but should not accept those answers at face value.

Like interest, ability matters. There is a substantial, significant correlation between rate of advancement and ability (Selover, 1962). In a meritocracy like the U.S., the most able should be getting ahead and they are. How can we spot ability? Employees who will advance most rapidly received higher grades in college. They were more active in college extracurricular activities and held leadership positions in those activities. They held fewer jobs before applying to work for you and score better on tests of arithmetic and vocabulary. They have a higher need to achieve, are better informed about the job in the company, and have higher-quality references (Keenan and Wedderburn, 1980).

The manager selecting productive people should look for individuals who show a total life pattern of success. People who will be productive in the future usually have been successful in the past. They did well in a good college, evidenced leadership, project a positive self image, and are confident and assertive. These qualities are related to effectiveness, regardless of the functional specialty. Certain personality traits are important, too.

Personality characteristics of top performers have been identified by Charles Garfield of Peak Performance Center, a company specializing in the identification of high achievers. On the basis of his interviews of over 300 executives, Garfield (Larson, 1983) thinks top performers have certain key characteristics. In top management, these people exhibit the following behaviors.

1. They strive to transcend previous performance.
2. They avoid getting too comfortable in their jobs.

3. They enjoy the artistic part of their work.
4. They vividly rehearse coming events in their minds.
5. They do not place blame for mistakes either on others or on themselves.
6. They examine the worst consequences before taking action.

For middle management, Garfield adds six more important characteristics.

7. They take time to plan.
8. They are adept at selling their ideas.
9. They seek responsibility.
10. They champion new ideas.
11. They do not strive for perfection.
12. They seek quality rather than quantity.

Of all the personality characteristics affecting productivity, motivation is the single most important one, more important than all the other characteristics combined. Motivation rivals actual ability in importance. In a study by Harrell and Harrell (1974), motivation and interest were compared to intelligence and scholastic aptitude as predictors of earnings. The Harrells followed a large sample of MBAs from Stanford University five and ten years out of school. They found that motivation and interest were more important than brains in determining what MBAs earned.

This brief review of the literature tells us that interest in the job, cognitive ability, and need to achieve are the core personality factors that correlate with productivity. What about noncore personality traits—such superficial aspects of the individual as height, weight, physical appearance, and dress? Do such superficialities matter? Do companies consider such things in selection, and if they do, are they justified in doing so? A number of researchers have attempted to answer these questions. Listen to Sands (1963): "Considerations such as height, weight, and general appearance are often given more importance than many companies like to admit.... Some of the companies studied indicated that an individual's height is very important, while to twice as many it is not important if within the standard range. Some companies feel a candidate's weight is an important characteristic; almost as many do not. In the balance between height and weight factors, the weight of an individual seems to cause more concern among companies than his height" (p. 45). A candidate's appearance does affect how managers will view his or her suitability for employment. Better-looking candidates are considered better potential employees (Cash, Gillen, and Burns, 1977). This tendency to generally prefer the more attractive candidate may develop with work experience, with age, or with both. Beehr and Gilmore (1982) asked undergraduate students to choose applicants for jobs in a simulated selection process. The students chose attractive applicants only when they believed that attractiveness was important for the job (in sales, for example).

If prettier and handsomer is better, how about taller? Do taller people have inherent advantages in their working lives? The data is mixed. Some studies have found that supervisors did not have negative attitudes toward shorter employees (Sheehan and Lester, 1980), while in other studies height did determine the reaction of others (Talbert and others, 1974). Shorter people are perceived as less authoritative. Among graduates of the University of Pittsburgh, men over six feet tall make 10 percent more in salary and bonuses than shorter men.

Bridgewater (1983) sums up fairly well the general findings on appearance: "Years of research have shown that the odds are stacked against unattractive people when it comes to forming first impressions. . . . They are consistently rated as less intelligent, less interesting, and less talented than their attractive counterparts." Only when looks are clearly not important to job performance—when a job does not involve much people contact—does the advantage of the good-looking individual disappear from the process.

Dipboye and others (1975) has summarized the selection literature findings on the most-preferred applicants. The preferred applicants are usually males over females, attractive people over unattractive people, and the better educated over the less educated. These preferences exist regardless of the sex of the selector or the selector's own personal attractiveness. The most-preferred person is the qualified, attractive male. The least-preferred person is the unqualified, unattractive female. Managers doing selection should be aware of these typical biases. The most-preferred candidate may not be the best qualified. It is here that a careful analysis of the résumé becomes especially important.

Résumés

Biographical data have consistently been a useful tool in the selection process. Historical data—a record of what the individual has done in the past—are one of the best predictors of what the individual is capable of achieving in the future (Worthington, 1951). According to Taylor and Nevis (1961), "The weight of evidence seems to indicate that biographical information items of one kind or another remain one of our best predictors."

We are lucky that using biographical data is a valid selection tool, because at least 50 percent of all job applicants are evaluated primarily on the basis of either a résumé or an application form (Goldstein, 1971). Biographical information, like that in a résumé, is a good predictor of the productive person. Nevertheless, those doing selection do not review biographical data carefully, nor do they have much sense of what to look for. Many interviewers merely skim biographical data before interviewing candidates and then make their selection decisions (Tucker and Rowe, 1977).

A piece of practical advice for managers is to take the time to read carefully the résumé or the application form. Assuming you do read it carefully, what should you look for? Acuff (1981) says that one important factor to observe when screening a résumé is omissions. He feels that these are always significant. Additionally, he suggests looking at salary progression, which is an indicator of success, and at academic records, which he interprets as indicators of intelligence. Earlier studies correlating biographical data with executive success suggest that you look for these biographic items: the candidate should be married, have a better than average school record, have siblings, and have a better than average work record (Freeman and Taylor, 1950).

Some candidates supply references as part of their biographical material. The literature says, and my experience confirms, that references seldom improve the validity of a selection decision. References are worthless, because all references are positive. Only the degree of positiveness varies, and the variance is related not to the quality of the candidate but to the personality of the referee. In view of the increase in litigation associated with giving references, many individuals and almost all companies have a policy of refusing to give any type of reference at all. They will confirm titles and dates of employment only.

In a résumé or an application, what other biographical factors are important? Education is a good general indicator of intelligence. Regarding education, look for quality, quantity, and consistency, in that order. A degree from the University of Chicago means more than a degree from the University of Cincinnati. A master's degree means more than a bachelor's. In general, stay away from holders of the doctorate, unless such a degree is an advantage for the job in question. Income increases with the earning of a master's but declines with the achievement of the doctorate. Moreover, there is an optimum level of intelligence and scholarship for business, and the doctorate is generally not advantageous. In some sectors of business, there is a negative bias against Ph.D.s. I myself have frequently encountered such bias and have even had people tell me I should hide the fact that I hold the degree.

A college degree is no longer very impressive. It is not uncommon now to meet college graduates working as machine operators, secretaries, switchboard operators, or accounting clerks. This was not always so. In 1900, only 28 percent of business executives had college degrees. In 1950, the figure was 62 percent, and by 1964, 75 percent of executives had college degrees (Campbell, Dunnette, Lawler, and Weich, 1970). Education is correlated with executive success up through the master's degree—the more education, the more success.

Biographical data have long been valid predictors of productive people. In reviewing biographical data, look for three things: evidence of intelligence, a need to achieve, and a continuity of interests consistent with the job you are trying to fill.

Interviews as Selectors

The personal interview is the most widely used selection technique in business, despite its being called inefficient, invalid, and costly for the results that it produces. In a survey of 852 companies, Scott and others (1961) found that 98 percent of the companies used the interview as part of the selection process. Often the interview is the key input into the final selection.

How valid is the selection interview? The findings are not encouraging. Different interviewers do not agree much in rating applicants (Scissons, 1978). Inter-relator reliability varies between .05 and .64, which is not much better than chance and is essentially nonagreement. Untrained interviewers are about as accurate as supposed experts (Stein, 1977). Why are interviews such a poor selection technique?

One reason is that candidates who are savvy about interviews can manipulate the evaluator's perceptions of them. If you want to get a job, the best way to handle yourself as an applicant during an interview is to show a sense of identification with the hiring organization, be relaxed, agree with the interviewer, offer suggestions and your own opinions, and volunteer information (Sydiaha, 1961). At the same time, be careful about volunteering negative information, and never do so in the latter stages of an interview. Interviewers react more readily to negative than to positive information and are especially sensitive to negative information revealed late in the interview. Candidates who fail the interview ask for a lot of information, ask for the opinions and suggestions of the interviewer, argue with the interviewer, are tense, and behave in ways that make the interviewer provide them with support and encouragement.

Most interviewers are not skilled in the task of interviewing. They spend most of their time talking about the job and the company (that is, selling the position) and too little time probing the candidate's qualifications, especially past performance (Keenan and Wedderburn, 1980). When asked which types of interviewers are most likely to induce them to accept job offers, job seekers mention interviewers who are careful about the personality they project, are accurate and complete in communicating about the job, and conduct themselves in an impressive manner (Schmidt and Coyle, 1976). Job applicants prefer companies with personalities that they feel match their own (Good and others, 1974).

The Interview

Despite the prevalence of the interview as the method of choice for selection, interviews are haphazard and ineffectual affairs. In a 1970 review of the literature, Campbell, Dunnette, Lawler, and Weich wrote, "In our review of current practices for selecting and promoting managers, it was apparent that nearly all decisions are based on personnel interviews or on judgments made from knowledge of a manager's past job performance. Psychological tests and standardized biographical data blanks are used not nearly as frequently as it has often been supposed. . . . Little research has been directed toward understanding more fully what goes on in personnel interviews" (pp. 469-470). In the interim since these remarks, there has been a little more research on the interview process. What does the research show? In the psychological literature, Clowers and Fraser (1977) found only thirty-six references on the employment interview for a period covering nine years— four studies per year for the key decision in the employment cycle. The research involved mostly white-collar workers, and the factors emphasized were impressionistic, not objective. Characteristics evaluated in the interview varied from political and social trends to the culture of the company. One strong finding was that interviewers were most influenced by a good first impression based on appearance, approach, and the ability to make conversation. Decisions about acceptability were based on a lack of negative impressions, on stereotypes, and on the applicant's job knowledge. A particularly frightening finding was that a decision about the candidate was frequently made within the first four minutes! This first impression was the basis for the most important decision in the entire employment cycle.

Other researchers have found that the selection process based on an interview is often quick and superficial. Webster (1964), viewing decision making during the employment interview, found that an interviewer has in mind a stereotype of what the ideal candidate is expected to be like. The stereotype is based on the interviewer's own personality and perceptions of the job's demands. During the first four or five minutes of the interview, the interviewer forms a quick impression of how well the candidate matches the stereotype. The interviewer depends most heavily on the most recently received knowledge. Unfavorable information carries more weight than favorable information.

The successful employment candidate is one who makes a quick, positive impression and then avoids contaminating that impression during the rest of the interview.

Quick decisions are made not only about candidates who are viewed negatively but also about candidates who are viewed positively. Tullar, Mullins, and Caldwell (1979) found that low-quality applicants get ruled out fast, usually in the first fifteen minutes. There is a correlation between the length of the interview and how favorably the candidate is perceived. High-quality applicants get longer interviews. Thus, the decision-making process in an interview appears to be this: A quick favorable or unfavorable impression is formed within the first five minutes. There is a truncated interview for an applicant who makes an unfavorable impression and an extended interview for an applicant who is initially perceived positively and who does not communicate negative information during the remainder of the interview and otherwise avoids contaminating the initial favorable impression.

What is the interviewee doing during the interview process to create a favorable impression, beyond those behaviors already mentioned? One additional important variable is body language. Interviewees create positive or negative impressions with body language, depending on the gender of the person doing the interviewing (Sterrett, 1978). In interviews with men, high-intensity body language makes a favorable impression and is interpreted as ambition. When women are doing the interviewing, high-intensity body language makes a negative impression and is interpreted as lack of ambition. Interviewers of both genders prefer applicants who make eye contact. Tessler and Sushelsky (1978) studied sixty interviews. They found that it is advisable for interviewees to maintain eye contact during the employment interview. It creates the impression of being suited for the job and makes the interviewer like the applicant.

Most interviewers lack skill in selection and need training in this area (Bayne, 1977). Fear (1984) has written an entire book on the evaluation interview that is worth reading. The next several chapters will also provide guidelines on what to look for during interviews.

Summary

In this chapter we have considered selection, the first step in the employment cycle. The manager's challenge is to select the person who will be productive in the future. To do so, managers should remember that interests and abilities are correlated with those who are successful. In the selection process, it is best to (1) insist on congruence between the person's interest and the job's responsibilities, (2) find evidence of intelligence, and (3) determine the strength of the individual's motivation to achieve.

Three techniques are commonly used to make selection decisions. Two of them are valid: psychological tests and biographical information. The most frequently used selection method is the interview. Given the way most managers perform the task of interviewing, the validity of the selection interview is highly questionable. At a minimum, the conscientious manager conducting an interview will take time to analyze the applicant's past record of achievement and will resist the temptation to formulate a quick and superficial first impression. Beyond this, it is recommended that managers acquire additional skill in conducting evaluation interviews or avail themselves of psychological appraisal techniques shown to be effective in predicting productivity. Psychological tests are the subject of the next chapter.

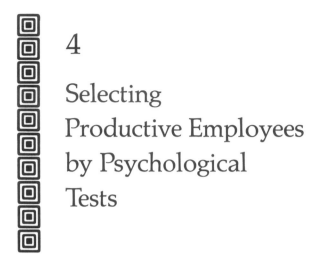

4

Selecting Productive Employees by Psychological Tests

In the last chapter I reviewed the selection of potentially productive people through biographical data and interviews. Most managers, in applying these tools, are indifferent and inept. Another available tool for the manager hoping to select good people is psychological assessment. This is a procedure with an honorable past, a shaky present, and a morbid future. I am devoting an entire chapter to psychological assessment because I believe that it has much to offer managers in making people productive.

Psychological assessment is the administration of a test for the purposes of making a personnel decision. The literature on psychological assessment grows smaller annually because the field is in decline. Each year there are fewer book-length treatments of the subject (Dunnette and Fleishman, 1982; Bass and others, 1979). This is a regrettable state of affairs, since no one is better equipped than psychologists to provide management with help in selection. "Nobody does a better job of assessing personality than psychologists do, and the use of our methods, imperfect as they are, is preferable to uninformed opinion" (Peterson, 1983, p. 785). The decline in psychological assessment is the fault of psychologists themselves as well as of the federal government. I will show why in a moment, but first let me briefly present the honorable history of psychological tests in the workplace.

A 1959 survey by *Industrial Relations News* of more than 200 companies found that 65 percent of them used some sort of psychological testing to screen job applicants. Even among the 35 percent of the companies that did not use tests, a full 60 percent indicated that tests were nevertheless useful. Only 2 percent of the nonusers considered the tests of little value. About a decade later, Campbell, Dunnette, Lawler, and Weich (1970) again found extensive use of psychological assessment as a tool for selecting potentially productive people: "As an overall figure, it is reasonable to estimate that as many as 60 to 70 percent of the companies in the United States use ability or aptitude tests, with considerably fewer firms using personality tests" (p. 26). Of the companies administering tests, fully 90 percent of them used them for initial selection, the entry of the employee into the company. By 1980, my own estimates were that average usage had fallen to about 10 percent, with about half for employment and half for promotion decisions.

The most obvious and natural use of psychological assessment is with individuals about whom management has no direct personal knowledge. When interpreted by someone skilled in their use, tests add valuable information to biographical data and interview impressions. Campbell (1971) reported that the most frequently used tests were cognitive tests, both verbal and arithmetic. I gave hundreds of psychological tests in the 1970s and found cognitive tests to be indispensable in the initial hiring process. After cognitive tests, Campbell reported a next-highest use of standardized personality and interest tests and then of projective tests (those that have no standard answers). Again, from experience I confirm this.

By the middle of the 1970s, despite both the large number of tests produced each year and research reports supporting their use, the decline in interest in testing on the part of business had become obvious (Cleveland, 1976). In the public's mind, because of federal intervention into testing, psychological tests were erroneously thought to be illegal. This perception was a misinterpretation of the stricter requirements the government imposed on the use of tests. The decline was also the fault of psychologists themselves. Fewer universities offered training in psychodiagnostics. Fewer skilled psychologists could be found who still believed in testing's usefulness and were willing to use the tool in their industrial/organizational consulting practices.

Lewandowski and Saccuzco (1976) maintain that the status and use of psychological testing actually began plummeting as early as the middle 1950s. Attacks on assessment came from within the psychological profession, as well as from consumer and regulatory groups. Among psychologists, the causes included shifts of interest in methodology in university training programs, as well as reports in the research literature about the nonvalidity of assessment. The net result was to make the public hostile to psychological assessment and psychologists nervous about using tests. By 1980, fewer than 10 percent of companies used testing as part of the selection process. This total was down from the 70 percent of less than a decade before.

Despite the attacks, tests are still popular with members of the American Psychological Association (Wade and Baker, 1977). Objective as well as projective tests are widely used. Psychologists use tests they know best, filtering the results through their experience. They use tests because they feel a need for them, because they feel confident in their value, and because they feel there are few practical alternatives.

Organizations that have stopped testing are depriving themselves of an important tool in the selection step of the employment cycle. For organizations interested in resuming testing, what kinds of tests are best? In 1970, Campbell, Dunnette, Lawler, and Weich believed that the measures with greatest potential for predicting managerial effectiveness were general intelligence tests, specially developed personality and interest profiles, and biographical inventories. On the basis of my experience, I believe that is still a fair summary in 1985. The use of testing is about equal for both executives and non-executives, but we shall be concerned here only with assessment of executives.

A pioneer in the use of tests to select executives was William Henry (1949), who used projective tests to identify high-potential executives. Henry thought that the characteristics of successful executives, determinable from the Thematic Appreception Test (TAT), included high need for achievement and a positive attitude toward authority. While attending one of Dr. Henry's classes, I heard him remark casually that one of the best determinants of an executive's potential level of success was what that individual was thinking about at five o'clock on a Friday afternoon. Although offered casually, the observation has face validity. At five o'clock on Friday, executives who were still working were more likely to be successful than those who were thanking God it was Friday.

The TAT remains one of the most widely used and best projective tests for selecting executives (Klopfer and Taulbee, 1976), although it is almost always used in combination with other tests. Psychologists use multiple tests to improve their confidence in their conclusions. Phelan (1962) reported that combined use of the Rorschach and the TAT was better at predicting success for first-line supervisors than using either instrument alone. I use both the Rorschach and the TAT in my selection work.

Testing for Intelligence

Testing cognitive ability is one of the oldest and most successful specialties in psychology. Despite heated debate over the validity of testing minorities, the opinion of most psychologists is this: Human intelligence is a characteristic that does exist in different amounts in different people, and psychologists are capable of identifying and quantifying it. Furthermore, psychologists believe that *general intelligence predicts job performance across a wide variety of jobs with a uniform degree of validity* (Dipboye, 1983). *Cognitive tests are valid predictors of performance in all jobs and all settings* (Hopkins, 1983). *Cognitive ability tests are equally valid for majority and minority groups.* Using cognitive ability tests can reduce labor costs. The point for managers to grasp is this: intelligence matters, and psychologists have proved it. Don't let anybody bully you into believing differently.

The nature of intelligence, and the amount of work that has gone into testing for it, has made it relatively easy for psychologists to identify those intelligence aspects of an individual that correlate with successful job performance. It is easier to identify these than to identify the personality aspects. Most psychologists speak with cautious forcefulness on the subject. "Some personnel tests, particularly intelligence tests, have sufficient validity to warrant their use as predictors of managerial effectiveness" (Dudek, 1963, p. 471).

If there is one thing psychologists are sure of, it is that to be successful you have to be reasonably smart. For executives, a minimum level of intelligence, probably an IQ of approximately 120, is necessary to succeed in a business career (MacKinnon, 1968). Higher intelligence test scores go along with a higher-level position in the organizational hierarchy. Higher-level managers are smarter than lower-level managers (Dubruszek, 1975). The idea of a range of intelligence and its relationship with productivity has been articulated by Gilmore (1974). "In general the person with an IQ of 125 will be more productive than one with an IQ of 95. . . . The person with an IQ of 150, however, may actually be less productive than the one with an IQ of 125" (p. 11). Professional jobs require more intelligence than semiprofessional ones, and semiprofessional jobs in turn require more intelligence than nonprofessional positions (Khoury, 1980).

One of the most convincing pieces of research on the validity of intelligence as a variable in determining career success was the work done at Stanford by Terman, who tested gifted children and followed them longitudinally until they were in their thirties and forties. As children, these individuals were certifiable geniuses, scoring on IQ tests in the top 1 percent of the general population. Terman showed it was brains that clearly separated this group of highly successful individuals from their more average peers, but within the group of the highly gifted the factors that ultimately differentiated the most successful from the least successful, even at the genius level, were stable goals, self-confidence, and perseverance (Terman and Oden, 1959).

Terman's findings are important, and it is useful to stop here and consider their implications. Intelligence is unquestionably a valid criterion for predicting who will be productive in business, but the research literature also is empathic on these points: Given sufficient brains, an intense need for achievement and a consistent application of intelligence will ultimately determine who will be the most successful.

Intelligence does matter, and it should be an important criterion in selecting people who can be made to be productive. What is necessary for success in management is a certain minimum level of intelligence, an IQ in roughly the top 10 percent of the general population. Both middle and top management are above average in intelligence (Ghiselli, 1959). What distinguishes top from middle managers is that the top executives have more drive, a higher need to achieve. Despite the importance of intelligence tests, testing either just intelligence or just personality is not enough to select good managers (Flanagan and Krug, 1964). Both types of tests are necessary, since they make largely independent contributions to the prediction of success.

Predicting Executive Success

Over the course of several years, I conducted a study to demonstrate that psychological tests are a valid tool in predicting executive success. The group I studied consisted of 268 male executives. I personally gave each of them a battery of intelligence and personality tests. For this group of men intelligence, vocabulary, and psychological strength predicted executive level in the organization. I also found a significant correlation between psychological strength and income.

At the time of the testing, these executives were employed by ten major industrial and financial organizations. Each one held a job I could classify into one of the following categories: administration, data processing, research and development, manufacturing, marketing, general management, sales, finance. Intelligence and personality were important, regardless of the type of job held.

I used a number of different instruments. Part of my battery consisted of:

- *Biographical Inventory.* Résumé-type information, such as age, title, annual income, education, and jobs held.
- *Wechsler Adult Intelligence Scale.* An intelligence test from which four subtests were selected. The *Information* subtest is a series of information questions tapping general knowledge. The *Comprehension* subtest is a series of questions assessing common-sense reasoning ability. The *Similarities* subtest measures a person's ability to identify the way things are similar. The *Block Design* subtest is a performance test in which the individual must recreate patterns.

Biographical Predictors

There are a few biographical predictors of executive success (Campbell, Dunnette, Lawler, and Weich, 1970). There is a correlation between age and success, with level in the organization being correlated with sufficient age. Success takes time to achieve. Beyond a certain age, success can be inhibited by age. The relationship between education and level in the organizational structure is also positive up to a point. There is a significant positive correlation between education and income, up to the top 5 percent income bracket for males (Mahoney and others, 1963). For the very rich, however, there is an inverse correlation between education and income. Education beyond the master's degree does not help much and can actually hurt.

The Role of Intelligence

The relationship between intelligence and success in business is well understood and documented (Wade and Baker,

1977). A certain degree of intelligence is necessary but not sufficient for success in business (Mahoney, 1963). The correlation between intelligence and success in business is positive and significant up to an IQ of approximately 125. For lower-level technical and professional positions (such as accountant, auditor, or production supervisor), an IQ of 110 to 115 is sufficient. For officer-level positions it helps if, compared to the general population, intellectual ability is in the top 10 percent minimally, in the top 5 percent preferably. Beyond an IQ of 125, additional intelligence is of value provided it is of a practical nature. To lead others, it can be useful to be somewhat brighter than followers, but this is not always the case. Intelligence beyond the top 1 percent of the general population (an IQ over 135) may be a handicap in business. Really smart people may be happier in careers outside business.

In some functional areas—sales, marketing, law, and personnel—verbal intelligence is more important than nonverbal intelligence. Other jobs are more dependent on nonverbal or performance intelligence for success. These include finance, data processing, engineering, manufacturing, and research and development. There are some positions for which a balance of verbal and nonverbal ability is important—general manager, for example.

I was interested in the mental aptitudes of my executive group as well as in their raw intelligence. IQ has a heavy genetic component that is fixed by the time one is an adult. Mental aptitudes, however, are more malleable and can be developed along with other aspects of the personality.

The literature on mental aptitudes and skills and executive success is fairly clear. The two most important mental skills an executive can possess are both verbal. The first skill is a broad fund of general information: The more an executive knows about more things, the better able he or she is to function and the more confidence he or she inspires. The second important skill is vocabulary. Command over language is the variable that has the highest correlation with the level an executive will occupy in an organization (Ghiselli, 1959). Like a book judged by its cover, executives are judged by their use of words.

Interests

I asked each executive to take the Kuder Preference Record, a test of vocational and personal interests. The Kuder uses a forced-choice format to ask individuals to make decisions about what they most enjoy versus what they least enjoy. The items on the Kuder Preference Records assess an individual's interest, corrected for sex and age, in the following categories: out-of-doors, mechanical, computational, science, persuasive, art, literature, music, social service, clerical, working in groups, stable situations, dealing with ideas, avoiding conflict, and authority and responsibility.

The literature on individual interests relative to success in business is correlational but not predictive (Harrell and Harrell, 1974). Because people tend to be interested in the things in which they do well and to do well in the things in which they are interested, there is a relationship between interest in an activity and success in doing it.

Clusters of interests are typical of people who make certain job choices. For example, above average interest in working with machinery, in science, and in being active outdoors, coupled with below average interest in literature and social service, is typical of individuals in manufacturing, research, and engineering jobs. Individuals in the finance and accounting area show high degree of interest in working with numbers, as well as above average interests in science and in art. Sales executives typically show intense interest in persuasive activities and in the cultural cluster: a preference for art, literature, and music (Eysenck, 1967). The sales area requires an extensive use of verbal skills, and sales executives' interests are more verbal than visual in orientation.

A general manager has the most clear and consistent pattern of personal interests, with other functional heads varying from the general manager's profile. The typical general manager shows a high interest in working with groups, low interest in stable situations, and a preference for variety and change. The general manager prefers working with ideas and enjoys jobs in which conflict is inherent (Nash, 1966). The general manager also likes being in positions of authority and responsibility. The typical general executive is a sociable person who thrives on variety and conflict, is at home in a world of ideas, and seeks responsibility.

Functional heads in staff jobs have slightly different profiles. The head of finance is more likely than the general manager to have a preference for stable situations, may be less interested in dealing with ideas than with facts and figures, usually does not seek out or enjoy conflict, but is no less eager for responsibility. The successful head of manufacturing, like the general manager and the head of finance, is likely to enjoy working in groups but prefers more stability than the general manager does. Like the head of finance, he is slightly more at home with facts and figures than with ideas. Like the general manager, however, he is not afraid of conflict and enjoys responsibility.

Personality and the Rorschach Test

The primary personality test I used in my research was the Rorschach. Piotrowski (1963, 1965) has published two books on the use of the Rorschach Ink Blot instrument in identifying successful executives. Piotrowski has developed a quantitative method of analyzing the Rorschach Test that makes it possible to predict executive success. He calls his method the Perceptanalytic Executive Scale. In my research, I called Piotrowski's total-scale score a measure of psychological strength.

The Piotrowski Scale has three parts. The first part deals with the executive's perception of human movement. The theory behind the perception of human movement is that to perceive movement in the cards requires a certain degree of intelligence, imagination, and risk taking. The theory of projection says that what the individual perceives the human in the card to be doing reflects his or her own self-image and inclinations. Executives who perceive people in the cards acting in positive ways have positive self-images and will interact with others in constructive ways. To have positive human movement perceptions is to see human-type forms engaged in social, confident, self-assertive activities, regardless of purpose. Piotrowski believes negative perceptions predict failure in business. A negative percept is to see individuals engaged in passive or frustrated activities. Reduced to common sense, the human movement part of the scale says this: If, in the Rorschach, a person sees people being competitive, social, or powerful, then the person is likely to act competitive, social, and powerful—that is, like an executive. In contrast, if the person sees individuals who are submissive, weary, or fatalistic, the person will act in that way and be beaten by the environment, the organization, or more assertive peers (Piotrowski, 1965, pp. 97, 153).

The second part of Piotrowski's scale is animal movement. For Piotrowski, the perception of animal movement is a deeper and more inherent aspect of the person's character. To Piotrowski, animal movement is the core of the personality, what is left of the person after socialization is stripped away. The same general concepts apply as for the perception of human movement. Correlated with success in business are perceptions of animals acting in assertive, energetic, or predatory ways. Correlated with failure in business are perceptions of animals moving and acting in ways that are submissive, frustrated, and under the control of others.

The final part of Piotrowski's scale consists of a number of miscellaneous characteristics. These signs are acquired personality traits, which can be learned and are more amenable to change than the core parts of the personality detected by the other parts of his scale.

General Hypotheses

In my own research, described here, I sought to show that there do indeed exist correlational relationships between success in business and various cognitive and personality variables, which can be discovered through psychological testing. I defined success in business as the executive's level in his organization's structure and his income. I defined three organization levels: Level 1, which includes such entry-level positions as individual contributor or first-level supervisor; Level 2, which includes such middle-management positions as manager or director; and Level 3, which includes such upper-level positions as vice-president or even higher positions. I defined income as the salary plus bonus (in 1970 dollars) being earned at the time of the test. For purposes of simplification, I used three levels of income: Level 1, under $15,000; Level 2, $15,000 to $30,000; and Level 3, over $30,000. For 1985, these figures would be approximately $45,000; $45,000 to $90,000; and over $90,000. The variables for which I predicted a positive correlation with success were intelligence (WAIS total score), vocabulary, personal strength (Rorschach scale), and persuasive interest (Kuder's score).

Results of the Study: Level in Organization

I found that the higher executives are in an organization, the greater their intelligence, vocabulary, and psychological strength. All three correlations were positive and significant at levels indicating that the results were very unlikely to have occurred by chance. My results are displayed in Table 3. The re-

Table 3. Predictors of Executive Success
(Criterion: Level in Organization).

Predictor	Significance Level	Number of Subjects
Intelligence	0.0000[a]	260
Vocabulary	0.0110[a]	261
Psychological strength	0.0000[a]	236
Persuasive	0.8210	258

[a]Highly significant; unlikely to have occurred by chance

sults indicate that the cognitive values of intelligence and vocabulary can be excellent predictors of how high an executive will rise in an organization. With practice, a selecting manager can develop a good feel for how smart candidates are and how well they use the English language.

The other variable I found that can be used to predict success is personal strength, as measured by Piotrowski's scale applied to the Rorschach. This variable is impossible for the selecting manager to detect without the help of a management psychologist skilled in the application of Piotrowski's technique. Persuasiveness, the one personal interest that I thought might predict success, proved to be insignificant.

Results of the Study: Level of Income

My other results were that intelligence and vocabulary were not significantly related to income, but psychological strength was. These results are shown in Table 4. Why was in-

Table 4. Predictor Correlations by Level of Income.

Predictor	Significance Level	Number of Subjects
IQ	0.2523	260
Vocabulary	0.1143	261
Psychological strength	0.0001[a]	236
Persuasive	0.3028	258

[a]Highly significant; unlikely to have occurred by chance

come not significantly related to intelligence and vocabulary? The pay practices of the ten companies varied greatly, and the statistical analysis performed did not attempt to control this variance. Perhaps that was the reason. Another explanation is that my research may have imitated life: The richest people are not necessarily smarter, but they are tougher and more driven to excel.

Summary

Using psychological tests in the selection phase of the employment cycle can significantly improve productivity. Tests can identify the intellectual, personality, and motivational attributes that correlate with success. Once popular, tests are now used infrequently and represent a forgotten resource for improving organizational effectiveness.

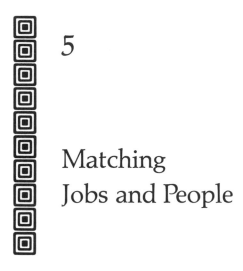

5

Matching
Jobs and People

This chapter continues the theme of employee factors that make people productive, individual attributes related to getting the job done. The focus is on the person doing the work, not on managers or on the organization. The purpose of this chapter is to show how individual differences and job families affect productivity.

The manager concerned with selection is dealing with individuals who have already made their career choices. As a manager, what you need to know is whether candidates will be successful in the jobs that you are trying to fill. Whether they made the correct career choices is their problem; you do not want it to become yours. There are only three steps you need to take to have a happy, successful career. First, find out what it is you most like to do, then commit yourself without reservation to making a living by doing it, and then do it very well. Anything else will take care of itself. Doesn't that sound easy? But it is one of the hardest things in life to do. People choose careers out of expediency. They become dentists not because they enjoy poking around in people's mouths, but because their parents wanted them to become dentists or because they read that there is a shortage of dentists or because they heard that dentists make good money. Even when we are fortunate enough to identify what we really like to do, many times we are afraid to do it. We lack the courage to starve in our chosen line of work; instead, we become affluent but miserable mercenaries.

Choosing the Right Person for the Job

In this chapter, I want to give selecting managers more ideas of what to look for in interviewing applicants. One useful way to find out which person is likely to be the most productive is to find out how important work is to him. Individuals who have work as their central life interest are more productive than those whose central life interest lies outside of work (Dubin and others, 1975). Hobbies, the community, the church —these things all are important; but the most productive people make their jobs the most important thing in their lives.

Another productivity predictor is the individual's financial need. Work involvement is highest in individuals in whom financial need is greatest (Gould and Werbel, 1983). The most productive person is likely to be the sole provider of income to dependents. Historically, this has been the husband with a non-working wife; now it is just as likely to be a divorced mother with a nonfinancially contributing ex-husband. The least committed and, therefore, least productive individuals are likely to be partners in childless couples in which both individuals work. In my experience as a partner in an international consulting firm with a large staff of associate consultants, the hardest workers were men from modest backgrounds who supported children and nonemployed wives. The least productive were single men from affluent backgrounds. Women fell in between. Their marital status appeared less relevant to their energy and commitment.

The selecting manager reviewing résumés to predict future productivity will naturally consider the individual's past working experience and how it relates to the job at hand—the tenure, task similarity, and performance achieved in previous

positions—but the relationship between these factors and productivity is unclear. Some studies have found a relationship between performance and years of experience, but other studies
have not (Gordon and Fitzgibbons, 1982). The best predictors
of future performance are, first, past performance, and then
interjob similarity. This does not mean that seniority is irrelevant, just that years of experience in similar work is not necessarily important. The value of experience is not related to its
length. To predict productivity, look first at past performance,
then at experience in a similar job, and only then at years of
experience.

Here are more tips helpful in the selection process. First-
borns achieve more than other children (Berger and Ivancevich,
1973). If you are hiring someone for a position with extensive
and intensive personal contact, look for someone who came
from a warm, loving home (Wittmer and others, 1974). An individual whose relationship with her parents was emotionally cold
is more likely to do better in an occupation that has limited requirements for interpersonal skills. Even participation in athletics can be a useful predictor of job behavior. Later occupational success can be predicted from earlier athletic participation.
A fifteen-year study of graduates from Boys Town found that
athletic participation had a positive effect on occupational aspirations and attainment (Otto and Alwyn, 1977). Love of vigorous and active sports, not spectator sports, differentiates between highly productive and less productive males.

Personal Predictors

There are gender and age differences in job behavior.
Women more than men prefer people-oriented jobs (Weller
and others, 1976). Compared with men, women are more sensitive, less self-assured, less relaxed, more disciplined, and more
shrewd (Osman, 1973). There are three significant gender differences in attitudes toward work. Males are more work-oriented in their central life interests. Women care more about
extrinsic work features and care less about the nature of the
work itself. Age makes a difference in the way in which people

work and how well they work. A study on age differences conducted by the National Council on Aging disconfirms some popular stereotypes about middle-aged and older workers. The physical demands of most jobs are well within the physical capacities of most older workers. Indeed, when properly placed, older workers are more productive than younger workers. They are more stable, have fewer accidents, and take less time off from work than younger workers (Meier and Kerr, 1976). Management style varies with age (Pinder and Pinto, 1974). Younger managers, those between the ages of twenty and twenty-nine, are more impulsive, autocratic, and have poorer social skills. They have an emotional orientation. Managers between the ages of thirty and thirty-nine are more consultative and factual and have a moralistic value orientation. Middle-aged managers and those between forty and forty-five are pragmatic and the most productive. Risk taking declines with increasing age. Entrepreneurial behavior, more typical of younger rather than older executives, peaks at age forty (Vroom and Pahl, 1971). Most successful entrepreneurs I know personally started their own companies between the ages of thirty-five and forty-five.

What about middle-aged people who change careers? Because whole books have been written about them (Levinson, 1976), I do not need to say much about them here except that the psychological research literature does not reflect favorably on midlife career changers. The literature says that people who change careers in middle life are incongruous, maladjusted, afraid of failure, confused, and inconsistent (Vaitenan and Weiner, 1977). They rate lower on the traits of ascendancy, dominance, responsibility, and endurance. Do not hire mid-career changers. It is not worth risking your business to let them try something new. Let them assume the risk by starting their own businesses in their new lines of work. When you hire someone middle-aged, you want the advantage of their accumulated experience in their earlier line of work.

Self-Esteem

Self-esteem is causally related to productivity. To function productively, people need to possess favorable attitudes toward themselves and their capabilities (Gilmore, 1974). This favorable attitude consists of self-acceptance, self-respect, and confidence. Productive individuals like themselves but are not conceited. In their language and bearing, they convey a sense of self-esteem to others. They respect themselves and expect others to respect them. Self-esteem is the psychological trait that is fundamental to the productive personality. It appears to be the one characteristic that differentiates the productive person from others (Gilmore, 1974).

People with higher self-esteem are able to achieve more. They understand their own interests and are less influenced by the opinions of others. High achievers have positive attitudes towards themselves, their environments, and their futures. High achievers possess a clear sense of identity. They know who they are and where they are going. Gilmore believes that because self-esteem and productivity are causally related, we can make people productive by increasing their self-esteem: "An essential process in the development of productivity in any individual is the enhancement of his self-esteem. This process may be initiated at any age."

The Harrells (1974) found that ascendancy, a variant of self-esteem, differentiated between high-earning and low-earning MBAs. Waetjen, Schuerger, and Schwartz (1979) found that self-esteem is not always related to productivity. In their research, they found that the individuals with the highest self-esteem were women who had failed as managers. Next in order, and following Gilmore's self-esteem hypotheses, were successful males, successful females, and unsuccessful males. Apparently, the failed women used their unrealistically high self-esteem as a defense mechanism, a form of denial, to protect themselves.

Other Personality Predictors

Other personality factors predict productivity. One factor is attribution, or locus of control. In attribution, we ask the rhetorical question "Who does the person believe is responsible for what happens to him?" The most effective and productive person is the one who believes that her experiences are controlled by herself, rather than externally (Heisler, 1974). She blames herself for failures and claims credit for her own successes.

How important is the characteristic of attribution in selecting people? Very important. One of the most exasperating types of employee to manage is the individual who is always personally responsible for any success but never personally responsible for any failure. He constantly overevaluates his own competence, claims credit for work done by others, and always has an excuse for poor work or missed deadlines. Individuals who attribute the causes of personal failure to factors outside themselves will bring you nothing but heartache and misery. Do not hire them.

An employee who will bring you joy is the high-energy workaholic, the so-called Type A personality (Mettlin, 1976). The Type A personality is concerned with time, is polyphasic, works under self-imposed time pressures, and is compulsively hardworking. Hire workaholics who blame themselves if things go wrong. They make life easier for managers.

More than any other individual attribute, energy and a willingness to work hard is what separates the highly productive from the merely mediocre. Talent is common. Discipline and dedication are rare. An enormous potential for hard work is the key to success in any job. Distinguished performance is achieved by singlemindedness of purpose and an unrelenting application of energy. Anything less can result only in mediocrity. The consistent application of energy in the pursuit of one goal separates the exceptional from the common.

The manager selecting for energy can look for a number of things. Does the person look, act, and talk energetically? How active is she? One measure of energy is the number of activities in which the individual is engaged. The more activities, the higher the energy level. A better measure is the number of hours she spends working. The typical top executive works about sixty hours a week. Most sales representatives put in a similar work week. Contrast this with the typical clerical or blue-collar worker logging between thirty-seven and forty hours. Energetic, productive people work longer hours or pack more into the same number of hours. Working harder is far and away one of the most important personal characteristics in the ultimate determination of success.

Jobs and People:
The Research-and-Development Function

So far in this chapter I have provided research data about individual differences that predict productivity. This has been part of the emphasis so far on selecting the right person for the job. Now it is time to get specific about job families.

The first of these job families is research and development. Research-and-development personnel are employed in technical positions, working on matters of basic or applied science. If we define technical management as comprising managers with technical degrees (regardless of the functions they are performing) plus all those in technical functions (regardless of their degrees), then six out of every ten managers in manufacturing companies can be said to belong to the technical profession.

To be successful as a scientist, Roe (1960) believed, five personality traits are needed: a sense of curiosity, a marked need for independence and autonomy, persistence, a high but not necessarily genius level of intelligence, and a high energy level. Another researcher (Rowe, 1973) found successful research and development employees wanted seven things: research autonomy, research facilities, administrative opportunity, financial reward, job security, university access, and advantages of the residential communities in which they were working. In a study using fifty-two different criteria to predict success among research scientists (Taylor, Smith, Ghisselin, and Ellison, 1961), the best predictors were grade point average and level of aspirations. Less effective predictors of success (as measured by number of research publications and ratings of supervisors) were ability tests and creative tests.

Successful research-and-development employees are characterized by a strong professional identification with the research area and moderate interest in everything else. In hiring research-and-development people, the key criterion to look for is intrinsic work motivation. Money ranks low as a motivator to these people, and they are not too concerned about advancement into the management ranks. Peer recognition in terms of status, awards, and prizes is important, however. For the typical scientist, interesting work and a solid reputation as a scientist among peers are the factors viewed as most important. To select the most productive scientists, look for these motivators, as well as an excellent grade point average from a prestigious university.

Engineers

Engineers are allied with scientists but are different from them. After a review of the literature Kerr, Von Glinow, and Schriesheim (1977) decided that engineers are different from scientists. Using engineers to test hypotheses about scientists will lead to erroneous conclusions, they believe. Engineers possess an above average interest in physical science and in other technical areas. According to a number of research reports (McMahon, 1962; Montgomery, 1962), superior engineers have superior cognitive abilities. They score high on tests of mathematics, mechanical comprehension, and verbal abstraction. Any good engineer is skilled in science and math. People working in different engineering specialties excel in unlike activities. Industrial engineers are the most like general businesspeople—technically less sophisticated than other engineers, but with stronger human relations skills. Mechanical engineers are natural tinkerers, often brighter and better educated than industrial engineers, but without the abstract capability of electrical engineers, who have the best abstract thinking skills and are more like mathematicians and physicists in their interests and skills. Civil engineers enjoy working outside on large-scale projects. In terms of interest and skills, civil engineers are most like architects (Krausz and Izraeli, 1980).

Some companies have two career tracks for engineers, a professional track and a managerial track. Those choosing the technical track remain interested primarily in engineering work and gain additional layers of experience and skill with time in grade. Those choosing the managerial track broaden their inter-

ests to include management and business and add human relations skills to their repertoires. Successful engineering managers
resemble other successful managers more than they do other
engineers. To be successful as an engineer, you need in-depth
technical know-how in your specialty field, as well as the ability
to solve problems within that discipline. To be successful as a
manager, you need human relations skills and the willingness
and ability to accept accountability for results (Clemens and
others, 1970).

When hiring engineers, make sure they have the interests
and skills typical of their specialties. When hiring engineering
managers, do not worry about their engineering skills. Make
sure they are like other successful managers, whom I will describe later.

Manufacturing

Manufacturing executives are responsible for making the
product. We know less about the personalities of successful
manufacturing executives than we do about their other functions (Moberly and Buffa, 1948; Finley and Ziobro, 1966).
Manufacturing executives are tougher and more aggressive than
executives in research and development or in engineering. They
can even be more physical. Their accountability is to produce,
on time and within budget, a quality product. In manufacturing, the goals are cost reduction, automation, and other operating efficiencies. If in research the emphasis is on getting the
right idea, and if in engineering the emphasis is on making the
idea work, then in manufacturing the challenge is to produce a
quality product at an acceptable price. Manufacturing executives are less theoretical, less perfectionistic, more pragmatic,
more profit-oriented, and tougher than engineers and scientists.
In my consulting work, the manufacturing managers I see fit
this mode, including the women. Both genders are blunt, fair
and physical. During an interview with me, a vice-president of
manufacturing once said about his plant manager, "I told him
he had better do it right the next time or I'd knock his god-
dam head off. I was so mad I could've killed the son of a bitch."
I believed him.

Personnel

Compared to other managers, personnel managers are softer, placing more value on forgiveness, harmony, and wisdom (Sikula, 1973). The successful personnel manager has a touch of the social worker. Personnel people are less aggressive and tough-minded than their counterparts in manufacturing, marketing, or finance. Miner (1976) compared the personalities of 140 industrial relations managers with personalities of 194 managers in other functional areas, using a sentence-completion test to measure motivation. He concluded that personnel and industrial relations managers were lacking in motivation, noncompetitive, nonaggressive, and lacked a sense of responsibility. To Miner, the main characteristic that differentiated personnel managers from other managers was lack of assertiveness.

Increasingly, we are seeing a feminization of the human resources function. Can it be that human resource development is becoming women's work? There are more women in the professional and management ranks in personnel than in engineering, manufacturing, marketing, or finance. Why? Perhaps it is because not so many women are interested in running factories and because, historically, few women have chosen to be scientists and engineers. Similarly, mathematics, the basic job content of finance, has been viewed as something that men are good at but women are not. Success in sales and marketing, too, requires aggressiveness and a willingness to travel (nevertheless, more women are going into sales and doing well at it). Consequently, some women have been placed in the human resources function by default. It is a function that does not require a technical degree. A highly assertive personality is less useful than skill in negotiation, cooperation, and service. Regardless of the reasons, the human resource function is one in which many women are doing well.

Sales

More has been written about the psychology of salespersons than about people working in any other functional specialty. If Drucker (1974) was right and the first requirement of any business is to have a customer, then the amount of research devoted to individual differences in sales success is justified. No company will survive if it cannot sell, regardless of the quality of its products or the efficiency with which they are made.

In my experience as a consultant, I have been intrigued by the difference in emphasis that companies give to the sales function. I am more fascinated by how few companies are truly sales-oriented. Reflecting on my current active clients, I can classify them as a building-materials company that is finance- and accounting-oriented, a health maintenance organization that is physician- and claims-oriented, a pharmaceutical company that is sales-oriented, a computer manufacturer that is industrial engineering–oriented, an electronics company that is product engineering–oriented (the vice-president of engineering of this company said he did not think the sales function was important because if the engineers did their job right, the product would sell itself), a bank that is rate- and federal funds–oriented, and another bank that is loan-oriented, in terms of both quality and review (this client, with whom I had worked for a decade, refused to issue me a credit card unless I submitted copies of my income tax return, and the executive vice-president apologized for being unable to make an exception to the bank policy).

Besides not being sales-oriented, American companies belittle the role of the sales representative. People outside the sales field think of the job family the way Arthur Miller did in *Death of a Salesman*—as populated by Willie and Wendy Lomans. True, the in-depth technical knowledge required in sales often is less than that required in other job families, but selling is a tough job, tougher than making the product or keeping score. Sales is where the risk is. Those who disparage the sales function usually have not tried it. It is harder than it looks.

Despite the importance of sales and the amount of effort that has gone into selection, picking sales representatives gives management one of its biggest headaches and is one of the most complicated problems in selection (Lippsett, Rodgers, and Kentner, 1964). There are many different kinds of sales, calling for different combinations of aptitudes, abilities, and interests.

The point of view that there are no commonalities for

success in sales continues to be held by some researchers in the field. This viewpoint, if true, would be unfortunate because of the large numbers of people employed in sales and the importance of their work. According to the *New York Times,* there are well over a million traveling sales representatives, who, compared to Willie Loman, are better educated, cover less territory, see more clients, earn more money, and stay away from home less. Although they suffer from loneliness on the road, most like the selling profession (Rhode and Peterson, 1972).

There is a best age for selling. Sales effectiveness rises to a peak at age thirty-eight to forty and then drops off again. What Jung called the meridian of life is the time when experience, interest, energy, and toughness are present in the amounts to produce the best results.

Those who have sold understand that a thick skin helps one cope with the inevitable rejection involved in the selling process. Greenberg and Mayer (1964) found only two personality factors that correlated with sales success. One factor was empathy, the ability to understand someone else's point of view. The other factor was ego strength, self-confidence and resiliency.

Other studies have found multiple factors predicting successful sales performance. In a study of sales managers, willingness to learn, cooperation with other employees, planning and organization skills, drive and dedication, ability to train, and intelligence made for success (Fallis, 1967). Fallis's factors are not sales-specific and are what we would expect of a successful manager in any function. This generality of predictors of managerial success is similar to what we saw in the engineering job family. Individual differences in job families are most pronounced at the entry level.

Cross-cultural studies of sales representatives suggest that some success predictors are universal. Like their American counterparts, successful Japanese car sales representatives are more motivated and have more confidence than their less successful colleagues (Motoaki and others, 1972). Canadian sales representatives are also strongly shaped in their behavior by their attitudes toward money. In this research, sales representatives worked just enough to obtain the level of income they desired.

This finding has pragmatic implications for planning. A manager budgeting a certain level of sales volume needs to tie that volume directly to the desired opportunity of the sales force. You must not allow the sales force to earn enough before you hit plan. Ask your sales representatives what they would like to earn. Then tie those compensation dollars to the volume you need from each person.

Measurements for predicting success in sales include questionnaires and other forms of psychometric tests. Lamont and Lundstrom (1977) had seventy-one sales representatives complete a special questionnaire, which measured dominance, endurance, social recognition, empathy, and ego strength. They then correlated these measures with the sales manager's performance ratings. The best sales representatives exhibited a great endurance. Positive performance as a sales representative was related to high endurance, low empathy, and low ego strength. This means that the best sales representatives are insecure, insensitive, and work like hell.

Positive sales performance correlates with drive, as measured by motivation and self confidence (Oda, 1982). Success in sales (as in any other functional area) depends more on sustained interest and continued application than on incremental differences in ability (Ferguson, 1960). This finding should be emphasized: Success is more the result of sustained interest and application than of differences in talent. Productive people are not necessarily the most able, but they are the most motivated. The ideal employee is one who combines ability with both interest and a capacity for hard work. In the long run, interest and the capacity to work hard will win over undisciplined talent.

What do successful sales representatives do? Productive sales representatives oversimplify, to enable prospects to accept the benefits of a product or a service, and gloss over the less pleasant consequences of accepting a sale (Uris, 1955, 1957). They make it easy for prospects to say yes. They follow the six rules of persuasion: building a backlog of good will, describing the benefits, identifying the potential objections, stimulating motivation to buy, making compliance easy, and assuming the sale has been made.

Successful sales representatives instill a feeling of confidence in potential purchasers, who feel confident about the sales representative and confident about the product or service (Bennett and Harrell, 1975). Two researchers (Byzzotta and Lefton, 1981) asked over 400 customers to describe the best and worst sales representatives with whom they had dealt. The best sales representatives were reported to exhibit a great deal of warmth. The worst exhibited high dominance, high submission, or hostility. To be successful in sales, you should be warm, continually pleasant, and careful not to come across either too strong or too soft. You need to keep your prospect's needs constantly in mind. Customer-centered sales representatives are more effective than those who are product-centered or company-centered (Rao and Misra, 1976). They will sell the most by focusing on prospects and what they think and want, rather than focusing on themselves, their products, or the companies they represent.

Carey and others (1976) documented the importance of the personal touch, studying 440 customers of a jewelry store in a small Texas town. The customers were divided into three groups. All subjects were past customers of the store. One group of customers was simply called and thanked for their previous business. The emphasis was not to sell them anything, but to show appreciation. A second group was called, thanked for their business, and told of a special sale. The emphasis here was to couple a personal contact with an attempt to sell. The third group of customers, the control group, was not called at all. Future purchases made by customers in the control group remained unchanged from the baseline, but among customers who were called, there was a 27 percent increase in sales over the previous year. The most exciting part of the research was that customers reacted more favorably to calls simply thanking them for their business than to calls thanking them and telling them about the upcoming sale. The moral of the story is: Successful sales representatives contact their customers and clientele frequently, but do not always use that contact as an opportunity to sell. They use softer, more indirect techniques.

The psychological literature has other interesting things to say about productive sales representatives. Sales representatives are more effective in selling to clients in their own social class or to clients in a lower class (Hmid and Stringfield, 1973). It is harder to sell to a prospect who is in a higher social class than oneself. Referrals from other customers have long been accepted as a standard selling technique. These are sometimes called buyer testimonials. In dealing with a prospective buyer, however, technical expertise in the product line, and in selling generally, is more effective than referrals when it comes to producing trust and the intention to buy (Busch and Wilson, 1976). Discounting is not a good way to induce people to buy. Discounting from an established or expected price creates mistrust and suspicion in the potential buyer. The results can be explained by cognitive dissonance theory: "If it's cheap, it can't be good."

Productive sales representatives are strongly motivated to earn money through selling. They expend great energy and maintain optimism in the pursuit of this objective. Successful sales representatives are technically knowledgeable in their products and in how to sell. They are careful not to alienate their prospects or show any hostility or arrogance. They are also careful to be neither too dominant nor too submissive in approaching their prospects. They contact prospects frequently and sell on the basis of personal relationships with prospects, not on the basis of the products or services or companies they represent. In their contacts with prospects, they sell softly or not at all. They communicate to prospects that they are at least equal to them socially, and they avoid price cutting to close a sale.

Successful sales representatives must have above average energy levels to look for and identify potential new customers. They need above average amounts of aggressiveness to uncover prospects, approach them, and ask for an order. They need the determination to keep after prospective customers, even when the initial response from them is rejection. Many sales are made after the prospective customer has said no five times.

The average sales representative is not much brighter than any other member of the general population. An IQ of 110 to 115 is sufficient for most sales positions in which the product or service is of moderate technical complexity. Mainly, the sales representative needs practical verbal intelligence. This group is not especially well educated, nor does it enjoy learning for its own sake. Instead, sales intelligence is characterized by common-sense reasoning ability, in which thinking on one's feet, or being shrewd, is more important than book learning.

Sales Managers

First-line sales supervision requires an IQ of only 115 to 120 to handle the problem-solving demands of that job. An IQ of 125 (top 5 percent) is adequate to handle most officer-level sales jobs, although levels of intelligence in the top 2 percent (IQ 130) are more typical of marketing executives in large corporations.

There is no doubt that sales managers are above average in intelligence, compared to the general population. The more interesting questions are whether they are less able mentally than executives in other functional areas and whether lesser intelligence is an asset in sales work. One study found sales managers scoring slightly higher than sales representatives and lower than other executives, but only eleven managers were included in the study (Turnbull, 1976). Another found that sales executives who were rated as promotable were higher in intelligence than sales executives who were rated as only adequate (Greenberg and Mayer, 1964). Harrell (1961), researching the same question, reports a mixed finding. Other studies of successful sales executives have yielded findings that are consistent with popular stereotypes. Sales managers are assertive, sociable extroverts who are people-oriented. They are more indifferent to criticism and are more confident and self-assured than other executives. Sales managers are less knowledgeable than other executives but are more convincing because of their aggressiveness and verbal skills. Of all executive groups, the ones in sales are the most dominant and optimistic.

The sales manager is interested in persuasive activities and is competitive (Lipsett, Rodgers, and Kentner, 1964). The sales executive's major shortcoming is spending too much time selling and not enough time managing (Harrell, 1961). Sales managers are highly verbal and aggressive. They are the most mentally healthy of all the executive groups, being more optimistic and dominant than other managers.

Finance

The functional specialties in finance include accounting, controlling, treasury, tax, audit, financial analysis, budgeting, and forecasting. The financial function is a support position. It exists to facilitate the work of the organization, to provide it with its monetary structure.

In finance jobs, the individual needs above average intelligence and the ability to think nonverbally as well as verbally. Financial people are far less gregarious than sales people and are more like research-and-development people. They prefer more fact-oriented relationships with people and like to avoid conflict.

Financial managers live in the dry world of facts, figures, laws, and regulations. They, too, feel pressures, but for timeliness, accuracy, thoroughness, and objective interpretation. Financial executives are more likely to value education than sales managers are and to compensate for inadequate social skills with technical know-how. The ability to think logically without the aid of words is especially important in the financial function, as is a capacity for working with details. Careful, accurate attention to detail is important to success in finance.

In summary, successful financial people will be well educated and brighter than other executives and will have special aptitude for nonverbal thinking and reasoning. Interests will include working with numbers and clerical detail. There will be an above average ability to do arithmetical computations and generate accurate quantitative estimates from limited information.

General Managers

General managers are responsible for heading up several different functions. They may be divisional heads responsible for profit centers or chief operating officers responsible for the direction of entire corporations.

The characteristics essential for success as a general manager are good judgment under stress, a high energy level, a desire to advance, interest in authority and responsibility, good verbal skills, above average intelligence, and a desire to organize the disorganized. Younger general managers have a higher degree of aggressiveness and egotism in their makeup and are likely to have more trouble dealing with authority than older general managers do.

While general managers are high in mental ability, they usually are not demonstratively or significantly brighter than other executives. The brightest people are usually in such staff jobs as finance, engineering, and law. Wald and Doty (1954) tested thirty-three general managers and found them to be in the ninety-sixth percentile, compared to the general population. Mental ability is higher for higher-earning executives than for those earning less money (Dunnette and Kirchner, 1958). The hobbies of general executives are action-oriented, take place in outdoors settings, and indicate that general managers have more energy than the average person (Morrison, Owens, Glennon, and Albright, 1962).

Summary

This chapter is about matching individuals to jobs and about how that process in turn relates to productivity. It is about the contribution that employees themselves make to the input/output productivity equation. It describes the types of traits known to be efficacious in employees generally, as well as in specific job families. Successful people produce something, demonstrating a mastery over the situations they face.

Productivity predictors can be gleaned from a résumé. Background and prior work experience are important. Past achievement is more important than job-specific experience, which in turn is more important than years of specific experience.

Certain personal attributes predict performance; appearance, marital status, age, and work as a central life interest all affect productivity. Good-looking, mature sole-wage earners for whom work is life are most likely to be productive.

Internal attributors will bring you success. External attributors will bring you nothing but grief. Hire people who blame themselves for failure.

A high level of energy is a trait uniformly found in highly productive people. In the long run, sustained interest and continuous application of energy win over differences in talent. Hire high-energy workaholics obsessed with the need to succeed.

Different job families—research and development, engineering, manufacturing, personnel, finance, general management, and sales—have their own personalities. Sales has received the most research attention, perhaps because if you can't sell your product, you don't have a business.

The next chapter is about training and begins our coverage of what to do with individuals once they are on the job.

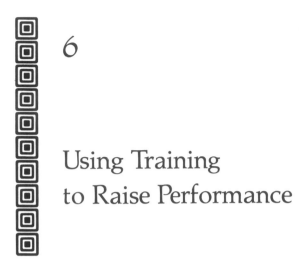

6

Using Training
to Raise Performance

In this chapter, we are going to look at the effects of training on the productivity of individuals. After setting the context for productivity, I stressed the importance of starting with the right person in the right job. With training, our focus is both on the individual and on a management technique. As a manager, you have selected the best person available for the job and are now about to provide him with a one-time experience—training—aimed at improving his effectiveness. In later chapters, we will look at providing him continuous productivity-improvement experiences.

Given the scope I have chosen for this book, I can provide only an overview of what psychological research has to say about training. After a brief introduction, we will turn to a very important question: Does training really work? To answer this question, we need to look at measures of training effectiveness and the differences between effective and ineffective programs. Next, we will examine various types of training programs: lectures, simulations, role playing, visualization, and behavior modification, with specific examples. The next section of this chapter will be about a specialized form of training—career and self-development. The final section offers specific, research-based guidelines for use in your own training programs.

Introduction

Not only is training good for business, training is also good business. As early as the mid-1950s, half of all major companies had some form of training program, many of them spending as much as a full week (forty hours) putting employees through the training paces. By the late 1970s, 75 percent of all major companies (those with over 5,000 employees) had stand-alone training departments offering full-range programs (Campbell, 1971).

If you add up all the costs associated with it, training is easily a multibillion-dollar business. Of all the money spent for consulting in the human resources field, 35 percent is spent on training, and consultants who specialize in training earn over a total of a billion dollars a year. American business has a heavy investment in training and relies on it, perhaps more than on anything else in human resource management, to help improve productivity.

As an experience, training stands apart from the other things that management does for employees. It is a special, time-limited experience. Unlike compensation, which occurs every two weeks, or managerial effectiveness and techniques, which are experienced at least a few times a week, training is an infrequent vacation from work. Going through training is like being on holiday. Most working adults like training experiences because they are fun, a break from the continuous responsibilities of the job.

If people were completely trainable, interchangeable parts of the organization, everything we have covered in the previous chapters on selection and individual differences, and everything that we will examine in the forthcoming chapters on managers and their techniques, would be irrelevant. Individuals' abilities and motivational patterns would not matter, because everyone could be completely trained to be effective on the job.

If most people could not be trained, however, then selection would be the cardinal consideration in ensuring a productive organization. This is the hoary nature/nurture, heredity/environment debate. In the real world, of course, neither extreme occurs. Training is important to productivity because most people can be trained to be more productive.

To make training relevant to productivity, we need to decide what to teach. Training content typically consists of one of five subject matters: factual content, usually personnel management or business administration; problem-solving and decision-making techniques; attitudes; interpersonal skills; and self-knowledge.

The question of what to teach begins with the employee's induction into the company. At all levels of management, job orientation and coaching are the two most popular methods of training (Maggison, 1963). The lower one is in the organization, the more likely it is that job orientation and on-the-job training will be one's sole training experience. Companies send middle-level managers to formal in-house training programs. Upper-level managers go away from the organization to attend special training programs. Top management usually leaves the organization for training, which typically takes place in a university or resort setting (Campbell, Dunnette, Lawler, and Weich, 1970).

Does Training Work?

For as long as companies have trained, researchers have investigated the effectiveness of training. I have said that training is a pleasurable experience for the participants. People who go through training report favorable experiences, and participants generally believe that training works (Andrews, 1957). Still, most companies that go to the considerable expense of training want something more than good feelings to come from it. They want to be sure that it works, that is, that it facilitates the learning of job-related behavior on the part of their employees (Wexley and Latham, 1981). Most industrial and organizational psychologists believe that job-related training works, although some are more reserved than others in advocating it as a major cure for the ills of poor productivity. Miner (1965) conducted an extensive review of the management training and development literature, keeping in mind the central question "Does training work?" Here are his general conclusions. First, in terms of volume, there has been a great deal of research done on the impact of training. Second, most of these research studies present positive evidence for short-term changes in behavior resulting from management training; however, and this is important, there is less evidence to support claims of permanent changes in behavior. Third, the change that occurs most readily as a result of training is the acquisition of human relations attitudes. Fourth, approximately 80 percent of all the research on the effectiveness of training yielded significant results showing that it works.

What does all this mean to the practicing manager? It means that you can be very confident that most training works, and that you should definitely support training in your organization. Training is a potentially powerful tool for improving productivity, but you must also be sensitive to the limits of training, and you should not try to use it as a cure for people-job mismatches, poor management, or ill-conceived compensation plans. Training is not a quick fix (Borenstein, 1983). As a manager, while you can be fairly sure that training will have a positive effect, in each of the training programs you put on in your own company you should still include a step to measure training effectiveness.

Measures of Training Effectiveness

Techniques for evaluating the effectiveness of training include opinion surveys, attitude changes, and objective examinations. It may help you to think of measures of improvement from training programs as hard data or soft data (Philips, 1983). Hard data include measures of quality improvement, output increases, time savings, and cost savings. Soft data include measures related to work habits, new skills, work climate, number of promotions, and improved attitudes and feelings. Other ways to measure improvement using soft-data techniques include pre-

and postcourse exams, asking for feedback about the program from participants, and simple observation—seeing if the work is being done better as a result of the training.

Over the past twenty-five years, concern about the effectiveness of training programs has increased, while confidence in the effectiveness of training has decreased (Neider, 1981). If you share these feelings, how can you know if your training program is effective?

First of all, avoid deficiencies common to many training programs. Bad training programs share these characteristics: They start with limited resources, they make no attempt to decide what constitutes improved performance, they do not offer the opportunity to actually develop new skills during training, and they provide no incentive for improved performance (Gilbert, 1978). Other common, reccurring, and avoidable errors in training are failure to tie the program to long-term goals, failure to qualify participants, inappropriate training methods, failure to focus on individual as opposed to group development, no follow-up or post-training support, and no evaluation of results (Miles and Briggs, 1979). To evaluate the effectiveness of your training program, you should conduct a needs analysis, establish some sort of baseline data, select an evaluation method and strategy, and develop some program objectives (Philips, 1983). There are at least six different ways to evaluate training effectiveness: Compare a control group to a trained group, count critical incidents, compare performance appraisals, do a time-series analysis, compare training costs to outcome benefits, and do an informal "over the shoulder" evaluation (Salinger and Deming, 1982). If you have done all this, how do you know if you have a successful program? For managers seeking guidance on how to do it right, here are ten commandments for putting on a good training program:

1. Focus on the behavior, not on the personality.
2. Train for results, not for the process.
3. Relate training to its context.
4. Remember that not all problems are training problems.
5. Have criteria and training objectives.

6. Match the technique to the training need.
7. Break the total training into successive stages.
8. Require that the learner produce some action during the training.
9. Give the trainee feedback and make it fast, specific, and positive.
10. Measure training against goals.

Like other aspects of human resource management, training succumbs periodically to fads. Too often, the selection of a training program is based on the interests of the trainer or on what happens to be popular at the time. It seems so obvious as to not require mention, but in developing and implementing your training program, the first thing you should do is conduct a survey of training needs. Ask managers and employees to identify shared areas of common need (Kirkpatrick, 1977). Consider your available resources and the skills of your trainers (Wehrenberg, 1983). Ask yourself why you are doing the training: Are you training to meet a proven performance need? Try to get off to a good start by creating favorable attitudes before the training begins; a favorable set of expectations creates a favorable set of end results (Kohn and Parker, 1972). To improve your chances of getting your training program and its recommendations accepted, do these four things (Hultman, 1981): Define your objectives, collect data on the needs and preferences of key managers, anticipate potential obstacles, and devise a way to evaluate your results as compared to your objectives. Once you have done this preliminary groundwork, you are in a position to select an actual training model. You have a number of types to choose from.

Choosing a Training Program

Two problems in selecting the proper vehicle for training are the wide variety of training programs available and the rapidity with which their popularity changes. The training field is mined with fads, gadgets, and amateur psychology (Deterline, 1978).

The human resource field in general, and training in particular, follows predictable cycles. First, a pioneer develops a new technique or resurrects an old one. Then the pioneer and a few advocates describe its successful use in a number of situations. They publish descriptive articles and maybe a book describing their successes. Then a second and larger wave of advocates gets busy and makes numerous applications and modifications of the technique. This group publishes a few empirical studies to show that the training technique really works. Third, there is a backlash. Vocal opponents criticize the universal application of the new technique and poke holes in the research data that support it. Their criticisms make absolutely no difference. What dilutes and eventually replaces the fad in the fourth stage is the emergence of a new technique and a repetition of the cycle.

In addition to the short-term cycles of specific training techniques, there are bigger, broader, and slower cycles. For many years, the trend in training was to provide people with experiences intended to help them become better leaders and develop better human relations skills. This trend was replaced by one that moved away from training for management skills and toward training for skills and a common body of knowledge or technology. Its emphasis was not on training for social skills, but on training for factual content. It ran parallel to the trend in general education back toward the classical fundamentals, emphasizing core subjects and skills. The trend now is away from general management training and toward learning experiences tailored specifically for the job (Divingston, 1983).

The most common type of training is employee orientation, and next is on-the-job training. The newcomer is introduced to the tasks and accountabilities of the job and provided with coaching, feedback, and encouragement. The coaching can be job-specific or it can involve mentoring of an informal or formal nature (Phillips-Jones, 1983).

Beyond on-the-job training, coaching, and mentoring, which all companies do, the most common type of training method is the conference method. In the conference method, a group of people with similar interests gets together and discusses a subject. The conference method can be used for any subject matter. The emphasis is on small-group discussion, with the leader providing guidance and feedback rather than drilling the conferees in a particular set of skills. The objective of the conference method is to present new or complex material, to impart general concepts and ideas, and to develop awareness. The trainee actively participates, mainly through verbal discussion with other group members. Occasionally, the trainee has a paper-and-pencil exercise to do. Criticism of the conference method centers around its inability to cover much of substance, its lack of organization, and its emphasis on verbal skills (Yoder, 1962).

Close in structure to the conference method, and close also in popularity, is the lecture method. This is the method of instruction that most of us experienced during college. It is the traditional method of teaching. Its benefits include its information-giving ability, its wide acceptance, its economy, and its role model of scholarship. Its weaknesses are its lack of provision for individual differences in learners, its requirement that the leader be skilled, and its lack of opportunity for feedback to participants, unless the leader gives a test.

The conference method and the lecture method are well received and at least moderately effective, particularly in transferring information. They are not good at helping people develop new skills, nor are they intended to be.

One training method intended to develop skill, especially skill in human relations, is the modality of T groups, or sensitivity training. In T groups, or sensitivity groups, the subject matter for discussion is the actual behavior of individuals in the group. Group members discuss why they said certain things, why they acted in certain ways, and what they think is actually going on in the group. They talk about one another's abilities to communicate, about their defenses, about their self-images, about their needs to attack or support one another, and about any subgroups that may appear. The trainer acts as a resource person, a behavior model, but is nondirective. T groups have fallen out of favor as a training tool because of evidence that they may actually harm some of the more vulnerable members

in the group, and because the data suggest that they are not effective ways of improving performance. In a study involving
225 personnel and training directors in large manufacturing
firms (Kearney and Marten, 1974), these practitioners concluded that sensitivity training is inappropriate, in many cases,
and is less effective than other techniques. On-the-job training,
business games, and simulation are all seen as more effective.

Another form of training that has also fallen from favor,
not from lack of effectiveness but because of the laboriousness
of the process, is the training modality called the "in" basket
technique. This technique consists of presenting the trainee
with a description of a role he is to assume and an "in" basket
containing documentation and examples of tasks typical of that
role. The object of the "in" basket technique is to teach decision-making skills. Trainees generally go through the "in" bas-
kets on their own and then discuss the results with the trainer.
The "in" basket technique requires a skilled trainer who can develop materials that make sense. It is time-consuming and consequently expensive. As with other attempts to teach decision
making, results have been disappointing (Lopez, 1966).

A fancier and more successful version of this technique,
one in which two or more people participate, is the business
game. Some business games teach decision-making skills, while
others teach information. Business games are effective in imparting both information and skill to the trainee. Their special
strength is that they make the training process fun. Because
business games are standard packages, they are cost effective. If
the games are carefully designed, so that they have high content
validity and give the participants a simulated real-life experience, they are an effective tool for training and team building
(McCall and Lombardo, 1979).

Also enjoyable for the trainee, although less so than business games, is programmed learning. The programmed learning
technique involves deciding what information is to be learned,
breaking it down into small components, and deciding on the
optimal sequence of presentation. A trainee is required to be
highly active and must emit a correct response to each slide or
frame before proceeding with the program. The advantages of

programmed learning are its recognition of individual differences, the need for the learner to be active, and the breaking down of the topic into meaningful elements. Programmed learning is fun because of its constant feedback. The disadvantages of programmed learning are its high initial cost, the time required to develop the program, and the need for special hardware or packaging. There is also the risk that the material, if not interestingly packaged, can become tedious for the trainee. With the proliferation of personal computers in the workplace, some of these disadvantages can now be overcome. Computer-based instruction holds great promise that has yet to be fully realized (Dossett and Hulvershorn, 1984).

To offset the disadvantages of programmed learning, off-spring programs were developed. These share the same advantages of active trainee participation in mastering the information or skill, but they do not require the meticulous and potentially tedious step-by-step approach. These newer techniques are simulation methods and modeling.

Simulation methods are techniques in which the trainee is presented with a simulated or artificial representation of the behavior and tasks to be mastered and is asked to react as if it were the real thing. Examples of simulation methods include case studies, critical-incident methods, role modeling, and visualization. With the exception of research on case studies, the research on the effectiveness of simulation as a training method is positive (Miner, 1980). It is an effective method of imparting information as well as of developing a skill. In a role modeling training program, the major elements are observing models, rehearsing their behavior, getting feedback on how close one came to the desired behavior, and getting social reinforcement for the transfer of training (Sims and Manz, 1982). Modeling works (Miner, 1980). Arguments for case studies are not so convincing. According to Argyris (1980), the problem with the case method is that it does not do a very good job of relating classroom behavior to behavior back home. My own problem with this method is that it does not ensure the trainee's grasp of the principles or the facts that the case supposedly illustrates.

Another effective and sometimes overlooked training method is reading. A reading program mainly imparts information. The information must be acted on for skill development to occur. The reading can include discussion, as in a graduate school tutorial, and it can also require evidence of mastery of information, as in a correspondence course (Hook, 1963). It can also be self-paced, with no feedback, as in reading this book. Reading is an effective means of development, especially of self-development (Nash, 1972). For some people, reading is the single best training method for acquiring both information and skill.

Career and Self-Development

A special type of training is career development. Career development means the evolution of an individual's job over time. Career development presupposes an upward progression, or at least intentional rather than haphazard change. Career development is a continuing issue in our working lives because occupation, and our success or lack of success in it, is closely related to identity and sense of self-worth (Skovholt and Morgan, 1981). Career decisions made early in life are difficult to reverse (Phillips, 1982) because the same motives, attitudes, and values tend to influence people's vocational decisions throughout their lives (Super, 1982). For example, the motivation to manage occurs early and strongly in those who are interested in management (Miner and Crane, 1981).

Companies that recognize the importance of career development provide their employees with structured guidance in this area. Gutteridge and Otte (1983) conducted structured telephone interviews with forty U.S. companies that had career development programs. They found that career development meant different things to different companies. Conventionally, career development means succession planning and management development. Progressively, it means career planning workshops and career counseling. The vigorous expansion of interest in career development and career counseling comes as the result of more and more managers becoming middle managers and middle-aged. It is in career counseling and career planning, not in promotions, that the most opportunity exists for helping individuals recapture and revitalize their productive capacity.

Part of career development is a reassessment of career goals. Setting career goals has a positive impact on your present adjustment to working life. People who occasionally think about their future working lives are better adjusted, as are people who can see the relationship between their present job activities and their future goals. The most unfortunate people are those who lack career goals or who feel that what they are doing is unrelated to their career goals. The need for congruence between current activity and future aspirations has been confirmed by Gottfredson and Becker (1981). They evaluated 1,394 white males and found that the men had a strong need for congruence between their aspirations and their jobs. Career congruence for most was achieved by modifying aspirations. They lowered their aspirations to match what they were doing. Males of higher socioeconomic status were no more successful in achieving their aspirations than were lower-class males. The authors did not blame these men for their failed careers and broken dreams. Rather, the authors believed that opportunity, or lack of it, played the major role in what the men had achieved.

A literature is developing on career planning. There are general books on the subject (Bursk and Blodgett, 1971; Jennings, 1976; Hall and Lerner, 1980; Gutteridge, Gallson, and Zimmerman, 1981), which can be read profitably by everyone. There are books for training career counselors (Sredalus, Marinelli, and Messing, 1982) and books specifically written on how to get ahead in your own career (Whitehead, 1959; Stryker, 1960).

To get ahead in your career, you should specialize and be proactive, not reactive. Specialization is particularly on point and parallels the positioning and doing one thing well that mark the successful corporation. It helps to enjoy one's chosen work. Vocational compatibility is directly related to satisfaction and competence but not necessarily to salary (Heath, 1976). Successful people choose their careers early and stick with one thing (Louis, 1982). Success in a career goes to those who are fortunate enough to find their work early, enjoy their work, and stay in the same field, all over a considerable span of chronological age.

Age is the single most important factor in considerations of career development. Successful managers act their chronological age (Ghiselli, 1964). When young, they act young and aggressive; when old, they act old and wise. In midcareer and midlife, people are most likely to run into difficulty. In a survey of 874 British and Australian managers, Hunt (1981) found that 37 percent of the men between the ages of forty-one and forty-five were depressed about their jobs. Many individuals reach career plateaus in their middle and late thirties (Dawson, 1983). There are only two options for people in this predicament. One is to hunker down and keep at it. The other is to break loose and do something different. In breaking loose and doing something else, people often revert to behaviors or vocational choices earlier discarded as impractical. While hunkering down and keeping at it may seem the more mature thing to do, it does not necessarily get you farther ahead in your career than reverting back to earlier behaviors (Phillips, 1982). Sometimes you can't win.

One of the more encouraging findings in career development is the value of guided imagery in bringing about successful career progression and change. Relaxation training and guided imagery are helpful in career counseling (Morgan and Skovholt, 1977). Research has also shown the usefulness of fantasy and daydreaming in career planning and career counseling (Morgan and others, 1966). Both spontaneous fantasy and guided imagery can be used in helping people develop their careers.

Tips for Trainers

Managers who have primary responsibility for training employees in their companies will be interested in research in psychology that can make them more effective in the trainer role. To present that research in a useful way is the purpose of this section.

You do not need a trainer to conduct an effective training program. For some kinds of training, self-instruction works just as well as instructor-based training (Glasgow, Simkins, and Guerrieri, 1981), but instructor-led training is preferred by most people. It is felt to be more fun, and it relieves people of the burden and responsibility of training themselves.

You do not have to have a custom-made training program in order to have a good program. The evidence is that standard programs can be just as effective as customized ones, provided the standard programs meet certain minimum requirements (Bass, 1977). The standard program should be based on current research in the area of instruction. It should outline the dimensions of behavior to be changed. It should provide rapid and meaningful feedback and have reliable and valid measures of effectiveness. The standard program should have a built-in mechanism for follow-up and evaluating change.

Remember that training means a planned effort to facilitate the learning of job-related behavior. The key idea in this definition for trainers to keep in mind is that, for training to be training, it must be planned in advance, must be directed at enhancing the work of the organization, and must result in a change in behavior (Wexley and Latham, 1981). No training effects are permanent. Estimates are that average office workers will need to be retrained from five to eight times during their careers.

A weak area in many training programs is needs assessment, which should be part of the planning process. Trainers should consider needs assessment as providing important answers to three questions: Where in the organization should training be placed? Who needs to be trained? What should be the content of the program? Trainers may fail first to identify weak organizational units that could benefit from training, or they may assume that training is the best way to strengthen the unit, rather than using other methods of organizational intervention (Moore and Dutton, 1978).

Since one definition of training is the acquisition of job-related behavior, a thoughtful trainer will first try to establish the content validity of a training program by matching relevant job tasks with program material. This is not an easy task, but the use of subject-matter experts, often from within the company, is one good way to identify the knowledges, skills, abilities, and other personal characteristics required for productivity in a job (Ford and Wroten, 1982; Lawshe, 1975). Having developed some sort of content validity index, the trainer will then be better prepared to ensure that the training program will indeed result in the learning of job-related behaviors.

If effective training requires learning, how can a trainer maximize an employee's learning? What can trainers do about trainability, the employee's ability to acquire the requisite knowledges, skills, and other behaviors needed for competent performance within a given time period (Robertson and Downs, 1979)? Trainability is a result of individual ability and motivation. Trainability can be predicted from how a person performs in a miniature training and evaluation testing session (Siegel and Ghiselli, 1971). More companies are beginning to use this technique.

Research shows that trainers should not only require employees to practice what is being taught but also be careful to require the right amount of practice. An optimum number of task repetitions leads to learning, and too much practice can be harmful (Hagman, 1980). Determining where the fine line is between enough practice and too much is tricky because other research has shown that overlearning something initially is better than first underlearning it and then taking a refresher course (Schendel and Hagman, 1982).

Trainers should design programs that provide feedback to trainees. Although there is still a debate among psychologists regarding feedback versus goal setting, studies of training effectiveness indicate that performance improves more with feedback, provided that the feedback is information the trainee can use (Matsui, Okada, and Kakuyama, 1982).

In putting on training programs, remember to keep an upbeat attitude and to communicate expectations of positive change. The Pygmalion effect happens in the training room just as it does in the classroom. Positive attitudes in trainers result in more positive behavior change in trainees (Eden and Shani, 1982).

Try to be sensitive to the individual needs of the people being trained. Training research studies have found that employees come to programs with different cognitive styles and respond differently to structured versus unstructured approaches. If you have large numbers of people who need to be trained, it may make sense to group participants by cognitive style and to provide the groups with training tailored to their preferred modalities (visual, auditory) and styles (lecture, group discussion, reading, and so on).

Summary

Training is a proven and powerful means of making people productive. Over 80 percent of all training programs have been found to be effective. Still, managers should not assume a causal relationship between knowledge or skills trained for and significant improvements in productivity. Training is defined as facilitating the learning of job-related behavior. The content of the training program needs to match the content of the job. The use of subject-matter experts can help identify valid knowledges, skills, and personal characteristics that trainers can teach.

Organizations should train either for information and job-specific content or for role modeling. They probably should not try to train for problem-solving skills. It is possible to train for human relations skills, but the effects are not permanent. Futurists predict that employees will need to be trained many times during their careers. Most people enjoy training experiences and look on them as helpful to their careers.

There are numerous ways to train, ranging from suggested readings to role modeling. All methods work, to some extent, but the most effective methods appear to use role modeling, in which individuals identify and practice the behaviors of people who are successful at a job.

Research in training has resulted in guidelines that can help make trainers more effective. It is important that trainers do a needs assessment to be sure that the right people in the right units of the organization receive the right kinds of training. A preliminary task analysis and the use of subject-matter experts will ensure optimum return from limited training resources.

Not all employees benefit equally from training. Trainability can be predicted from miniature trainability and evaluation sessions. Some companies, when hiring many people for the same position, are beginning to make trainability evaluations part of the selection process. Also, if large numbers of people must be trained, it may be efficacious to separate them into groups according to their preferred sensory modalities and cognitive styles.

Feedback will improve training results, as will sufficient practice of the behavior to be applied on the job. Through the Pygmalion effect, positive expectations and attitudes in trainers produce better-trained employees.

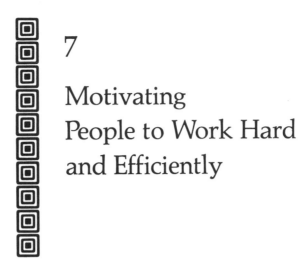

7

Motivating People to Work Hard and Efficiently

In this chapter, we will cover various theories and research studies about what motivates people to be productive. Our focus here is not on what managers can do to motivate people to be more productive. We will cover that subject in Chapters Eight and Nine. Here we are concerned with what the employee brings to the workplace—the internal, already developed, in-place drives that make people try to do their best. Also, we will touch only briefly on economic motivators in this chapter, because we will deal with them at length in Chapter Eleven.

The review of motivators begins with a quick overview of some general observations about motivation and moves on to major theories of motivation in the work force, the theories of Herzberg and Maslow. After that we will consider expectancy theory, which is a psychologically sophisticated version of the power of positive thinking. Next comes a review of the work on motivation fantasy begun by Murray. In his work on the analysis of fantasy, Murray was the first to identify a need for achievement. The remainder of this chapter deals with the construct of need for achievement, the single most explicative variable in determining why some people are much more productive than others. To describe and document the relationship between need for achievement and productivity, we will draw on the work of McClelland.

How important is motivation to individual productivity? If you select the right people, understand their individual differences, and provide them with training, isn't that enough? Attempting to determine how much motivation influences performance is a tough task (Ghiselli, 1968).

It is easy for us to mislead ourselves about the role motivation plays in productivity. With the advent of the human-potential movement and the arguments of people like Herzberg, Maslow, and McGregor, we were told that people work primarily for feelings of self actualization and fulfillment. These views held sway from the Second World War until 1980. In the 1980s there has been a return to the fundamental belief that people are motivated by money and will respond to incentive compensation. Still, we produce more bad ideas than good ones about what motivates: "There is more nonsense, superstition, and plain self deception about the subject of motivation than any other topic . . . . Motivation is a favorite nostrum offered as a cure for incompetence" (Gilbert, 1978, p. 308). Theories of work motivation are numerous (Snyder and Williams, 1982). Among them are theories of equity, self-consistency, reinforcement, attribution, expectancy, and goal setting. (We will consider equity theory in Chapter Eleven. We discuss goal setting in Chapters Nine and Ten.) This chapter covers expectancy theory because the research literature seems to support it as a valid explanation of work motivation and because my personal experiences have shown it to be a powerful shaper of work-oriented behavior. First, though, let us put to rest some lingering misconceptions about what motivates people to work.

Major Wrong Theories: Herzberg and Maslow

Many managers will be familiar with the ideas of Herzberg and Maslow, although they may not be able to match either man to his concept. The purpose of this section is to help managers recall a few details of these well-known theories and to remind them that while the theories are interesting, they are not valid. Consequently, we treat them as major wrong theories.

Herzberg postulates the existence of two classes of work motivators (1966), satisfiers and dissatisfiers. Extrinsic satisfiers are the outward characteristics of work, including pay, security, working conditions, and the like. Extrinsic factors can only dissatisfy. To Herzberg, intrinsic factors are the real satisfiers and motivators. Intrinsic factors include achievement, recognition, responsibility, advancement, and all the elements of the work itself. Despite the popularity and appeal of these notions, they have not been helpful in explaining why people work (Miner, 1980).

Maslow's (1965) theory is more complex than simply an inside/outside view of the nature of work. Maslow postulates a hierarchy of human needs, incorporating several levels. According to Maslow's theory, the needs of the lower levels of the hierarchy must be largely satisfied before the needs of the higher levels become operative. Here is Maslow's hierarchy:

1. *Physiological Needs:* hunger, thirst, and so on
2. *Safety needs:* freedom from bodily threat; feelings of security
3. *Affiliation or social needs:* the need for friendship, affection, and love
4. *Esteem needs:* the need for self-respect and for a stable, positive evaluation of self
5. *Self-actualization:* the need to become what one wants to be, to achieve one's life goals, to achieve the potential of one's personality

Maslow had a good idea. There is a logic to his progression of needs, from the lower-order needs (physiological) to the higher-order needs (self-actualization). The needs themselves make sense; they have face validity. We all recognize physical needs in ourselves, the need to be with others, and the need to feel that we are doing what we are capable of doing. These needs are present in everyone to some degree at some time. The problem with Maslow's needs hierarchy is that it cannot be turned into a practical guideline for managers who are trying to make people productive. The research evidence is just not there to support such rules of thumb as "If you satisfy people's physiological and safety needs through job security and a competitive compensation program, then you can assume they will be motivated mainly by needs for affiliation and for self-actualization." It would be very helpful if this advice were accurate, but it is not.

For years, Maslow's concept of self-actualization held the attention of academicians, consultants, and other advisers to American business, but they have let go, and so should managers.

Major Correct Theories

Expectancy theory says that individuals have cognitive expectancies regarding the outcomes that are likely to occur as a result of what they do. Individuals also have preferred outcomes. Thus, people have preferences and expectations about the likely consequences of their acts. The expectancy theory of motivation says that the anticipation of reward energizes behavior, and the perceived value of the outcome gives the behavior its direction. Expectancy theory says that what drives people to work and to produce is the belief that if they behave in certain ways, they can then expect positive results. They act in the belief that there will be a connection between their behavior and the end result, that they can cause an outcome, and that the attribution of the effect lies within themselves, rather than in the hands of management or with fate.

Elements of expectancy theory are contained in research about achievement motivation, attribution research, and risk-taking decision making (Shanteau and Bristow, 1983). The core concern of expectancy theory is the relationship of expectations to actions and their expected outcomes (Feather, 1982). People behave intentionally because they expect their actions to produce outcomes with positive value. The quality of the person's performance depends not only on expectations and on the strength of the valence of the outcome, but also on the degree to which the individual believes that he has the skills necessary for success. Self-efficacy belief, a belief that one does possess the necessary skill, predicts performance (Barling and Beattie, 1983). Belief in self-efficacy can be developed. Eden and Ravid (1982) found that repeated affirmations of possessing the necessary skill increase self-confidence and improve consequent performance.

Advocates of self-development through guided imagery have long recognized this truth. One of the tenets of guided imagery is that individuals should make repeated affirmations to themselves that they already possess the requisite skills and the outcomes they fantasize. Belief in one's self-efficacy sets up a self-fulfilling prophecy. It becomes a self-prescribed placebo. Belief about outcomes and expectancy are significant and powerful predictors of actual outcomes (Nash and Zimring, 1969). Positive expectation means a positive, trusting attitude about the experience to be undergone and a belief that there is a relationship between what one does and the end results (Cammann and Lawler, 1973).

Do not underestimate the power of self-expectancy. Expectations are more important than ability. Gilmore (1974) found that a person's concept of his or her own ability is a better predictor of achievement than IQ is. This is a strong, supportive finding for the validity of the power of positive thinking. What you get depends more on what you believe you will get than on ability.

Our thoughts not only mold our own behavior, so that we get what we expect, but they also mold the way others perceive us, so that they aid us in achieving the outcomes we anticipate. This is the Pygmalion effect, another example of the self-fulfilling prophecy: "The Pygmalion effect, or the self-fulfilling prophecy, states that when one predicts an event, the expectation of the event changes the behavior of the 'prophet' in such a way as to make the event more likely to happen. . . . This reflects the well-known principle that one person's expectations can influence the behavior of another" (Ross, 1977, p. 45). As managers your expectancy is a Pygmalion effect. Eden and Shani (1982) looked at the causal interplay between managers' expectancy and evaluations of employees' leadership, ability, and performance. In their work, they found that managers' expectancy explained an astounding 73 percent of variance in performance. Higher performers do better because they and their managers expect them to.

The Japanese are better known for their proclivity for participatory decision making and for quality circles than for their equally strong belief in expectancy theory. Rehder (1983), in comparing U.S. and Japanese training systems, pointed out that the Japanese emphasize continuous education and believe in the self-fulfilling prophecy for employee motivation.

What does this mean for the practicing manager? The most productive people are those who have high expectations of themselves. Such people may present themselves ready-made at your office or plant, or you can remake them that way: "If a high level of performance is to be achieved, it appears to be necessary for a supervisor to have high performance goals and a contagious enthusiasm as to the importance of those goals" (Ross, 1977, p. 45).

One of the best predictors of individual performance is the self-image the individual holds of herself in her mind and the perceptions of her that others have. The value of this finding to the practicing manager is that it is possible to shape motivation through the simple device of repeated affirmations that you expect high productivity from the individual. If the individual, through repeated suggestion, convinces herself that she possesses the skills necessary for success and expects to be successful, the chances are good that there will be a highly productive outcome. The practicing manager seeking improved productivity should be a Pollyanna, not a Cassandra. The manager should talk positively, not negatively. This is not Babbittry, but sound management practice: You get what you expect. If you want success, anticipate it. If you don't want failure, don't think about it. This is a simple, invaluable rule of thumb.

Murray's Motivation Mathematics
and the Analysis of Fantasy

In this section, I tell about a line of research that has predictive value equal to expectancy theory but is much more complex to analyze. It is the impact that fantasy has on the motivation to work, its pervasive influence on workers' needs for affiliation, power, and achievement.

The initial research on the evaluation of motivation through the analysis of fantasy was done by Murray and others (1948) at Harvard University. He used the TAT, in which the individual is shown a picture and is asked to make up a story that goes along with it. He is asked to give the story a beginning, a middle, and an ending and to tell what the people in the picture are thinking and feeling. The stories are analyzed for themes and for what they reveal about the individual's core motivations, as shown in the fantasy creations. Murray's work led him to postulate that people have about twenty basic needs. Among the more important are the needs for achievement, aggression, autonomy, affiliation, sex, and nurturance. Of these, three have the most relevance for work: the need for achievement, the need for affiliation, and the need for power.

The Need for Power

Murray, McClelland, and others have looked at the relationship between need for power and success in business. The need for achievement and the need for power are both related to managerial success in employees, supervisors, and top managers. Veroff and others (1960) found that managers score higher on TAT measures of power than nonmanagers do. The need for achievement is the single best predictor of success in business, and it is this motivator to which the remainder of this chapter is devoted.

Achievement Motivation

I was first formally exposed to the idea that successful and productive people had a high need to achieve during a course I took from William Henry, then a professor of human development at the University of Chicago. In his class, as described in a previous chapter, Henry taught that the successful executive had a high need for achievement, felt positively toward authority figures and expected them to be helpful, and at five o'clock on a Friday afternoon was one of only a few people who would still be thinking about work. About the same time, at Michigan State University, Jennings (1965) was saying that the successful executive had a high need to achieve but gained only secondary satisfaction from the results of that need. Things such as money, status, or power were not goals in themselves, but benchmarks showing degrees of achievement. Jennings's research on successful executives showed that they were emotionally separated from parental figures but retained positive feelings toward them, which were transferred to superiors and to the corporation. McClelland continues to write on the achievement motive (1982), and there are now entire books of research devoted to the subject (Fryans, 1982; Rosen and others, 1969).

The relationship between need for achievement and productivity has been investigated experimentally, especially in India, where McClelland trained people to be entrepreneurs. Mukherjee (1968) found that achievement motivation is related to productivity among Indian scientists when the measure of productivity is number of publications and that Indian farmers with high needs to achieve produced more than farmers with low needs to achieve. In the United States, Durand (1975) found that among minorities (in this case, blacks), need for achievement is correlated with high performance. A strong need for power can be helpful when it is found along with the need for achievement, but when it is present alone, need for power predicts failure (Varga, 1975). Before need for achievement can work, it must be focused on a job that involves the individual, one that the person enjoys. With this brief review of some of the more recent literature, it is time to turn to McClelland's seminal work on need for achievement.

The Achievement Motive

The need for achievement is the pre-eminent motive in increasing productivity in business because it produces more goods and services for society as a whole than any other motive. If business wants to increase production, it should recruit high-need achievers and train other employees to acquire a high need to achieve.

The material presented here draws from the work of McClelland (1961, 1985). McClelland believes that business can teach people to want to achieve. McClelland's work in his own words, is the "broadest possible test of the hypothesis that a particular psychological factor—the need for achievement —is responsible for economic growth and decline." McClelland makes an important distinction between the profit motive and the achievement motive. The profit motive is a drive for wealth. The force behind organizational growth is the desire to improve and become more excellent. This is the need for achievement. To understand the role of the need to achieve in making people productive, we need to understand how McClelland measures this motive.

Measuring Need for Achievement

To measure need for achievement, McClelland and his associates use the TAT. Need for achievement is present if the testee shows the desire to achieve a goal; experiences frustration because movement toward the goal is blocked, either by his own weakness or by the environment; and has an emotional reaction to the eventual outcome of the effort. It is not important whether the person making up the story gives it a happy (goal achieved) or unhappy (goal denied) outcome. All that is important is that emotion be expressed regarding the outcome— that the outcome be invested with the energy of affect.

Historical Examples

McClelland's (1961) distinguished contribution to the psychology of productivity lies in his analyzing historical examples of the relationship between need for achievement and economic growth. Voltaire believed that the historical periods in which achievement flourished most were the Golden Age of Greece under Pericles, Renaissance Italy under the Medici, and France under Louis XIV. McClelland agrees with Voltaire and adds the Spain of the late Middle Ages, England from Tudor times to the Industrial Revolution, and the entire historical span of the United States up to its most recent past.

McClelland used the imaginative literature of Greece as the data for determining its need for achievement. As the index of economic activity, McClelland used the number of pots and jars that could be dated to the trading area of the Greeks, measured in millions of square miles. The count of containers per million square miles is a measure of olive oil and wine exports, which in turn are measures of economic activity. The data show that high levels of achievement motivation precede economic growth and that lower levels of achievement motivation precede economic decline. Economic growth occurred when Greece valued impulse control and self-discipline, prerequisites of strong character. During the period of economic climax, the emphasis shifted from impulse control to moderation and merely avoiding excess. Aristotle's Golden Mean was the rule. Finally, during the period of economic decline, impulse control was not valued at all, either for building character or for avoiding trouble.

Gibbon, in *The Decline and Fall of the Roman Empire,* tells how Rome built its empire with men who valued nobility of character. The capacity to endure hardship was gradually replaced as the nation's primary value by the stoicism of Marcus Aurelius. Finally, when Rome fell, its citizens were locked in a passionate embrace with hedonism. Apparently, no nation or organization has escaped this cycle.

Spain in the late Middle Ages provides the next major example of the relationship between need achievement motivation and the economic success of a nation. Spain rose and declined as a power from 1200 A.D. to 1700 A.D. The measures of its economic activity used by McClelland were Spain's shipping exports and the sheep population. For need achievement, McClelland's group analyzed literature from fifty-six authors, who wrote during three general economic eras. Included as forms of imaginative literature were fiction, poetry, short stories, and history. The first economic period, occurring between 1200 and 1492, was one of growth. The period of economic climax extended from approximately 1492 to 1610.

Then, between 1600 and 1700, Spain gradually declined as a world power. Spain continued to weaken over the next century until, by the year 1800, its influence on world affairs was negligible. The research findings for Spain were the same as for Greece. Achievement motivation was highest during the first period of economic growth and had dropped off by the time of economic climax. A decline in need for achievement foreshadowed subsequent economic decline.

The findings sugest that nations become bored with the achievement motivation culture after an extended period of time and take for granted the general affluence that achievement need creates. Eventually a reaction forms against high achievers, and intellectuals begin to argue that the best investment of one's life is in the service of others, particularly the poor. Once general values of social service, equality, and pleasure seeking become widespread, economic decline is inevitable. Thus, in the flowering of the achieving society are the seeds of its own shriveling away. Once decline begins, there is no arresting it. The economy rots and productivity putrefies. The nation becomes a haven for has-beens and neer-do-wells.

During the 400 years from the time of the Tudor kings to the Industrial Revolution, England's achievement motivation drove its economic development. As the index of economic activity for England, McClelland chose shipments of grain and coal to London. These were tallied and correlated with counts of achievement imagery in the dramas, accounts of sea voyages, and street ballads of the day. Again, motivational changes preceded economic changes by thirty to fifty years. Approximately one to two generations were required for national attitudes to affect the national economy.

Finally, McClelland addressed himself to the achievement motive in the United States: What would it say about our future productivity? He looked at the period from 1800 to 1950. His measure of achievement motivation was the imagery on every third page of the four leading American reading textbooks from every twenty-year period from 1800 to 1950. For his measure of economic activity, he used the number of patents granted per one million people.

What did McClelland find? Has the United States reached its productivity peak, its apex of economic growth? Will it follow Greece, Rome, Spain, and England into decline? McClelland does not know. He did find that the patent index in the United States coincided closely with achievement imagery in textbooks. While changes in achievement imagery occurred somewhat ahead of similar changes in the patent index, there was not enough of a time difference to enable him to assume a probable connection between achievement need and technical innovation. Perhaps the problem lies in his choice of economic activity. McClelland did find the beginnings of a decrease in achievement imagery as expressed in the American literature and music of the 1950s, the time when his book was published. This is also the time when humanistic theories of personnel management replaced scientific theories. Our decline continued unabated during the 1960s and 1970s. If it runs on through the 1980s, we can assume that the United States has entered the period of irreversible decline as an economic power. If, instead, the resurgence of entrepreneurism is strong enough, there may still be hope for us.

Need for Power

The need for achievement is not the only motive that moves people to work. Also important are needs for power and needs for affiliation.

Power is the ability to produce an intended effect. A need for power is a need to control, to influence other people. Power exists in interpersonal relationships when one person has control over another. Power is about the pleasure of winning, the anger of losing, being weak or being strong, and getting your own way.

People whose needs for power are stronger than their needs for achievement may not reach their goals. A manager with a high need for achievement will accept whatever is necessary, including temporary submissiveness, to achieve a goal. The same manager, driven by power, can become so engrossed in power struggles that it prohibits him or her from achieving the goal. The same manager, if motivated primarily by the need for affiliation, will want to stay on friendly terms, regardless of the cost. The goal may not be achieved if it must be reached at the expense of other people. All three motives—achievement, power, and affiliation—are present in everyone at any given moment, but the need for achievement is the one most directly related to individual productivity. The need for power, when coupled with the ability to control aggressiveness, is called the Leadership Motive Syndrome and may be related to effective management (McClelland, 1985).

Need for Affiliation

A need for affiliation is a need for warmth, companionship, and friendship. Friendship is a major source of job satisfaction. When scoring imaginative literature or the TAT for affiliation need, characters in the stories establish, maintain, and restore positive relationships with others.

People with high needs for affiliation want approval. They need to be liked. Business executives with high needs for affiliation choose friends rather than experts to work with them. Managers with high needs for affiliation have fewer employees who quit than do managers with high needs for power. Managers with high needs for achievement experience different rates of turnover, depending on the kinds of employees they have and whether the need for affiliation or need for power is the manager's second most dominant need.

The need for achievement and the need for affiliation are related, but the relationship is not statistically significant. Employees with high needs for achievement are also likely to have high needs for affiliation, but productivity declines as an employee's need for achievement is replaced by a need for affiliation. This would explain the decline in profitability seen after the introduction of McGregor-type Theory Y techniques.

Humanistic personnel management stresses affiliation over achievement. As opinion leaders pushed affiliation as a major management style in America, productivity declined. It is possible for a company to emphasize both high needs for achievement and high needs for affiliation, but only the need for achievement spurs productivity. There is no connection between productivity and the need for affiliation.

The implications for management are clear. When interest in need for achievement declines, productivity declines will follow as surely as sunset follows sunrise. To sustain high levels of productivity, an organization cannot abandon a value system that places high status on the need for achievement. A humanistic approach to management may make people feel good, but it will not make them as productive as achievement-oriented management.

Childrearing Practices

Assuming managers want to sustain achievement motivation, they need to know something about how the need to achieve is created. One key to need achievement is childrearing. Affluent families have an unfortunate tendency to decrease achievement-oriented childrearing, although the economic aftermath is not noticed overnight. It probably takes at least three generations of either rising achievement motivation or falling achievement motivation for a detectable change in productivity to occur.

Achievement-oriented childrearing emphasizes self-reliance training. Self-reliance fuels the need for achievement, providing the energy and confidence necessary to stimulate productivity. Although individual differences in a child's need for achievement can be detected as early as age five, the most important period for creating the motive is between the ages of eight and ten. Mothers as well as fathers are influential in creating the need for achievement. High need-for-achievement children are expected to become independent of adults. They are expected to look after themselves, not get in the way, and quickly become self-reliant.

People who produce high-need achievers emphasize that they expect the person under their direction to meet standards of accomplishment that are not beyond the individual's ability but certainly test them. The individual is expected to internalize standards of excellence and, as goals related to these standards are achieved, to set standards for successively higher levels of performance.

The mothers and fathers of high achievers set higher standards of excellence than parents of low achievers do. Parental standards of low-achieving children permit carelessness, indifference, or self-indulgence. The parents have lower expectations or few expectations at all. Parents of high achievers, in addition to expecting their children to do well, support their children's efforts with encouragement and affection.

Parents of high achievers are more domineering, but the dominating behavior does not interfere with the development of the need to achieve, provided that it is the mother who dominates and not the father. Fathers should arrange to leave home periodically. This happens naturally in families when the father holds a position that requires travel. The most inhibiting environments are those in which the father is a high achiever but has an occupation that does not periodically remove him from the home. Such occupations can include the law and medicine. The best situation is one where both parents have high standards of excellence, where both show some affection, and where too much dominance is avoided by periodic paternal absence. For single-parent families to produce high achievers, the parent must be warm as well as demanding.

A country produces the largest number of working adults with high needs for achievement when it has childrearing practices that encourage intact nuclear mother-father-child families, self-reliance training, high standards of excellence, warmth from the mother, partial absence of the father, and mastery training (McClelland, 1961).

Characteristics of High-Need Achievers

Common sense suggests that need for achievement and income should go together. This is true, but only in certain situations. There is a positive relationship between need for achievement and salary at the lower and middle levels of business organizations, but not at the higher levels. In the upper levels of large U.S. corporations, salary is not correlated with the need to achieve. There is evidence to suggest that those with the highest needs to achieve leave the organization as middle managers. They realize that few people reach the top of the corporate ladder or get rich while working for someone else, and so they leave and become entrepreneurs.

High achievers do not work just for money, but money is important to them as a symbol of higher achievement. Even though high achievers are not motivated solely by money, they believe in higher rates of pay than do lower achievers for accomplishing difficult tasks.

Besides money, high need achievers value autonomy. They prefer situations where they can control the environment. They want to act on their environment rather than being acted upon by it. People with a high need for achievement are not gamblers, nor are they typically competitive in athletics. They are interested in sports but do not strive to excel in them. People characterized by high need for achievement are more likely to be upwardly mobile, willing to move from one geographical locale to another to better themselves, and have a tendency to travel more.

High need for achievement is associated with independence, encouragement of self-reliance, and disdain for tradition. Individuals with high needs for achievement gain satisfaction from initiating action that is successful. They do not particularly care whether they receive public recognition for their accomplishments. High-need achievers are happiest when they decide to do something difficult and then do it. People in the public eye, such as celebrities and politicians, are not necessarily those with the highest needs for achievement. They may be those with a high need for power (politicians) or a high need for affiliation (actors and entertainers).

High-need achievers are optimistic, self-confident, practical, and liable to overestimate their chances for success. When there are no facts on which to base an estimate, people with high needs for achievement overestimate the probability of a successful effort. This is a result of their greater self-confidence. When facts become available, high-need achievers become practical and base their judgments on facts. High-need achievers work best when they are given concrete task feedback regarding their performance, rather than feeling-level feedback. Feeling-level feedback works better for people who have high needs for affiliation.

People with high needs for achievement work harder when they believe their own efforts make a difference in the outcome. They work hardest at tasks requiring mental manipulation or originality, not at routine tasks. Because they are not concerned with efficiency, they make poor bureaucrats. They are concerned with achieving more and with challenge. As the task becomes easier or less risky, its incentive value drops for high-need achievers. In their attitudes towards work, high need achievers show the following characteristics: they work to achieve excellence rather than money, prestige, or power, and they work hard to achieve more, not to make more money. They respond better to opportunities for excellence than to opportunities for publicity or prestige. They are indifferent to whether they work alone or in groups. They pick experts over friends as coworkers, and they become successful entrepreneurs more often than they become professional managers.

Training the Need to Achieve

The achievement of organizations is the total achievement of the individuals who compose them. Most organizations want to improve productivity. Increasing the achievement motive of employees is one way to do so.

The best way to create an organization full of high achievers is to recruit entrepreneurial people or to train people in need achievement. Most of the work in teaching people how to learn to achieve has been done by McClelland. He believes that the need to achieve is gained early in life, but that "if achievement motivation is encouraged and developed, it will continue throughout a person's life . . . achievement motivation is within everyone" (1985, p. 4). In a workbook developed for school-children, he has broken learning down into six steps (see Table 5). The concepts are also applicable to adults in work settings.

McClelland has also taught adults how to be entrepreneurs

Table 5. The Six Steps to Achievement.

Step 1: Study Self
   Know own strengths and weaknesses.
   Be aware of past achievements.
   Be reasonably self-confident and self-reliant.
   Respect self and abilities.
   Have self-control.
   Try new things and try to improve.
Stpe 2: Consider Goal Ideas
   Use brainstorming to get ideas for goals.
   Think about strengths and weaknesses to get ideas for goals.
   Think about past achievements to get ideas for goals.
   Think about activities of interest and new things to try.
   Devise goal ideas that are challenging but possible.
   Develop many goal ideas to achieve, both short-range goals and long-
      range goals.
Step 3: Set a Goal
   Set both short-range and long-range goals.
   Make sure goals are based on strengths, weaknesses, and past achieve-
      ments.
   Make sure goals are responsible.
   Make sure goals are medium-risk—challenging but possible.
   Make sure goals are specific enough to be measured.
   Make sure goals have a time limit.
Step 4: Plan
   List tasks necessary to achieve goals.
   Arrange tasks in order.
   Find and use help that strengthens.
   Plan how to deal with obstacles.
   Revise plans, as necessary.
   Choose methods that are responsible.
Step 5: Strive
   Check progress on list of planned tasks.
   Compete with self, with others, or with a standard of excellence to
      keep striving.
   Keep striving and imagine feelings of success and failure.
   Keep striving and remember past achievements.
   If necessary, get encouragement from experts or by thinking of achieve-
      ment heroes.
   Use other striving methods, as needed, to reach goal.
Step 6: Evaluate
   Be realistic about whether or not goals are achieved.
   Feel good about goals achieved.
   Review goal setting, planning, and striving process.
   Learn from successes and failures.
   Consider whether goals were achieved responsibly.
   Think about how achieved goals may lead to future goals.

Source: Adapted from Johnson, 1984.

by putting small groups of ten to fourteen businessmen through intensive ten-hour daily training in a retreat setting. The inputs into the training are shown in Table 6. He reports that businessmen trained in achievement motivation showed significantly more activity in certain key measures of business success, in-

Table 6. Training Inputs in Courses for Business Entrepreneurs.

Purpose is to increase:		
Motive Strength (n Achievement) M	*Perceived Probability of Success* P_s	*Incentive Value of Being More Entrepreneurial* V
1. Learning achievement motivation theory	1. Prestige suggestion that they could change and become more entrepreneurial	1. Realization that chosen occupation requires it
2. Practicing moderate goal setting; getting excited about achievement	2. Commitment to concrete goals and plans (increased effort)	2. Realization that chosen occupation fits in with life goals
3. Following behavior of attractive entrepreneurial models (vicarious satisfaction)	3. Keeping track of progress toward goals; using feedback to increase self-confidence	3. Clarification of how this value fits in with other values that might conflict with it
4. Visualization experiences	4. Receiving warmth and respect from trainers during confusion and failure	4. Retreat setting to dramatize importance of life change
	Gaining confidence from experiences in course	
	Gaining confidence from self-knowledge and from knowing how to change	
		5. New reference group of trainees to give reminders and reinforcement after training

Source: Adapted from McClelland, 1985. Reprinted by permission.

cluding creation of new jobs, monthly sales, profits, and personal income.

It is clear that achievement motivation is related to productivity, and that people can learn to have higher levels of the achievement motive. To date, however, organizations have done little systematic training in this area.

Summary

This chapter is about the internal attributes that motivate people to work.

Managers will be most familiar with the work motivation theories of Herzberg and Maslow. Herzberg postulated the existence of two classes of work motivators, satisfiers and dissatisfiers. Extrinsic factors, such as pay and working conditions, can only dissatisfy. Intrinsic factors, such as achievement and the work itself, can satisfy. Researchers have been unable to verify Herzberg's theory, and managers should not rely on it.

Maslow believed that work motivation consists of a hierarchy of needs. At the lower levels are physiological and safety needs. At the higher levels are needs for affiliation, esteem, and self-actualization. Researchers have also been unable to verify Maslow's theory, and managers should not rely on it either.

Managers can rely on expectancy theory. People behave in ways in which they expect themselves—and their supervisors expect them—to behave. Successful, productive people are fulfilling self-prophecies of high levels of achievement. Belief in self-efficacy can be developed through repeated affirmation and guided imagery. Self-expectancy has more predictive power than ability does for productivity and achievement.

People are motivated by the needs that dominate their fantasies. Three common motivational needs at work are affiliation, power, and achievement. Only the need to achieve is clearly significant for productivity, although the need for power may be related to leadership success. The achievement motive is significantly higher in economically successful individuals, companies, and countries. While the need for achievement is formed early in life by childrearing practices, there is some evidence that the trait can be developed in adults through special training.

8

Developing
Effective Managers

Effective managers share a common set of traits and behaviors and a common set of accountabilities. One of these responsibilities is to make their people more productive.

Understanding effective managerial performance requires asking and answering several key questions: What are the demands on the individual in a managerial job? What type of individual is most likely to be an effective manager, and what type is most likely to fail? What must managers do generally, and what must they do specifically? What makes someone a productive manager?

According to Banks and Gleck (1984), most discussions of effective management focus either on the determinants of leadership and on matching leaders to situations, or else try to show how leaders can contribute to organizational effectiveness (Hackman, Lawler, and Porter, 1983). In this chapter, we will try to do a little of each, presenting various definitions of management and using the critical-incident method to outline what successful managers do. This chapter also will list characteristics correlated with managerial success, show why such lists can be reduced to a few core traits, look at research on top-level leaders (the supposed paragons of managerial excellence), and cover the subject of managerial style, especially the question of whether being task-oriented or people-oriented produces the best results. Finally, this chapter will consider why some managers fail.

Just how important is effective management? Even with properly selected, trained, and motivated employees, here in the United States we act as though managers and their techniques are more important than individual employees in achieving the objectives of organizations. Americans are not alone in our belief about the importance of management. Haire, Ghiselli, and Porter (1982) studied opinions about management in fourteen countries. In each country, there was a low opinion about the capabilities of the average employee, coupled with a high opinion of the necessity for effective supervisory practices.

While other countries share our opinions about the importance of management, Americans are more optimistic that effective management can be learned. In the Haire, Ghiselli, and Porter research, Americans, more than any of the other fourteen nations, supported this statement: "Leadership skills can be acquired by most people regardless of their particular inborn traits and abilities" (p. 30). We produce an unending stream of books, most of them without any foundation at all in research, providing advice on how to manage better. We demand a lot of our managers, expecting them to produce organizational efficiency, high productivity, profit maximization, organizational growth, business leadership, organizational stability, employee welfare, and social welfare (Campbell, Dunnette, Lawler, and Weich, 1970).

What Is a Manager?

"Who," the caterpillar asked Alice when she was in Wonderland, "are you?" If we asked that question of managers, we could expect over 350 answers to our question (Bennis, 1972). Since managers manage and workers work, at least we know that there are fewer managers than workers. About 10 percent of all the employed people in the United States are managers. The term *executive* is used interchangeably with *manager*

(Sands, 1963). The term *top management* includes chairman of the board, president, executive vice-president, and all corporate officers and executives who report directly to the president or to the executive vice-presidents. Besides there are middle management and first-level supervisors. Lack of agreement on who is a manager and what the job consists of makes it difficult to create a list of desirable managerial talents. The concept of management includes technical and administrative skills, as well as an understanding of human relationships and organizations.

The word *management* does not make semantic sense unless it includes a direct responsibility for people. Being a manager means having people work for you. In most companies, the word *executive* is more specific than *manager,* referring to heads of departments and even higher people, including upper-middle as well as top management personnel. A manager is anyone from a first-level supervisor up to and including the chief executive officer of the organization. It is acceptable to use the words *manager* and *executive* interchangeably. It is not acceptable to use the word *manager* for someone responsible only for activities or projects and not for people. A manager is accountable for the selection, training, and work direction of other individuals. An executive without subordinate direct reports is not a manager.

The differences between types of managerial jobs are not so profound as those between managers' jobs and nonmanagers' jobs (Porter and Lawler, 1968a). Managers at the same organizational level are more alike than different, regardless of functional specialty. And even managers at different organizational levels are more alike than are managers and nonmanagers. Across industries, managers are more similar than they are different (Lau and Pavett, 1980), and the same is true across cultures. All managers are alike in that they all are able to manage people (Jones, 1976; Rim and Frez, 1980). What else do they do?

What Managers Do

Lists of what managers do vary from single responsibilities to hundreds of duties (Flanagan, 1954; Williams, 1956). What managers do has long been the subject of hundreds of publications (Carlson, 1951; Wallace and Gallagher, 1952;

Brooks, 1955; Bellows, 1962; Lamb and Turner, 1969). The literature is diverse, from brief articles to doorstop books (Drucker, 1974). For example, Campbell, Dunnette, Lawler, and Weich (1970) say that effective managers do thirteen things: manage work and people, plan and organize, set realistic goals, derive decisions, delegate, rely on others for help in solving problems, communicate, stimulate others to act, coordinate, cooperate with others, act consistent and dependable, win gracefully, and express hostility tactfully.

How do Campbell and his colleagues (or anyone else, for that matter) know what effective managers do? There are only three ways to find out. First, you can follow a manager around and observe what he does. Second, you can ask the manager to keep a record or a log of his activities during the day. Finally, you can ask the manager to estimate how he spends his time, provide him with a checklist of duties, and ask him which are more important (Stewart, 1967).

Kelly (1965) followed 1,800 managers around. He concluded that 50 percent of managers' time was involved in planning, 25 percent in technical matters, and only 10 percent in dealing with people. Haizer (1972) was less ambitious than Kelly. He asked only 100 line managers and 100 staff managers to analyze what they did when they were effective and what they did when they were ineffective. Five managerial actions were effective: planning, technical conference, delegation, task emphasis, and group process. Ineffective actions were satisfying personal needs, acting like supervisors, and emphasizing authority.

What else can be said about what effective managers do? Quite a lot. The critical-incidents method (Flanagan, 1954) identifies important aspects of the managerial role. Critical incidents are behaviors that are especially effective or ineffective in helping managers do their jobs. On the basis of responses from over 3,000 Air Force officers, Flanagan concluded that five factors and forty-four critical incidents described almost all managerial behavior. The five factors he found are supervising people, planning and taking action, accepting organizational responsibility, handling administrative detail, and accepting personal responsibility.

Flanagan's first factor, supervising people, has thirteen critical incidents. The incidents are matching people with assignments, delegating authority, giving instructions, ensuring comprehension, giving reasons and explanations, supporting approved action, encouraging ideas, developing teamwork, setting a good example, assisting subordinates in their work, evaluating subordinates, showing concern for subordinates' welfare, and maintaining relationships with subordinates.

Flanagan's second factor, planning and taking action, has eight critical incidents. They are taking responsibility, solving problems, calling on past experience, planning for the future, taking prompt actions, suspending judgment, making decisions, and making forceful effort.

Flanagan's third factor, acceptance of organizational responsibility, has six critical incidents. The critical incidents are complying with orders and directives, accepting organizational procedure, subordinating personal interest, cooperating with associates, showing loyalty, and taking responsibility.

Flanagan's fourth factor, handling administrative details, has nine critical incidents. They include understanding instructions, scheduling work, getting information from written material, getting information from others, checking accuracy of work, writing letters and reports, presenting finished work, keeping records, and keeping others informed.

Flanagan's fifth factor, accepting personal responsibility, has eight critical incidents. They are attending to duty, attending to details, reporting on time for appointments, meeting commitments, maintaining a businesslike appearance, being fair, adapting to associates, and adapting to the job.

Two years later, Williams (1956) published a collection of 3,500 incidents and six factors that were critical for managerial effectiveness. Williams finally reduced the list to eighty critical incidents and six factors. They are listed in order of importance.

William's first factor is technical competence. It has ten incidents critical for managerial effectiveness: displaying knowledge of management principles, applying knowledge of management to the job, deriving cause-and-effect relationships from available information, utilizing all available sources of information, providing information that is accurate and reliable, contributing ideas outside one's own area, demonstrating ingenuity, seeking ways to improve productivity, performing effectively outside one's immediate area, and anticipating effects of judgments and decisions.

Next in importance is Williams's second factor, coordination and integration of activities. The ten critical incidents are providing necessary physical materials, maintaining physical materials in good order, assuming responsibility for achievement of objectives, applying one's own and others' experience in planning, overcoming obstacles to achieving objectives, persisting in efforts to reach objectives despite setbacks or opposition, making vigorous attempts to reach objectives, deriving general policies and conclusions from unintegrated facts, voicing support and carrying out company policy, and interpreting policy to subordinates.

The third factor is work habits. There are also ten critical incidents in this factor: working diligently on delegated and self-assigned tasks, working long hours when necessary, being punctual in keeping appointments and starting conferences, planning time so that it is not wasted by interruption and diversion, delegating responsibility when absent, being honest in all matters pertaining to company property, demonstrating pride and responsibility in work, making reasonable and reliable estimates of time required to achieve objectives, scheduling work of subordinates for efficient performance, and regularly reviewing organization and taking corrective steps.

The fourth factor is adjustment to the job. The number of incidents begins to increase, with thirteen listed: demonstrating by action that company objectives are more important than personal convenience, performing work without regard to personal advancement or compensation, supporting company policy and personal criticism, participating in community activities, assuming responsibility of associates when necessary to achieve objectives, fulfilling commitments promptly, improving proficiency by self-development, being honest in statements about work, maintaining a good attitude toward the job despite stress, making a good impression by manners and social conduct, maintaining a good physical appearance, performing effectively despite unusual demands, and improving the effectiveness of organization by friendly and cooperative relationships.

The fifth factor, relationships with associates, is the traditional "managers manage people" factor, with twenty-five specific critical incidents: establishing channels of communication, making knowledge available to associates, using knowledge and services of associates, persuading and influencing to support objectives, understanding jobs of subordinates and superiors, understanding capabilities and limitations of associates, matching subordinates with jobs, assisting subordinates with personal difficulties, showing interest in working conditions and personal welfare of subordinates, assisting associates in performing jobs by friendly advice and help, avoiding animosity or differences of opinion, making clear assignments of authority and responsibility for subordinates, explaining reasons for policies, supporting policies and actions of superiors even when not in agreement with them, supporting actions of subordinates, making sure subordinates understand policies and decisions and instructions, stimulating associates to each objective of the organization, encouraging associates to submit ideas and plans, guiding subordinates by commending good performance and offering frank discussion of inferior performance, stimulating subordinates by assigning increased responsibility, stimulating associates by competitive devices, stimulating pride in the company, keeping continuously informed of progress toward objectives, stimulating associates by good examples and work habits, and encouraging professional development of subordinates.

The sixth and final factor is planning, organization, and execution of policy. The number of critical incidents drops to a mere twelve: basing plans and actions on clear knowledge of the objectives of the company, formulating effective policies for achieving objectives, communicating and interpreting policy so that it is understood, anticipating difficulties to be overcome in achieving objectives, delegating authority and responsibility, using own and subordinates' experience, making prompt and explicit decisions, using ingenuity to achieve objectives, persevering in effort to achieve objectives, reviewing the work of the organization and making necessary corrections, ensuring that all available information is used, and initiating plans and actions promptly.

What must managers do if they are to be effective? Take your pick—one factor or six, four critical incidents or eighty. I myself like four, the classic ones. With accountability for people, managers must plan, organize, execute, and review.

The problem with writing about management is that it is a never-ending story. The research literature on leadership and management is voluminous (Meyer, 1982). Our concern here is what it contributes to managerial effectiveness. Ghiselli (1966) reviewed hundreds of studies that appeared between 1919 and 1965 on the subject of executive effectiveness. Ghiselli also reached three conclusions. Ghiselli concluded that only three factors predicted managerial effectiveness: intelligence, personality, and interest. On the basis of my own research, described in Chapter Five, I agree with Ghiselli. The best predictors of managerial success are an above average IQ, a strong personality, and a desire to achieve as a manager. McClelland calls this desire to manage the III B pattern, or the Leadership Motive Syndrome. It consists of a high need for power, a low need for affiliation, and high activity inhibition (McClelland, 1985).

Predictors of Effective Managers

The list of predictors of managerial effectiveness is just as old and almost as long as the list describing what effective managers do. Uris (1955) said that effective managers have these abilities: they stay calm when frustrated, encourage participation when others contradict their decisions, are self-questioning, live easily with competition and criticism, and keep mood swings small and accept victories and defeats in stride. In 1958, Dunnette and Kirchner said effective managers are more intelligent than those whom they manage and have stronger personalities.

In 1963, Sands expanded this list a bit. For her, the key qualities of successful executives are leadership personality, specific intellectual capabilities, highly developed social sensitivity, certain physical characteristics, and a certain life-style. Sands based her observations on top-level managers. She believed that a pleasant personal appearance was characteristic of effective executives, and she was not alone. Freeman and Taylor (1950), after studying 100 naval officers, also decided that personal appearance was an important leadership trait. "In leadership, personality traits are probably ten times as important as all aptitude and proficiency factors combined" (p. 18). They asked their 100 naval officers to list the traits most important for leadership. Here is the list:

1. Personal neatness and bearing—90 percent
2. Personal poise and tact—60 percent
3. Reliability and dependability—60 percent
4. Firmness and forcefulness—50 percent
5. Endurance—40 percent
6. Loyalty—40 percent
7. Intelligence—30 percent
8. Adaptability—22 percent

Because the percentages listed are percentages of the sample mentioning the trait as being important, the total is more than 100 percent. Most officers mentioned more than one trait. The traits have the virtue of being mostly easy to measure.

Another fairly measurable list is Mahoney's (Mahoney and others, 1963), who concluded that more successful managers were smarter, more dominant, better educated, had better-educated spouses, participated in more extracurricular activities, had interests similar to others in their fields, and were not like farmers or skilled tradesman. Other short, sensible lists are Ross and Dunfield's (1964)—successful executives show greater intelligence, dominance, and better job performance—and Vroom's (1965), which says that the more successful managers want to achieve more and exercise initiative.

McClelland and Boyatzis (1982) published the results of what they called a leadership motivation pattern. People motivated to lead show moderate to high needs for power, low needs for affiliation, and high energy. According to McClelland's new view, need for achievement is associated with success only at lower management levels, where individual contributions are more important than the ability to influence people. At top levels of the organization, need for power is more important than need for achievement. High-need achievers leave to become entrepreneurs (Allen and Panian, 1982).

Some studies have found that good managers are tough-minded. Effective supervisors are more willing to discriminate between high-performing and low-performing subordinates (Kirchner and Reisberg, 1962). Good managers are less lenient, especially with poorly performing subordinates. Nice managers get happy employees but mediocre results. At the U.S. Naval Training Center in Orlando, Florida, humane company commanders graduated recruits who felt satisfied with their training experience but were poor performers (Weller and Blaiwes, 1976). The most aggressive managers get the most from their groups, but their aggressiveness can stand in the way of their advancement to top management (Brenner and Tomkiewicz, 1980).

The Research of Bennis on Top Leaders

The research of Bennis (1981) is valuable for the information it provides about the personal characteristics of people who have reached the top of their fields. Bennis's subjects included ninety executives of *Fortune* 500 companies, as well as the heads of public organizations, university professors, and football coaches. Their average age was fifty-six; most (80 percent) were still married to the first spouse. They were stable in other ways, too, and had spent over twenty-two years, on the average, with the same organization and eight years in the current job.

Although Bennis catalogued 350 different definitions of leadership, he views leadership essentially as an art form. To him, leadership is the art of recruiting the right people and then getting out of their way and letting them have fun. For Bennis, leadership means doing the right thing at the right time. Like others before him, Bennis initially could not see any unifying or special personality characteristics in the leaders he studied. He studied and restudied the three hours of taped interviews with each subject, until finally this pattern emerged: Leaders are intentional. Leaders do not waste any time. They are results-oriented, consistent, focused, and intense. Leaders stay on course even when they have no apparent support and are surrounded by critics. They do not take things personally. They have a sense of vision and remain true to their dreams. Top leaders do not experience failure personally but see it as an opportunity to learn. Their focus is always on the outcome, the goal. Early in their careers, Bennis's leaders had determined what they liked to do and then pursued that interest with a fervent, unswerving passion. Bennis's elite leaders are similar to the elite in any profession. They share a single-minded drive to be the best in their chosen specialty.

Management Style

The style of Bennis's leaders was to pursue intensely a single goal. The literature on management style shows that this single-minded pursuit of a dream is but one of several different management styles documented in the literature.

There are probably four different management styles. These styles are telling, selling, participating, and delegating. Bass and others (1979) after studying 500 managers and subordinates, called the four styles by slightly different but similar names: direction—related to structure and clarity; negotiation—related to short-term objectives and authoritarian subordinates; consultation—related to long-term objectives and intergroup harmony; participation—related to clarity and warmth; and delegation—related to warmth and lack of routine tasks.

Is managerial style important? Yes, to some extent. Managerial style is related to employee satisfaction. A salesperson leader sells ideas or instructions. The consultant leader discusses plans and problems with subordinates. The authoritarian leader tells you what to do. The most satisfied employees have supervisors who use a consultative management style. The most dissatisfied employees have authoritarian supervisors. The salesperson management style falls somewhere in between. Thus, consultant-type managers are the most popular; but be careful. The trick is to ask others for their opinion and then ignore it. Supervisors who follow the opinions of subordinates can be viewed by them as incompetent!

Can the same style work equally well in all settings? A participatory or consultative management style might fit a partner in a law firm, but how would it work with a company of Marines? The question of whether one management style can fit all has been researched. Proponents of a single best management style include Blake and Mouton (1982), with their concept of the managerial grid. Blake and Mouton argue that there are two primary variables of leadership—people and production. They scale both of these factors from one to nine, so that number one indicates the manager with the least measurable amount of leadership or production orientation, and number nine indicates the manager with the most measurable amount of production or people orientation. Thus, we have two possible management style extremes (from one to nine) on two variables (production and people motivation).

The numbers 9,1 on the managerial grid describe a leader with a task-oriented style and no concern for people—a slave driver. The coordinates 1,9 depict a leader who has maximum concern for the welfare of people but is unconcerned about getting the job done—a social director. Blake and Mouton call the designation 1,1 an impoverished style, depicting a leader concerned about neither tasks nor people. "Middle of the roader" is the label given to the 5,5 style, and the designation 9,9 is called participatory management (although this designation does not appear especially apt). Blake and Mouton argue that the 9,9 style is the optimum—the single best style for ensuring productivity. It is a high-task, high-consideration approach.

There is a body of experimental literature that supports the validity of the structure-consideration approach to managing people. Its origins lie in the work of Fiedler (1967). Fiedler's theory of leadership effectiveness says that there are two extremes of leadership style. One extreme is a total task orientation; the other extreme is a relationship, or consideration, orientation. Fiedler did not believe that the high-task, high-relationship style per se was the best single style. Instead, he maintained that high-task leaders function best in extremely favorable or extremely unfavorable situations. High-relationship leaders get the best results in situations of intermediate favorability.

Increased consideration does correlate with increased productivity, according to some studies (Vroom, 1964). Consideration is defined as an act of the manager intended to develop mutual trust, respect for ideas, and sensitivity to feelings. Fiedler was able to show that consideration was positively correlated with productivity when situations were only moderately difficult. Moderately difficult situations are the ones that we encounter most of the time. Consideration and group productivity were negatively correlated, however, when the situation was either very unfavorable or very favorable. When conditions are very unfavorable, the best approach seems to be to emphasize the accomplishment of end results at all costs. The leader does not have either the time or the resources to worry about people's feelings. When the environment is highly favorable, perhaps the environment itself provides support and nurturance (consideration), and a simple focus on getting the job done is the best approach.

Most of us work the middle ground. In the middle ground, where the environment is somewhat unfavorable and people are somewhat uncomfortable, *managing both the job to be done and the feelings of the people is the approach that will ensure the highest productivity.* The more lenient your managerial style, the better your employees will feel (Johnson, 1974); but if you have to err either by oversupervising or by undersupervising, then it is better to supervise too much than not to supervise at all (Patchen, 1962). By oversupervising, you will get more productivity over the short term, while over the long term you will create poor morale.

In summary, the research on managerial style indicates that style is related to productivity. The worst style is to act like a boss, telling people what to do. The best style is to act like a consultant and ask people for their opinions, without paying too much attention to their opinions. An acceptable but less effective style is to sell your decisions. In weighing the merits of structure versus consideration, structure wins as the best technique for ensuring productivity. The style of a productive manager includes setting goals and objectives, defining the work to be done, holding specific people responsible, setting deadlines, and providing feedback about how the work is progressing. As a manager, if you do not provide some structure, you cannot expect much productivity, but you also need some consideration if you want your employees to be happy. As we will see later, satisfied employees are not necessarily more productive employees, but satisfied employees are cheaper in the long run, because you do not have to keep replacing them. To make people happy and maintain morale, you need to show some consideration. Blake and Mouton are right in arguing that high structure–high consideration is the most effective management style, but if you can do only one thing as a manager, then provide structure.

Why Managers Fail

If you can succeed by providing structure and consideration, how can you fail? Some managers fail because they are incapable of structuring the work of the people who report to them. They are poor planners and poor organizers. Others fail because of excessive turnover due to their inability to show consideration for people. Still others fail as managers because they lack intelligence, strong personalities, or the will to manage. Gaudet and Carli (1957) offer two broad explanations of why managers fail. The first reason concerns knowledge factors—lack of knowledge of the technologies, concepts, vocabulary, and techniques of any number of bodies of knowledge important for success as managers. In actuality, few managers really fail from lack of knowledge because, in business, technical knowledge is so easy to acquire; business is not physics or neurosurgery, but you can fail because you lack knowledge of how to manage. Nevertheless, most managers fail because of personality factors. These factors include (but are not limited to) inability to delegate, poor judgment, and abrasive personality. Managers fail, too, from timidity and laziness, from lack of the sustained drive necessary for achievement, and because they are too weak to withstand the continual pressure of responsibility. Mainly, managers succeed or fail because of personality factors.

Summary

This chapter reviews what makes managers effective. Understanding what makes managers effective requires, first, that we define what we mean by *manager* and, second, that we agree at least generally about what a manager does. From the hundreds of available definitions of *manager,* a practical and useful definition is "anyone who is directly responsible for getting work done through others." This definition includes first-level supervisors as well as chief executive officers. The managerial literature tells us that despite functional specialty, level in the organizational structure, or cultural context, managers are more alike than different. The primary job factor that makes someone a manager is the need to plan, organize, and control the work of other people. Exhausive lists of the critical incidents in a manager's job can run to over 3,000 incidents, but the essence of them is that the effective manager successfully produces work through guiding other people.

Successful managers are brighter than their followers, have stronger personalities, and are more motivated to lead and be successful. Elite managers—individuals who have reached the top of their organizations—have intense, narrow interests and a strong drive to achieve. High-achieving managers decide early in their careers what they want to do and pursue it maniacally. They sweep others along toward the goal, refusing to be stopped by criticism, lack of support, or temporary failure. The highly successful manager is no more able than more mediocre colleagues, but is definitely more motivated and has a higher set of self-expectations.

Managers have different styles, and at least four have been identified. The most successful style is the consultative style, followed by the one that emphasizes salesmanship. One style that does not work well is the authoritarian style of management. An effective manager structures the work to be done by identifying goals, distributing tasks, setting deadlines, and re-viewing results. The effective manager also shows consideration for people's opinions, feelings, and general well-being.

After years of research and thousands and thousands of articles about what makes a good manager, a fairly simple picture remains: A good manager is a cut above the worker in brains, personality, and ambition. The productive manager structures the work and shows concern for the welfare of the people who must do the work. That is the essence of an effective manager.

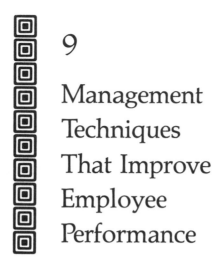

9

Management Techniques That Improve Employee Performance

In the last chapter, we looked at the core characteristics of effective managers. In this chapter, we look at specific managerial techniques that help make people productive.

The task of effective managers is to structure the work of those who report to them and to be considerate of their welfare. Structuring managers convert organizational objectives into action plans, set measures of achievement, and establish timetables. Considerate managers do three things well: They are warm, sympathetic, and friendly to subordinates and concerned about their feelings and needs; they are sensitive to individual differences and supportive of career development efforts; and they encourage participation by employees in decisions that affect them.

As Americans, we may overemphasize the importance of various managerial techniques in making people productive. We have a tendency to assume that what the manager does is more important than who the employee is: "Better management practice at all levels in the organization is the method increasingly accepted as the single best way to improve productivity" (Ross,

1977, p. ix). Is this constant search for magic management techniques justified? Let us see.

Goal Setting

In initiating structure, management must set goals (Nash, 1983). An organization without a set of goals is a ship sailing without a destination. The concept of productivity includes the assumption of goals. Productivity means goal-directed behavior, a drive to improve output.

What has research found about goal setting? Simplifying and summarizing, we can say that *any goal is better than no goal, quantitative goals are better than subjective goals, hard goals are better than easy goals, and shared and communicated goals are better than unilateral goals.*

Yukl and Latham (1978) published data showing that difficult goals lead to higher performance than easy goals. Organizations and individuals who perform well set difficult goals, have high needs to achieve, and are confident and have strong self-esteem. Latham, Steele, and Saari (1982), using college students at the University of Washington as subjects, found that students who were assigned hard goals had higher levels of performance than students who were assigned lower goals. Thus, the rule is "harder is better."

In addition to improving productivity, setting goals also makes people feel better. Ivancevich (1977) found that goal setting has a positive impact on employees' morale. For upper and top management, or for a well-educated work force, merely setting a tough goal is a valuable tool for ensuring high levels of productivity. Goal clarity and goal feedback are more important for improving the performance of the less educated (Ivancevich and McMahon, 1977). For the average employee, the most important thing in goal setting is for managers to be crystal clear about the goal to be achieved and to provide frequent specific feedback about progress toward the goals. Goal setting works best in companies where the culture emphasizes achievement. It is least effective in companies where the culture emphasizes power. In environments where the main cultural value is affiliation, its effects are intermediate (Srinivas and Long, 1975-1976).

Goal setting can even work in companies with unions. Union acceptance of the program makes the difference between successful and unsuccessful goal-setting experiences. If the union accepts specific goals, the result can be a significant increase in productivity. If the union withdraws its support of the goals, the result can be a strike (Latham and Saari, 1982).

Unions are an example of the power that employee groups can have over the achievement of goals. If a company wants to achieve an immediate increase in productivity, increasing pressure on the group will work over the short term, but eventually it will lead to lower job satisfaction and lower group performance (Bridgewater, 1983). Blake and Mouton (1981) believe that there exists a sociology of work groups and group norms. They argue that the thinking of people in small groups converges around norms. These norms exert a pressure on group members to conform. Blake and Mouton have a theory about the sociodynamics of work-group productivity. These are the basic tenets of their theory: (1) When people get together and discuss thoughts, feelings, and attitudes, their viewpoints tend to converge. (2) Once convergence occurs, it takes on the character of a norm (a rule, standard, model, or average). (3) Group members who deviate from the norm cause others in the group to exert pressure to bring the deviants back into line. (4) A group member who persists in deviation from the norm runs the risk of isolation and rejection. (5) Norms control the group and the individuals in it, even if the norms are outmoded, inefficient, or wrong.

Norms are important to productivity. To improve group productivity, managers must raise group norms. How is this done? For Blake and Mouton, the answer is participatory management: "The way to change norms is to involve those whose behavior is regulated by them in studying what the existing norms are and exploring alternatives that might serve corporate objectives better . . . the key is to involve those who are controlled by a norm to change the norm itself" (1981, p. 75). If managers want to use participatory goal-setting techniques to raise group productivity norms, how should they proceed? Blake and Mouton suggest the ten steps shown in Exhibit 1.

Exhibit 1. Blake and Mouton's Guidelines
for Setting Higher Productivity Norms.

---

1. Have everyone participate.
2. Make the leader the person responsible for the ultimate decision.
3. State the problem.
4. Ask what can be done about it.
5. Provide facts about the situation.
6. Let people ventilate.
7. Identify reasons for the problem.
8. Make implicit agreements explicit.
9. Set new norms.
10. Keep following up on the new norms.

Source: Adapted from Blake and Mouton, 1981.

Participatory Management

Blake and Mouton and numerous others recommend participatory management as the preferred management technique. I, too (Nash, 1983), have advocated participatory management. How useful is it, and why does it work?

Proponents of participatory management argue that the best way to improve productivity is through shared goals of managers and employees (Bain, 1982). Why is this so? Maier (1952) reasons that the effectivenesses of a decision is a product of the quality of the decision and the acceptance of the decision. He provides a formula for determining the importance of participation and acceptance. The formula reads $ED = Q \times A$. Here, ED = an effective decision, Q = the quality of the decision, and A = the acceptance of the decision. According to Maier, two types of decisions can be made. A Type One decision is where A is greater than Q, meaning acceptance is more important than quality. The Type Two decision is where Q is greater than A, meaning quality is more important than acceptance. According to Maier, decision acceptance is more important than quality 75 percent of the time. The best way to ensure acceptance of a decision is through participation. Participation does not have much of an effect on the quality of a decision, but it has an enormous effect on whether people accept the decision and will implement it. Participation is important because it increases the probability of achieving a goal if it must be accomplished through others.

Lehrer (1983) suggests that if managers want to use participatory techniques, they must be sure certain prerequisites exist in their organizations. Lehrer lists these as desire, opportunity, ability, clear objectives, management support, training, follow-up, staff help, and continuation of support. Kanter (1982) believes that employee participation works best when managers start with a small local issue, allow the group to decide what to discuss and what to avoid, assign tasks and define boundaries, and set time limits, accountabilities, and reporting relationships.

Top management generally does not favor participatory techniques (Buchholz, 1978), and I see this regularly in my consulting practice, too. Beyond their unwillingness to share decision-making power, top managers believe (and are correct in their belief) that a participatory approach is time-consuming and allows some managers to avoid taking responsibility or action. Top managers resist employee participation in the decision-making process because they fear being stuck with decisions they do not like. To limit or shape employee involvement, management may resort to withholding information or selectively communicating information (Van der Bruggen and den Hertog, 1976). Management is more likely to tolerate or encourage employee participation in decision making if the decisions are to be implemented on a trial basis (Rosen and Jerdee, 1978).

I did a consulting assignment for a large electronics company in which my mandate was to serve as an unofficial arbitrator between management and the union on matters of job evaluation and job rank. I urged a participatory approach to develop recommendations. The company was willing to allow the union to have a voice in these decisions only if management could reserve the right to override union viewpoints with which the company did not agree. The irony in this assignment was that while management refused to allow me to involve the union in developing my recommendations, it then ignored my recommendations and capitulated completely to union demands.

Management's fears about employee participation may be unwarranted. More often than not, workers are not interested in sharing responsibility for decisions about corporate strategy, investment and divestment, and other such weighty matters. At Verbatim, an electronics company in Sunnyvale, California, 1,200 office workers were asked what kinds of decisions they wanted to participate in. They emphasized three things: to help choose new office equipment, to attend sales presentations by vendors, and to pass ideas along via a suggestion box. These are hardly world-shaking matters.

Putting aside the potential risk, what are the benefits of participatory management? They are said to include better attitudes, better morale, increased job satisfaction, and less resistance to change. Participation makes people feel better: "The process of participation in solving work problems has been studied by many individuals, from many points of view. In general, research studies confirm the common-sense view that people, both individuals and groups, are much more supportive of effectively implementing decisions which they helped to shape than decisions which are supplied to them" (Lehrer, 1983, p. 290). Beyond worker satisfaction, participation is said to improve productivity and to lower costs: "Experience has shown that involvement in solving one's own work problem not only enhances individual productivity but produces improved quality of work life as well" (Lehrer, 1983, p. 2).

There is some evidence that participation improves productivity, but it is not overwhelming. Ivancevich (1977) found that participation in goal setting led to better performance and more satisfaction than did mere instructions to "do your best." Performance improvements began to dissipate after six to nine months, but satisfaction resulting from participation remained.

This increase in satisfaction from participation has been documented often by research. Participation produces improvements in perceived involvement, feedback, and attitude (Taylor and Zayacki, 1978). In one illustrative experiment, Seeborg (1978) conducted a job redesign study of two groups. Identical changes were made in job design in both groups. In one group, employees participated; in the other, they did not. The identical changes in job design were perceived to be better changes by employees who participated in the redesign. The evidence is quite clear that satisfaction increases with participatory management. These findings exist even across cultures. In Japan, managers trained in participatory management are more effective than untrained managers are (Misumi and Fujita, 1982).

Most managers, even advocates of participatory management, recognize the tool for what it is—a technique to increase satisfaction. They do not see worker participation as a means of improving the quality of work; they see it as a means of increasing morale, improving communications, and increasing acceptance (Dickson, 1982).

All management techniques, even good ones, will eventually be criticized if they are around long enough. Participatory management is no exception. Some critics see participation as manipulation, an indirect way of pressuring employees to produce more. Others are afraid workers may improve themselves out of a job. Still others ask what is in it for the worker or criticize management for ignoring employees' recommendations and proposals. When programs are first started, participatory management can stimulate skepticism and suspicion. Programs are easier to begin than to sustain. They often suffer from poor follow-up (Grunwald and Bernthal, 1983).

More damaging than ideological or methodological criticisms are published research findings that say participatory management does not work. Latham and Marshall (1982) used a government agency to test the impact of participatory goal setting. They found that participation did not help: There was no difference in degree of performance between those who set their own goals and those who set them with managers. There was no difference in actual performance between those assigned goals, those who set goals for themselves, or those who set goals in participation with management. Actually, the assigned group did somewhat better. Latham, Steele, and Saari (1982) also found that participatively setting goals did not result in higher performance than just assigning goals of equal difficulty.

Long (1981) is another researcher who is unimpressed

with the purported benefits of employee participation. Long studied an electronics company that introduced numerous formal participatory mechanisms, including employee representation on the board of directors, employee councils, and participatory ownership. Little change was found in perceived worker participation at the decision level, desire for worker influence, and distribution of influence in the organization. Employee ownership and increased participation did not result in any increase in motivation, general satisfaction, or feelings of trust. Long's results cast doubt on the value of participation, even for improving employee satisfaction. After surveying the literature, Toscano (1983) also concludes that the research evidence does not support claims that employee ownership enhances worker satisfaction or increases productivity.

The value of participatory management, once assumed, is now assailed. On the basis of the evidence accumulated so far, I also must conclude that most of the time, *participatory management probably does not improve productivity*. When it does improve productivity, the results are probably transitory. Most of the time, *participatory management probably does improve satisfaction*. If you are worried about employees understanding, accepting, and being satisfied with your goals and decisions, then use participatory techniques. If you are concerned mainly with the quality of decisions and your overall level of performance, then you can bypass the participatory step. Simply set tough goals, and tell your people to get to it.

Quality Circles

If employee participation in making a decision does not improve the quality of that decision, will employee participation in quality circles improve the quality of the product? Unfortunately, probably not.

Real research evidence in support of quality circles is shaky. The popularity of quality circles is derived from American industry's off-again, on-again admiration for Japanese management practices. The benefits of quality circles are said to include price reduction, team building, problem solving, improved communications, better attitudes, increased job satisfaction, and self-development. Nevertheless, there is little empirical research showing that quality circles work. Companies that use it say it is of questionable value. Quality circles are a form of participatory management. They may improve employees' sense of satisfaction, but they do not necessarily improve the company's bottom line.

Work Simplification

In 300 B.C., the unknown author of *Ecclesiastes* wrote that there is nothing new under the sun. Two thousand years later, Goethe reminded us that everything has been said before and that the trick is to remember what was said. Work simplification is an example of what they meant. Work simplification is a management technique that emerges from time to time under different names. It is now receiving renewed interest, but it is a concept that goes back to at least the early 1900s. It is Taylorism revisited. It has been called job simplification, methods research, administrative engineering, and other names, and it is a mixture of industrial engineering and participatory management. The term *participatory management* has a human resources ring to it. The term *work simplification* has more of the sound of industrial engineering: "For simplicity we will use the designation *work simplification* for the entire range of participative approaches, for participational work simplification was the earliest formalized approach to meaningful participation" (Lehrer, 1983, p. 2).

As a management technique, work simplification predates World War II and is a direct descendant of the industrial managerial techniques first introduced by Frederick Taylor (1911). In 1954, Sears Roebuck surveyed eighty-five other companies to see if they had work simplification programs, and 88 percent did, some of them already fifteen years old (Lehrer, 1983). The one major difference between work simplification and classical industrial engineering is participation: "A combination of participational work simplification and staff industrial engineering assistance is an extremely powerful tool" (p. 298).

Work simplification takes a nuts-and-bolts, paper-and-pencil approach to improving productivity. It does not trouble itself much with consideration of people's feelings. Its goal is to make the work of the organization more efficient. The goals of a typical work simplification program include reducing the number of steps in the task, arranging the steps in the best order, making the steps economical, reducing the number of handlings, combining steps, and shortening moves. Work simplification aims to lower labor hours, thereby increasing productivity. Work simplification can result in real cost savings. For example, in Buena Park, a city of 63,000 in Orange County, California, a work simplification program generated fifty-seven different suggestions, resulting in savings of one million dollars.

Time Management

Time management is a form of work simplification. Its goal is to get more done in less time. It is a direct frontal assault on productivity. It is structure, not consideration. For example, Standard Oil of Ohio teaches a three-way approach to time management, even at the hourly level. First, each department has both quiet time, for undisturbed work, and contact time, for meetings and phone calls. Second, employees are taught to use time management schedules for organizing daily, weekly, monthly, and annual plans. Third, each employee makes a daily "do" list, with high and low priorities.

One way you can have more time is to figure out how you waste it. Here are the reputed top ten time wasters for management: people interruptions, telephone interruptions, doing work others can do, meetings, a cluttered desk, "fire-fighting," doing unimportant things, procrastination, waiting for others, and the lack of objectives, priorities, and deadlines. The top time wasters for sales representatives are similar: long lunches and coffee breaks, unproductive phone calls, failure to delegate, time lost waiting or because of a poor schedule, long personal discussions, "fading" in the afternoon, and spending too much time on a project.

Exhibits 2 and 3 list timesavers, as recommended by ex-

Exhibit 2. Ten Favorite Timesavers.

1. Delegate.
2. Plan your work the night before.
3. Set priorities and deadlines.
4. Use the 80/20 rule: Find the 20 percent of your total task that gives you 80 percent of your results.
5. Mechanize recurring operations.
6. Stay on time.
7. Do unpleasant things first.
8. Work in private, where you cannot be reached.
9. Do not do everything but only important things.
10. Do it now.

Exhibit 3. More Time Tips.

1.	Think it through before you start.	13.	Make a time table and stick to it.
2.	Keep a time diary.	14.	Use a secretary.
3.	Keep communications brief.	15.	Impose time estimates and stick to them.
4.	Say no.		
5.	Group tasks that are alike.	16.	Do difficult jobs during prime time.
6.	Set deadlines.	17.	Do important things first.
7.	Focus on results.	18.	Write it down, then check it off.
8.	Limit interruptions.		
9.	Neglect the unimportant.	19.	Use waiting and travel time.
10.	Do one thing at a time.	20.	Use small time blocks as well as big time blocks.
11.	Finish what you start.		
12.	Handle any piece of paper once.	21.	Write less and phone less.
		22.	Visit selectively.

perts in the field. Time management is a structure technique and nicely complements a goal-setting program.

Employee Assistance Programs

So far in this chapter, we have reviewed selected techniques that emphasize structured, task-oriented approaches to improving productivity. Among these are goal setting, work simplification, and time management. We have looked at two management techniques that combine structure and consideration: participatory management and quality circles. In this section, we look at a technique that involves pure consideration: employee assistance programs.

American industry is showing increased willingness to assist troubled employees. A survey by the American Society for Personnel Administration (Manuso, 1983) found that employee counseling programs were popular with large companies. Of the 100 largest companies in the United States, 73 percent have career counseling programs, 71 percent provide assistance to employees with personal problems, 63 percent offer retirement counseling programs, 63 percent maintain alcohol and drug abuse programs, and 60 percent offer outplacement assistance.

Research has not shown conclusively whether or not these programs are effective. Only 15 percent of the companies using them attempt to evaluate their effectiveness in any way. Nevertheless, more companies are adopting these programs. Another survey of 450 large companies, conducted in 1983 (Mancuso, 1983), found that 33 percent had employee assistance programs, another 13 percent were developing them, and 18 percent were willing to offer assistance on an as-needed basis. Thus, about two thirds of all large companies use management techniques that involve pure consideration. They assume that a cared-for employee is a productive employee. Of these employee assistance programs, 40 percent are offered in-house, 45 percent are provided by outside agencies or consultants, and 13 percent offer combined sources of help. The four major employee assistance programs include treatment for alcohol and drug abuse, retirement counseling, career counseling, and outplacement assistance.

Do employee assistance programs improve productivity? I am not sure. The empirical evidence in support of pure consideration is scanty; research suggests that consideration is useful only when mixed with structure (Greene, 1975). Even leaders who show both high structure and high consideration are not necessarily more effective than other leaders (Nystrom, 1978). A good management style can show a moderate mix of each (Boeyens and de Jager, 1982; Glogow, 1979). In my own experience as a manager, I found initiating structure to be much more effective in achieving high levels of performance than showing consideration was. I think showing consideration may have been of some value in controlling turnover, but I am not certain of this.

Managers, here is my homily: Give structure. Establish goals. Show some consideration. There lies the shortest route to improved productivity. And remember, the best way to show consideration is not necessarily through participation or employee assistance programs. The best way is through positive reinforcement, a technique of behavior modification.

Behavior Modification

The use of behavior modification to induce more productivity is not well known outside a small circle of advocates. One survey (Hamner and Hamner, 1976) turned up only ten companies that used behavior modification techniques in any kind of systemic or intentional way. All reported positive results.

Managers who use positive reinforcement improve performance and subordinate satisfaction, while managers who punish subordinate behavior get mixed results. The enormous animal-behavior modification literature is very clear in its recommendation to use positive rather than negative reinforcement. Reinforcement need not be an actual reward. Reinforcement can also be information, or feedback. Wikoff, Anderson, and Crowell (1982) introduced behavior modification in a factory. They used both feedback (verbal and visual reports of individual efficiency) and feedback plus praise as rewards. There was no difference in effectiveness between these two methods; both feedback and feedback plus praise were moderately successful in improving productivity: "Improving information [about performance] generally has more leverage for improving performance than any other strategem we might apply—including incentives" (Gilbert, 1978, p. 309).

Giving feedback is an effective management technique, a form of behavior modification. The best type of feedback to give is impersonal, highly specific, and directed at the individual (Pritchard, Montagno, and Moore, 1978). Feedback like this can result in a 25 percent increase in productivity, as measured by both quantity and quality. Positive reinforcement of employees increases productivity and decreases discipline problems (Crawford, Thomas, and Fink, 1980).

Behavior modification as a management technique is unexplored and controversial. It shows promise for improving productivity, but we may never know its full potential and power because of strong prejudice against its use (Miner, 1980).

Summary

This chapter has reviewed research on techniques that managers use to try to make people productive. Setting goals definitely improves productivity. To be effective, a goal need only be specific, difficult, and communicated. It is not critical whether goals are assigned, developed on one's own, or established in a participatory setting. There are individual differences in how people respond to goals. Well-educated people and top managers merely need to be told what the goals are. Less educated people and lower-level employees have more of a need to have the goals explained and to be given periodic feedback. Goal setting is a continuous process that requires the use of variety to avoid plateauing and burnout. *Of all the productivity techniques available to management, nothing has been found that is as consistently useful as setting tough goals.*

Research results are mixed about the efficacy of participatory management practices. Most of the time, participation in decision making and goal setting does improve employee acceptance and satisfaction, but participation does not improve quality and seems to have only a limited ability to improve productivity. As a management technique, the primary value of participation is to improve employee satisfaction.

Work simplification, a variant of the techniques first introduced by Frederick Taylor around the turn of the century, is a useful management technique that emphasizes structure and task. Work simplification seeks to eliminate and simplify work and to improve productivity by reducing labor input. Another effective task-oriented technique is time management. Since productivity is directly related to time, more effective use of time is a worthwhile technique that managers can apply, both to themselves and to their employees.

Techniques emphasizing consideration for employees are based on two assumptions: that a cared-for employee is a satisfied employee, and that a satisfied employee is a productive employee. There is not much empirical evidence to support this viewpoint, but employee assistance programs are common in large companies and increasing in other companies.

In general, research indicates that management techniques emphasizing structure improve productivity, while techniques emphasizing consideration improve satisfaction. One technique for effectively combining consideration and structure is behavior modification. A small but generally positive body of literature suggests that behavior modification works, but its use as a management technique is unlikely to spread wide.

With this overview of structure and consideration as general management techniques, we are now ready to consider in depth two specific techniques that bear on productivity. The first of these is performance appraisal (Chapter Ten). The second is compensation (Chapter Eleven).

10

Setting Goals and Appraising Performance for Maximum Productivity

Let us summarize quickly the ground covered so far. The intention of this book is to provide managers with guidelines on how to make people productive throughout the employment cycle. The goal of this book is to present the highlights of psychological research literature on productivity throughout the employment cycle, from recruiting through separation. Exhaustive reviews of the literature are of no use to managers, but neither are nostrums or one-minute solutions. My goal has been and remains to selectively present those empirical findings of psychologists that are of practical use to managers.

In the first chapters, I established what productivity is and why it is a problem for American organizations. Then I showed how to evaluate prospective employees, first through interviews and résumés. Next, I told how psychological testing identifies those differences in intelligence, personality, and interests that affect employees' achievement. I presented my own validity research on the psychological assessment of managers.

People are not interchangeable, like parts of a machine.

Because I believe that putting the right person in the right job is the foundation of productivity, I worked at length to explain the individual differences related to employee effectiveness.

After selection, the next step in the employment cycle typically is providing employees with some sort of training. This training can be simple orientation, or it can be an elaborately structured management development program. The unstated ethic in American industry is that the unproductive employee is untrained or unmotivated, not congenitally unsuited for the job. Therefore, American industry spends billions of dollars each year trying to teach people to do the work they were hired to do. American business may expect too much of training and too little of selection.

After selecting people and training people, the next step in the employment cycle is to motivate them to do their work. I summarized the literature on motivators and said that I was most impressed by expectancy theory and need achievement as means of understanding what really makes people work.

At this point in the employment cycle, the employee was already hired, trained, and motivated, and we turned him over to the managers. Together, we then looked at the characteristics that make managers effective, in much the same way that we looked at effectiveness in individual employees. Finally, in Chapter Nine we took a hypothetical manager with the potential to be a good manager and asked her to behave effectively. We did this by looking at the techniques managers can use to make people work harder and more efficiently. One such tool—a technique of known value in inducing productivity—is goal setting and performance appraisal. It is the subject of the present chapter.

Introduction

This chapter delves deeply into goal setting as a management technique, coupling it to performance appraisal. Effective managers provide structure for those who report to them, and goal setting is one way of providing that structure. Performance appraisal is logically another way of giving structure.

Performance appraisal is essentially a mechanism for telling employees how well they are progressing toward their goals. By setting goals, appraising performance, and providing feedback, a manager is providing the structure that research says is correlated with higher levels of productivity.

Productivity can be improved through setting goals and providing feedback. Pritchard (1981) tested the effects of feedback and goal setting on productivity. His results are concrete and unusually helpful. He found that goal setting and feedback did improve productivity, personal feedback was just as effective as impersonal feedback, absolute feedback was just as effective as comparative feedback, goal setting with feedback was more effective than feedback alone, poorer performers were helped more than better performers by the process of setting goals and providing feedback, and morale improved when goals were set and feedback was provided. Pritchard's work is exciting because of its practical implications: By setting goals and providing feedback, you are helping to improve productivity. You need not worry too much about whether the feedback you provide is personal or impersonal, whether it is individual or specific, or whether it compares one individual to another. The important thing is to set goals and provide feedback. The people who need it the most—the poor performers—will be most helped by it.

The same is true of performance appraisal. There are numerous books devoted to it (De Vries and others, 1981; Carroll and Schneier, 1982; Latham and Wexley, 1981). Latham and Wexley's book is devoted entirely to performance appraisal and productivity, with chapters on a review of the literature and on performance appraisal and the law. For my purposes here, I will draw primarily on two chapters from a book of my own (Nash, 1983).

As with goal setting, that performance appraisal be done is more important than the exact method used to appraise performance. Managers searching for the perfect performance appraisal system will find only frustration. The perfect system doesn't exist. Performance appraisal by managers will always be a combination of intuition and calculation (Thompson, 1982). The exact system used to appraise performance does not matter too much. Massey, Mullins, and Earles (1978) looked at the performance appraisals of 120 Air Force noncommissioned officers. After comparing three different rating systems with the criteria of successful performance, they concluded that all three performance appraisal systems—a trait-oriented system, a work-oriented system, and a task-oriented system—worked equally well. Even the advantages of objective performance appraisal systems over subjective systems have been questioned, and some researchers (Keeley, 1977) believe that under certain circumstances a subjective approach may be better than an objective one.

For the most part, however, the newer objective performance appraisal systems are to be preferred over the older, more subjective ones, and the trend is away from personality traits and toward job-based criteria (Bhatia, 1981). Other trends in performance appraisal include increased disclosure, subordinate participation, legislation, and litigation (Williams, Walker, and Fletcher, 1977).

Goal Setting

One of the fundamentals of performance psychology is that setting goals activates behavior. It increases performance by focusing the person's efforts on specific goals. Research has shown that setting hard goals results in better overall performance than setting easy goals or no goals at all (Atkinson and Feather, 1966).

A number of specific things are known about goal setting. The more educated the employee, the more it is that challenging goals are related to actual performance (Ivancevich and McMahon, 1977). For the less educated, performance improvement depends on goal clarity and goal feedback. Sophisticated people can be motivated simply by having goals set. Less sophisticated people need clear, specific feedback on their performance relative to their goals.

Corporations that extend goal setting below the management ranks should provide formal, detailed educational programs for rank-and-file employees. For upper-level managers, briefer and more general training in goal setting is sufficient. Educated employees are able to fill in for themselves the details of the goal-setting process. Less educated or less intelligent employees need to have these details spelled out for them.

Variation in Need to Achieve. Goal setting does not work equally well in all companies with all people. Performance is significantly related to two factors (Fineman, 1975). First is the overall need to achieve. The greater the need to be successful, the greater the success you will have with a goal-setting program. Second, performance is positively and significantly related to the perception of the work environment. High-achieving people believe their companies are populated by like-minded individuals with high needs to achieve.

Seasoned, self-confident executives do best with tough goals for which they have a sense of priority. Motivated, confident individuals with a high need to achieve prefer challenges of intermediate difficulty, where the odds of success are 50/50 (McClelland, 1961).

Less confident executives, motivated by fear of failure, prefer either very low-risk tasks or very high-risk tasks because the outcomes are more predictable. In low-risk tasks, the chances of failure are small, and the individual predicts success. In high-risk tasks, the chances of success are small, and the individual can predict failure, which can then be attributed solely to the difficulty of the undertaking.

Difficulty. A universal problem in goal setting is that top management wants to set more difficult goals than the rest of management does. Who is right in the conflict between the higher goals imposed by top management and the lower ones sought by middle management?

In psychological terms, top management is more correct. Campbell, Dunnette, Lawler and Weich (1970), after a review of the literature on goal setting and corporate achievement, state categorically: "Specific difficult goals are better than specific easy goals" (p. 375). If performance is the criterion of rightness, then it is better for goals to be a little too hard than a little too easy. The hard goals result in better performance.

Time. The difficulty of a goal depends partly on the time allotted to achieve it. Faster goals are harder than slower goals.

Parkinson's famous law, which states that the volume of work expands to fill the time available to do it, has been proved experimentally (Bryan and Locke, 1967). Organizations can improve their overall performance by truncating the time frames they give themselves for accomplishing their goals. When goals are set without time limits, the work drifts and picks up unnecessary volume as the speed decreases.

Supervision. Interactions between supervisors and employees affect goal attainment. By merely providing information on how actual achievement compares to the plan, supervisors can improve performance (Burke, 1970; Kim and Hamner, 1976). Employees are most satisfied when they feel that their superiors are honest with them about performance, and that they in turn can be open with their superiors. Goal setting coupled with adequate supervision is correlated with higher productivity (Umstot, Bell, and Mitchell, 1976). Goal setting without effective supervision is correlated with employee turnover (Ronen, 1978).

Having set goals, effective managers need to appraise how well employees perform against those goals. Performance appraisal is a skill necessary for effective management and improved productivity.

Performance Appraisal

Participation. The reviewing of actual performance is just as important as setting goals. Part of effective supervision is encouraging employees to participate in performance appraisal (Greller, 1975). Self-review performance appraisal has been found preferable by a majority of managers who have tried it (Basset and Meyer, 1968). Self-review generates less defensive behavior in the employee than a manager's review does. Subsequent employee performance is significantly less likely to be rated below expectations by the manager. Low-rated employees are especially likely to show improvement in performance after a self-review discussion. The elements of openness and trust create a sense of employee satisfaction. Therefore, let your employees participate fully in performance appraisals.

Some people are more liberal than their bosses are in evaluating themselves, but others are surprisingly tougher. Heneman (1974) found that self-ratings of performance, as compared to boss ratings, were less lenient, had a wider range of scores, and showed more halo errors.

The wise manager never criticizes employees for anything. Let employees be self-critical, and then agree with a more lenient interpretation of that self-criticism. People are much more sensitive to criticism than most managers realize. There is no such thing as constructive negative feedback. (Nash's Law says, "Never say nothing negative to nobody about nothing.")

Reliability of Ratings. Realize that your opinion of people is likely to change over time. Performance ratings over time are not very reliable (Bass, 1962). When performance appraisals are close together (conducted six months apart), then the correlation between merit ratings is a significant 62, but when performance ratings are infrequent (forty-two months apart), then the correlation is an insignificant 29. This means that given enough time, your superior's current opinion of you will change, and so will your appraisal of those who work for you. Individuals initially rated as excellent performers will be viewed as progressively more mediocre the longer they stay with the company. Those initially viewed as poor performers will be seen as improved, provided that they survive for about three and a half years. There are executives who change companies every three years, perhaps intuiting that after a few years of good reviews, it is best to move on before things start to sour. Given enough time, all positive reviews decline. After two to three years, once-bright stars begin to fall in the corporate firmament.

Validity of Ratings

One goal of this chapter is to help you as a manager be more effective when you evaluate performance, by making you more careful. Performance appraisal systems are imperfect, and even the best of them are knocked off caliber by extraneous inputs from you and your employees.

Kipnis, Schmidt, Price, and Stitt (1981) examined the relationship between leadership style (democratic, authoritarian, laissez-faire) and actual production performance. There was no significant relationship between actual performance and the leader's evaluation of that performance, but there was a significant relationship between the evaluator's management style and evaluations of performance. Democratic leaders saw employees as more internally motivated to work. The more leaders saw employees as internally motivated, the more likely they were to evaluate performance positively.

Objectivity in performance rating can be increased by getting the opinion of the appraisee's peers. Gilbert and Downey (1978) found that in Army Ranger Training, formal peer ratings had a higher correlation with final class standing than any other measure did. Peer ratings are not practical in most for-profit organizations. If you are concerned about the fairness of your performance appraisals, however, then use a participatory approach. Distortions in appraisal occur more when goals are unilaterally dictated than when they are mutually agreed upon (Dossett and Greenberg, 1981).

Effective managers set goals and appraise performance because they understand that these steps are crucial parts of providing structure, but it is a difficult, exasperating process, and most managers hate doing it. Performance appraisal is a nuisance because it is hard to measure performance for many jobs, and it is unpleasant to tell people that they are not doing well.

Even if they are careful, managers can interject their personal values into performance appraisal. While managers accept the necessity of performance appraisal as a factor in determining salary increases for subordinates, they also believe that non-performance criteria should be used to establish their own increases (Dyer, Schwab, and Theriault, 1976). Managers rank those subordinates highest who have values like their own (Senger, 1971). Managers rate themselves higher than they are rated by their superiors (White, 1973). Older workers receive lower performance appraisals than younger workers, and blacks receive higher performance evaluations than whites. When blacks are given feedback about their performance appraisals, they receive higher performance ratings. When whites are given feedback about their performance appraisals, they receive lower ratings (Cleveland and Landy, 1981). Ivancevich (1977) reports a disturbing finding, which he calls "The Contrast Effect": In an organizational unit, the greater the percentage of actually unsatisfactory performers, the more favorable the superiors' performance ratings.

Employees have their own biases in the performance appraisal process. The lower you are in the organization, the more likely you are to feel dissatisfied with your supervisor's performance appraisal behavior and with the rating you are given (Burke, Deszca, and Weitzel, 1982). As an employee you will rate yourself more leniently than your superiors or your peers will (Holzbach, 1979). Employee self-ratings suffer from strong halo effects. It is harder to fool your peers, and peer ratings are especially valid in military and paramilitary organizations. Among police officers, peer rankings correlate highly with superior ratings, number of awards and commendations, and lack of on-the-job injuries (Love, 1983).

Employee Perceptions. Managers should expect that employees will not agree with their actual performance ratings. This is why performance appraisal is not fun. I have found overwhelmingly that managers hate to do performance appraisals and do them only because they must. Different perceptions about performance are a major source of conflict in performance appraisal. Conflict can be reduced but not eliminated by using quantitative goals as the basis for judging performance.

Managers who want to be seen as fair and accurate should evaluate performance frequently. They should be specific about what needs to be done to eliminate weaknesses. They should have firsthand knowledge of the subordinate's job duties and of his performance as measured against them. All these things have been found through research to be correlated with employee satisfaction (Landy, Barnes, and Murphy, 1978). Employees feel better about their appraisals when they have a chance to state their side of the issues, when the factors on which they are evaluated are job-relevant, and when objectives and plans are discussed with them (Dipboye and de Pontbriand, 1981).

Employees who leave organizations are not necessarily any worse or better performers than those who stay, but employees who are intelligent and also do not get along with their superiors are more likely to get negative performance ratings if they tend to be among the smarter employees. If there is harmony between the employer and the employee, then intelligence is unrelated to the performance rating. A personality clash between a smart, good employee and a less smart boss usually means that the good employee leaves.

Other factors affect performance appraisal. People with high anxiety perform less well than those with low anxiety (Srivastava and Krishna, 1980). Even looks make a difference. The more physically attractive you are, the more likely you are to get a good performance rating (Ross, 1981). High performers are judged competent regardless of their age, but if you are a poor performer, the older you get, the more likely you are to be subjected to pressure to retire. This is true regardless of the type of performance appraisal format used: trait scales, behaviorally anchored rating scales, or management by objectives (Rosen, Jerdee, and Lynn, 1981).

Changing Behavior. In surveys I have done, almost all managers say they appraise performance because they must, not because they believe it makes any difference in performance, but implicit in the conduct of a performance appraisal is the assumption that behavior can be changed by the process; and, indeed, it can. Pritchard, Montagno, and Moore (1978) found a 26 percent increase in quantity and quality when appraisal feedback to employees was individualized, impersonal, and highly specific. It did not matter whether this feedback was given in public or in private. The lesson to be learned here is this: To effect behavioral change through performance appraisal, be concrete and unemotional. Communicate exactly the specific behavior you want. Give negative feedback first, then positive feedback.

It is natural (Mitchell and Wood, 1980) to want to punish poor performance when the cause is believed to be within the person (internal attribution) or when the consequences of the performance are serious. Although the inclination to punish is understandable, extensive research in the psychology of learning forces us to conclude that negative reinforcement (punishment) is not an effective means of extinguishing unproductive performance. The correct thing to do with employees who are your poorest performers is to reward the desired behavior when it occurs (Crawford, Thomas, and Fink, 1980). If repeated attempts to do this fail to bring about the desired results, terminate the employee.

Performance Appraisal Techniques. In a survey by *Fortune* magazine of its 500 largest corporations, about 80 percent reported using formal appraisal for counseling, training, promoting, and motivating employees and for deciding whom to keep. The long-term trend is to evaluate the achievement of specific goals instead of individual traits. Another trend is more litigation over performance appraisal and its consequences (Cascio and Bernardin, 1981). It would be reassuring if using one particular method of appraisal would clearly indemnify the employer; unfortunately, although some systems are better than others, none is foolproof.

Although there are many types of performance appraisal techniques (Nash, 1983), the one I favor is goal setting. Goal setting consists of four basic steps: establishing organizational goals, establishing unit goals, securing individual commitment to these goals, and reviewing actual performance.

Despite the success of goal setting, it is far from being a universally accepted management technique. Some still consider it a fad; others see it as manipulation. For every ten companies that try formal management by objectives—a particular version of goal setting—five discontinue its use. The program becomes burdensome, boring, or frustrating. Goals are set too high and people fail, or else goals are set correctly the first year but then are left unchanged and become a problem in subsequent years.

My clients all tell me the toughest thing in goal setting is deciding how hard to make their goals. I remind them that the very act of setting goals improves results (Yukl and Latham, 1978), and so any level of scale will help. There is a natural inclination among top managers to set goals high, since high achievers set higher goals (McClelland, 1961). Goal theory postulates—and research has confirmed—that harder goals lead to higher performance than easier goals do (Matsui, Okada, and Mizuguchi, 1981).

Even though it is a good idea to set hard goals, it is also wise to set them realistically. Satisfaction is greatest when you achieve the goal level you expect (Locke, 1967). You can achieve admirably and still feel like a failure because you fell short of your goal. For example, in the 1984 Olympics in Los Angeles, a U.S. swimmer was criticized in the newspapers for acting depressed when he won a gold medal but failed to set a world record. To the world he was a winner, but in his own eyes he was a failure, because his goal was not the medal but the record.

Summary

Goal setting and performance appraisal are effective techniques for making people productive because they combine both the structure and consideration functions of effective management. Setting goals and appraising performance are difficult and unpleasant tasks because of the inherent potential for conflict, but perhaps no other technique is so directly related to organizational effectiveness as establishing and communicating the goals of the organization, parceling them out to individuals, and keeping track of which employees are doing their share.

Individuals vary in their needs to achieve and in their responsiveness to goal setting and performance appraisal. It is hard to know exactly how difficult to make goals, but tough goals result in greater productivity than easy goals do. Whether or not employees participate in the goal-setting process depends on the preferences of employees as well as on those of managers. Well-educated people, and those at the top of the organization, can merely be told the goals for which they are accountable. People lower in the organization, and the less educated, require considerable communication, clarification, and participation in order for the manager to be sure that they understand and accept their goals.

No perfect performance appraisal system exists, nor are

we likely to invent one. Any performance appraisal system has problems with reliability, validity, and the value systems of appraisers and appraisees alike. All that managers can do is to be aware of the more obvious pitfalls and take steps to avoid them.

While most managers appraise performance only because they are told to, the objective of performance appraisal should be to modify behavior. Behavior modification requires that managers provide employees with feedback about the employees' performance. Behavior will not change unless feedback is provided and the desired behavior is reinforced. The best way to change behavior is to provide information about the desired behavior and the way in which current behavior deviates from it. You cannot be too careful or too tactful in communicating negative information.

Companies without performance appraisal programs or with trait-oriented programs should establish a goal setting-based performance appraisal program. These companies can expect to encounter numerous problems in setting up and maintaining such programs, yet there is little alternative. Goal setting and performance appraisal are indispensable tools in making people productive.

11

Designing
Compensation
Strategies
to Boost
Performance

In Chapter Nine I sidestepped the subject of compensation because its importance requires that it be treated at least at chapter length. Prior to World War II, a chapter on compensation in a book on improving productivity would have surprised no one, but given the influence of the human potential movement on management psychologists, to suggest that people work for money has been considered, if not crass, at least scientifically naive. Everyone knew that people worked, not for money, but for self-fulfillment. By 1975, the pendulum had stopped moving to the left and had started to swing right again. Compensation as a management tool had regained respectability. A computer search of the last decade's psychological literature on the subject found 500 articles, enough material for a book of its own.

The first steps in utilizing compensation as a tool for productivity are to structure jobs and then to structure pay. Accordingly, this chapter will look first at job analysis and job evaluation, the foundation of any compensation system. Next, we will touch on some of the research on pay satisfaction, the factors correlated with being content with one's pay. At the core of the dialogue about pay and satisfaction is the concept of equity—perceptions of fairness about one's own pay relative to the pay of others. According to equity theory, perceptions of equity or inequity cause people to be more or less productive. Equity theory postulates that people behave more productively when they believe that their pay is related to their performance. We will look at two alternative ways of trying to meet concerns about equity: salary and incentive pay. The latter is a technique I believe to be especially effective in improving productivity. Equitable compensation programs are of little value unless employees believe they are equitable, and so we will turn finally to the issues of communicating compensation.

Background

Frederick Taylor, the father of modern management techniques, believed that money was a prime motivator of people's work efforts. His opinions prevailed from around the turn of the century until World War II. In the late 1930s, 75 percent of industrial companies made heavy use of incentives. By 1950, Herzberg, Maslow, and others began to argue that money did not matter so much as intrinsic and higher-order factors in explaining why people work. American productivity began its decline coincident with the decline in the belief that compensation was a motivator (Shapiro, 1978). The belief of academicians and personnel opinion makers has been that money is important, but only selectively so. Nonfinancial factors—especially self-esteem, affiliation, self-actualization, and the like—are really the reasons why people rise early each day, travel miles through congested traffic, and spend eight hours typing letters, cleaning floors, and working on assembly lines. The human potential movement theorists believed that for the great bulk of American workers, money was a matter of indifference, that workers could be induced to be more productive by enriching their jobs and providing them with opportunities to self-actualize.

More often than not, theorists who believe that people do not work for money are academicians whose own value systems or whose organizations' mores say that money is not that important. Writers more removed from the ivory tower have a different view: "Greed is more effective in promoting efficiency than power" (Gilbert, 1978, p. 321); "All the stereotype pep talks and management platitudes . . . are not going to stimulate much adrenaline in the veins of a factory worker who's worried about where next month's car payment is coming from" (Patton, 1982, p. 38); "In the long run, greed beats lust" (Crystal, 1984).

With more research, there is evidence of a renewed realization that money matters. For example, Hines (1975) conducted a review of the literature on money and motivation and found that money is important when it comes to achieving predicted levels of performance, money is only selectively useful for gaining improved levels of performance, money loses its incentive value and becomes a habit, and money should be varied and used imaginatively so that it retains its motivational value. Hitt and Morgan (1977) concluded that as far as productivity is concerned, money is the most important dimension of six organizational practices: adaptability, planning, work flow coordination, consistency, decision delay, and information distortion and suppression. Feldman and Arnold (1978) asked American and Canadian graduate students what were the most important factors they considered in choosing a job. Compensation ranked first.

Structuring Jobs

Whether money ranks first in importance, as some researchers now think, or whether it ranks only fifth or sixth in importance, as Herzberg and Maslow believed, properly structuring compensation programs will improve productivity. The first step in that structuring is to document job content and rank-order job importance. Managers need complete, accurate, and up-to-date job descriptions for their people. These descriptions can be written by personnel specialists, by supervisors, or by employees themselves. The practice I prefer is to have employees fill out job description questionnaires, which are then reviewed by supervisors. The format of the position is not crucial for purposes of job ranking. As long as the description contains the essentials of the job, most position-description formats will do. In 1982, researchers manipulated job descriptions, making them more or less interesting and providing more or less information. There was no difference in the final ranking of the jobs after job evaluation, regardless of the description. You can call a janitor an environmental services aide, but you usually will not fool a job evaluator.

Once jobs have been analyzed and described, they need to be ranked and matched to benchmark jobs in surveys. Through this method, management can ascertain whether or not its salaries are competitive. Perceptions of pay equity are based on employees' beliefs about how their salaries compare to salaries at other companies. These perceptions are not always accurate. Management, through salary surveys, should know the facts. Just as it does not really matter much which format of job description is used, it is also largely irrelevant what method of job evaluation is used to rank and price jobs. Snelgar (1983) evaluated jobs, using a number of different job evaluation technologies. The correlation coefficient between the different techniques ranged from .75 to .99, with an average correlation of .9. Snelgar concluded that there is a high degree of agreement among job evaluation methods, irrespective of job type and level within the organization. Almost any job evaluation method, correctly applied, will give the same results. A similar piece of research was carried out by Gomez-Megia, Page, and Tornow (1982). They compared traditional, statistical, and hybrid job evaluation approaches. All in all, they used seven different job evaluation techniques and evaluated 657 positions. Results indicate that traditional and hybrid systems are at least as accurate, reliable, and objective in predicting grade level as statistical methods. The moral is this: Be sure to describe, rank, and price your jobs. The method you use to do it is not terribly important.

Pay Satisfaction

Much of the experimental literature on compensation has been devoted to the issue of pay satisfaction. As we have seen, Herzberg thought that pay was an extrinsic factor, capable of satisfying but not of inciting increased productivity. Maslow, too, believed that pay was less important to workers than job enrichment was. Simonds and Orife (1975) researched this question: "What's more important, job enrichment or increased pay?" They found that when people were transferred from one job to another without a pay increase, no preference was found for the more enriched job, and that no statistically significant preference was found for more enriched jobs, regardless of whether or not a pay increase was included. In other words, at least in this study, pay seems to be the major satisfier.

People not only prefer pay over enriched jobs, they also prefer to have most of their compensation in straight salaries. Mahoney (1964) asked 459 managers how they would prefer to have their compensation. Most of them opted for straight salary and expressed little interest in benefits or incentives. I have confirmed this in my own research on compensation. When I survey executives on compensation preferences, I find that most would prefer all their compensation in salary if they could have it that way. When forced to choose the more traditional categories, the people in my survey indicated that they preferred 70 percent of their compensation in salary, 20 percent in benefits, and 10 percent in incentives. Once, deciding to test informally the pay-versus enrichment hypothesis during a speech I was giving, I polled fifty personnel managers in San Diego, most of them male. I asked how many of them, if they could retain their current level of pay, would give up their positions as managers and work instead as garbage collectors, and 90 percent of them raised their hands to signal that they would. The reasons the men gave were that for the same pay, they would prefer working outside to inside, would rather be more physically active, and would take the nonmanagement job because it involved less stress. Two conclusions are possible: that money was more important than the nature of the work for this group, or that this group preferred manual labor to enriched, higher-status jobs. Later, I found that another explanation was possible. The results could be due to gender differences. A client told me that someone repeated my survey with a female audience, and she found that few of the females would trade jobs with a garbage collector for the same money.

Pay satisfaction means how people feel about their pay.

To decide how they feel about their pay, people use three classes of references: other people's salaries in other companies, other people's salaries inside their own companies, and their own salaries compared with their performance. People who perceive their compensation as equitable have more favorable attitudes toward work and toward their organizations. They also have a lower termination rate than employees who perceive their compensation as inequitable.

Managers are more concerned with comparisons outside the company than inside it. Pay satisfaction is predicted better by the individual's standing within the entire industry than by their standing within the company. That's why it is important to do those salary surveys.

Other studies have found that managers are sensitive about how their pay compares with that of their subordinates and care more about this than how it compares with that of their peers or superiors. Small differences in pay between managers and subordinates are associated with pay dissatisfaction. The more money you make compared to those who work for you, the better you feel about your pay. Many people care as much about internal equity as they do about external competitiveness.

To be snugly on the side of safety, it is best to have a compensation program that is capable of satisfying equity feelings, both externally and internally. Make sure your pay practices are both competitive and fair according to job content.

In addition to needing to feel that they are paid fairly, as compared to their counterparts in other companies and to their peers, people need to feel that they are paid fairly relative to their performance. According to Porter and Lawler (1968a, 1968b), the best index of organizational morale is the correlation people feel between their pay and their performance. If individuals perceive the relationship between performance and compensation as strong, then morale can be assumed to be high. If they think the link between performance and compensation is weak, morale can be assumed to be low. This relationship shows the importance of paying people directly for their accomplishments. It is an argument in favor of incentive compensation over straight salary. When pay is controlled by someone else, people who evaluate their own performance highly are less satisfied with pay (Motowidlo, 1982).

Equity theory says that people will believe their pay is fair if they believe it is contingent on their performance. Greene (1975) found that merit pay programs are indeed related to satisfaction with pay but pointed out that satisfaction is a result of performance, not a cause. The relationship between merit pay and satisfaction is not entirely clear. Attempts were made to test a number of hypotheses for Lawler's (1981) equity model of pay satisfaction. It was concluded that without the inclusion of a variety of employee perceptions, only a small portion of pay satisfaction can be accounted for. The relationships are not simple. The only general predictor of satisfaction with pay is the individual's actual pay: The more money you make, the more satisfied you are with your pay.

Correlates of Pay

What can managers do to make pay programs more effective? As with most programs, participation in plan design and implementation increases both job satisfaction and pay satisfaction. Participation also increases pay program understanding and trust (Lawler, 1981).

There are other correlates with pay that the manager will want to keep in mind. You can expect the greatest demands for higher salaries to come from the poorest-paid people in the lowest levels of your organization (Singh, Mathew, and Das, 1977). The relationship between pay and talent is generally positive for younger managers but becomes progressively lower and finally negative for older managers (Siegel and Ghiselli, 1971). Other research on pay over the employment cycle indicates that what people are earning today does not necessarily predict what they will be earning later. Over a twenty-year working career, an individual's salary at the end of eighteen months correlates at only the .33 level with salary twenty years later. At the same time, salary at the end of four and a half years correlates quite high (.68) with salary at the end of ten and a half years. Some people are slow starters and late bloomers. Others begin well but then fizzle out. If you are not making much money now, do not worry. You may make up for it later on. If you are making good money now, though, do not let up. Chances are good you will wipe out later on.

Performance Contingent Pay

By 1984, over 80 percent of all companies were claiming that they followed a merit pay philosophy and gave salary increases only in the form of merit pay. In a merit pay program, high-level performers receive larger salary increases than average performers and poorer performers. The increases for better performers tend to be one and a half times as great as those for average performers. For example, if the average performer's increase is 6 percent, then the superior performer would get a 9 percent increase.

Despite the popularity of merit pay, not everyone agrees with the concept, myself included. Some researchers are critical of merit pay salary increases, thinking they demotivate rather than motivate because most employees will exaggerate their performance and then feel their salary increase is too small. Concurrently, managers make too small salary discriminations between individuals in the same jobs, regardless of performance. Others argue that an individual's pay ought to be based on tenure and, so long as the performance is satisfactory, it should increase at a fairly predictable rate. This is, of course, the way people are paid in the public sector, which now accounts for one third of our entire work force. Pay for tenure is a sensible system in tax-exempt service organizations. I agree that differential increases in salary are often demotivating and fail to differentially reward the superior achiever. I, too, would pay an average salary for tenure and satisfactory performance. I no longer support merit pay increases in salary; instead, I recommend the use of monetary incentives, variable-performance contingent pay, to reward special merit.

Merit pay, manipulation of the entire annual salary, is not the same as contingent pay, the awarding of additional money in the form of an incentive or bonus. True contingent pay programs are bonus or incentive plans. Contingent pay programs incite increased productivity, generating higher output but not higher quality (Vecchio, 1982). Under contingent pay plans, employees believe they earn the extra money and produce more work without feeling exploited (Greenberg and Ornstein, 1983). Merit pay awards a percentage of this year's salary to next year's salary. You pay a year late for performance and you compound your cost, since the merit pay is added to the salary base. Incentive pay avoids both of these problems.

Incentives

Contingent pay means incentives and bonuses, variable awards in addition to salary increases. I recommended paying average salary increases (not slightly higher merit pay salary increases) to all employees under incentive and bonus pay programs, and discontinuing merit pay plans for them. Only a few of my clients follow my advice. Most add bonus and incentive plans to salary merit pay plans. By doing so, they pay twice for the same thing.

The incentive research literature is limited but strongly supports the conclusion that incentive plans make people productive, improving their performance. For example, small daily bonuses paid for coming to work on time are effective in reducing chronic tardiness among industrial workers. Employees who are paid incentives perceive a higher linkage between performance and pay than those paid only salaries. Korman, Glickman, and Frey (1981) tested the influence of incentives on the decision to enlist in the Navy. Incentives were a $1,000 versus a $3,000 signup bonus, two years versus four years of free college, and a 10 percent versus a 25 percent bonus for exceptional performance. All the incentives were used through a four-year enlistment period. All worked, to some extent, but no significant differences were found by type of incentive and disposition to enlist; neither the number nor the magnitude of the incentives made a difference. Just offering a bonus helped. It did not matter whether it was a single small bonus or several large bonuses. Of course, the behavior incited was a noncontinuum, single-choice behavior—enlist or not. We cannot be sure about the effect of bonus size or numbers on continuum behavior.

Incentives are effective, not only with managerial jobs but also with such hourly jobs as maid, housekeeper, and bellhop (Anderson and others, 1982). With the introduction of incentives, productivity increases 20 percent over baseline, and output becomes more stable. Output is more stable and predictive when incentives are paid. There is less variance in output for workers under piecework incentive plans than for those paid a straight wage. The standard deviation in output is 20 percent under nonpiecework conditions and 15 percent under piecework conditions (Schmidt and Hunter, 1983).

A form of hourly incentive plan that does not pay individuals for piecework, but instead rewards a whole group of employees, is called gainsharing. Under these plans, groups of employees share in a pooled incentive rather than being awarded an individual incentive for their own efforts. The benefits of gainsharing programs include improved employee performance, better attitudes, improved productivity, reduced waste, better use of materials, improved processes and procedures, and better product quality. There are three common forms of sharing: equity participation, profit sharing, and gainsharing. In a typical gainsharing program, 50 percent of the money saved by increased efficiency goes to the employees, and 50 percent goes to the company. The range of gain shared with the employee is from a minimum of one third to a maximum of two thirds.

Communications

Before they communicate a compensation plan, effective managers take steps to be sure the compensation program makes people productive. They describe and assign jobs. They rank jobs fairly and price jobs competitively. They pay employees for performance, either individually or collectively. They pay incentives. Finally, they communicate the pay program.

How much of your pay program should you reveal? Both

too much openness and too much secrecy will cause problems. We know that communicating some information, even if ineffectually, increases pay satisfaction, but the relationships between pay disclosure and pay satisfaction are more complex than previously supposed. Futrell and Jenkins (1978) tested the effects of increased pay disclosure on 500 sales representatives, 150 in an experimental group and 350 in a control group. After one year, sales representatives in the open pay group performed better and were more satisfied with their pay. Managers under an open pay policy program also expressed more satisfaction with their pay (Futrell, 1978).

So, what should you communicate? Most companies communicate information about pay scales, either the salary grades for jobs and their accompanying ranges or the individual's own salary range. You should understand that this involves risk. Individuals who are low in their range frequently ask, "Why?" Individuals who are high in their range complain that they have limited opportunity for further salary increases because they are already bumping the ceiling in their pay grade. Outside the public sector, few organizations communicate information about the pay of other employees. If government regulations require that you publicly disclose details about the pay of specific individuals, you can do little other than comply. But don't do so voluntarily.

Summary

Compensation, especially incentive compensation, is an effective management technique for improving productivity. It deserves book-length treatment. The first scientists of management, people like Frederick Taylor, advocated the use of various compensation techniques, such as incentives, to make people productive. After World War II, with the advent of the human potential movement among management psychologists, compensation as a motivator fell into disrepute. Concommitant with humanistic psychology in the workplace, U.S. productivity declined. By 1980, coincident with alarm over U.S. productivity problems, compensation was coming back as a legitimate technique for stimulating worker output. The subject is still scantily treated in the research literature, and much remains to be learned about how money motivates.

Effective managers will take steps to ensure that they are using compensation to stimulate productivity. Consistent with their role of providing structure, managers will define job content in position descriptions and will establish a hierarchy of job value through job evaluation or job ranking. Research has shown that the exact techniques used to describe and rank jobs are not important. Most reputable techniques work equally well. Because employees are most concerned with how their pay relates to that of others, managers will see to it that salary surveys are made so that the company can communicate its competitive posture.

There are some known correlates of pay that the manager will find useful. The most important of these is that people produce more when they believe pay is contingent on individual performance. The majority of organizations still try to tie pay to performance through the use of differential salary increases on an annual basis. This is called merit pay. While popular, merit pay is not especially effective.

Incentive pay is psychologically more sound and pragmatically more efficient than merit pay. Incentive pay improves productivity at all organizational levels, among managers as well as hourly workers. While much remains to be learned about how incentives work, the general finding is that with incentives productivity increases of 20 percent are common. Output is more stable with incentives, and pay satisfaction increases.

Compensation programs must be communicated, and employee satisfaction tends to increase under conditions of open pay disclosure. Full disclosure, however, is inadvisable, and communications programs are best limited to general descriptions of the program's objectives and specific details about the individual employee's compensation opportunity.

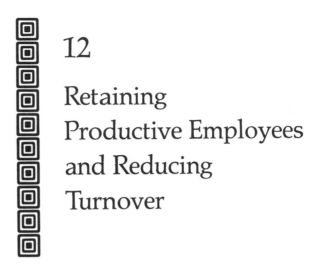

12

Retaining Productive Employees and Reducing Turnover

We are nearing the end of our review of guidelines from research in psychology about how to make people productive. Earlier, I defined productivity and explained why American organizations are having a problem with it. My stated goal has been to selectively present proven advice—derived from research, not opinion—about how to improve human resource productivity throughout the employment cycle.

In previous chapters, I described the impact of the individual employee on productivity. I presented data on selecting the right people through interviews, résumés, and psychological tests. Together we looked at individual differences, job family differences, motivation, and effects of training. Then I shifted the focus from employees to management—effective managers and effective management techniques. The most important specific techniques I described were goal setting, performance appraisal, and compensation.

Now we shall concern ourselves with outcomes. There are three possible outcomes from the efforts of employees and managers to be productive. The first is turnover, which we cover in this chapter. People can leave a job, and that ends the employment cycle, with the question of productivity answered largely in the negative. Except for promotions, turnover means that somewhere in the employment cycle mistakes were made. Turnover increases costs and reduces output, thereby hurting productivity. The next chapter is about the second possible outcome, job satisfaction. While people can stay put in a job and be reasonably happy with their lot, we shall see that this is no direct guarantee that they will be productive. A satisfied employee is not necessarily a productive employee. Nevertheless, if we do things right throughout the employment cycle and apply guidelines from research in psychology, we shall definitely improve our chances of making people productive. The third possible outcome is to have people who are productive and satisfied. This is the subject of the last chapter.

In an ideal world, an organization would find an individual matched for the job, give her whatever specific job-content orientation was required, set standards of performance for her, and then forget about her. Day after day, month after month, year after year, this competent employee would perform happily and productively. If the company chose not to promote her, she would still remain loyally and productively at her post until she dropped dead or retired.

The real world differs greatly from my ideal. People come and people go continuously, impairing your efficiency. People are less productive while they are tuning into an organization and less productive again while tuning out. Turnover is a nuisance. Turnover is unproductive. The individual who voluntarily leaves an organization creates a productivity problem. The individual who involuntarily leaves an organization was, by definition, a productivity problem.

The number of times someone will turn over a position is astounding. According to the Bureau of Labor Statistics, the average male worker in the United States will spend thirty-eight years at work. The average female spends twenty-eight years at work. In normal economic times, turnover runs about 20 percent a year in large companies and 25 percent a year in smaller companies. This means that, on the average, the organization will have to refill all its jobs every four to five years. It means that the average male worker, with a career life span of thirty-eight years, will turn over from seven to nine different jobs. The average woman will turn over five to seven different jobs. Seldom will these positions all be with the same company. The individual who stays with the same organization for an entire career is unusual. Only 10 percent of the work force does so. Just as the pattern of married life in the United States has become serial monogamy, so too has the pattern of employment become one of serial rather than continuous employment.

There are organizations where the average employee is long tenured and where turnover is low. Typically, these organizations are in the public sector or are quasi-public (for example, utilities and aerospace industries). They account for about one third of the work force. The rest of the work force comes and goes, is recruited and applies, resigns or is fired numerous times before retirement. This is why executive search firms and employment agencies make over a billion dollars a year. This is why the employment subfunction in personnel is the first position staffed separately when the company becomes of sufficient size to warrant more than one personnel professional, an event that usually occurs when an organization reaches about 100 employees. With 25 percent turnover typical in that company of 100 people, you say, "Welcome aboard" or "Goodbye" to fifty people a year—about one per week.

Since turnover is expensive, effective management means doing something about turnover. At a minimum, doing something means at least understanding how turnover occurs. It means managing people so as to create a stable work force. The departure, against your will, of people you want to keep is the most unproductive type of turnover. Some turnover is either unavoidable or even desirable, however. Promotions are a form of voluntary and positive turnover. Retirement and death are unavoidable. Eventually, we all turn over.

A certain percentage of all turnovers are firings. In sales, as an example, estimates are that the sales representative turnover rate each year is made up of 63 percent resignations, 7 percent retirements, and 23 percent firings. The probability of getting fired, while slowing because of litigation, is still high. By 1984, as another example, turnover among chief executive officers and chief operating officers of the 100 largest corporations in the United States had risen from a historic 3.3 percent to 9.8 percent. Much of this turnover is involuntary. The 10 percent turnover at the top of the pyramid is still less than the 20 percent turnover at the base of the pyramid, but it shows that the bell tolls eventually for many of us.

There are three things about firings the effective manager needs to know. One is how to fire so as to minimize the hurt it causes to the employee and to the company. The second is how to fire without getting sued. The concept of employment at the employer's will is rapidly eroding, and people who are fired are increasingly inclined to sue their former employers for wrongful discharge. The third thing managers need to know includes statistics and techniques to help those who have been told to look elsewhere.

Voluntary turnover, whether at the top of the organization or at the bottom, is never productive for the organization, nor is it really productive for the individual. People who change jobs frequently earn about the same income and reach about the same level in the organization as people who stay in the same company (Cherry, 1976). Persistent job changing does not result in any more or any less job satisfaction, pay, or opportunity to use one's skills and abilities. There is, however, research that indicates that frequent job changing is indicative of personality problems and lack of personal adjustment.

Although turnover is costly, both at the macro level and the micro level, there has been a surprising lack of comprehensive research on turnover, especially among executive and professional employees (Hinrichs, 1970, p. 544), but we are beginning to learn more. The research on turnover is confusing and contradictory (Muchinsky, 1983), even though there are now entire books on the subject (Mobley, 1982). Factors influencing turnover are sometimes beyond the control of management. The single factor that most influences turnover is the current level of unemployment. During the expansionary and inflationary years, from 1979 through 1981, turnover in some of my clients rose to 42 percent. During the height of the Great Recession, the years 1981 through 1983, turnover in those same clients dropped to 3 percent. Obviously, the recession had an enormous impact on turnover. People do not quit their jobs when they have no place else to go. Saying that is saying the obvious, but why do people quit when there is someplace else to go?

To understand why people quit, Dodson and Haskew (1976) suggest categorizing employees into turnovers, turnoffs, and turnons. Turnovers leave because they find no compelling reason to stay. Turnoffs remain for maintenance or external environmental reasons but are no longer motivated in their jobs. Turnons find their jobs satisfying and continue to strive. Dodson and Haskew's study of 600 government employees identified 57 percent as potential turnovers, 9.2 percent as turnoffs, and 34 percent as turnons. Their findings are consistent with other surveys. Estimates are that in any major organization at any given time, one third of management and professional employees are circulating their résumés and another third are thinking about doing so. Managers should realize that fully half of their employees are potential turnovers at any given time. Could you as a manager meet your goals if half your employees left at the same time?

Turnover statistics should motivate the effective manager to act. First, plan for 20 percent turnover per year—not to create a self-fulfilling prophecy, but so that you are not caught unprepared. Second, read on to learn why people quit and what can be done about it.

Quitting a job can be a symbolic act, part of a career decision in which the individual's work life takes a different direction. (I will describe the consequences of such decisions later.) Turnover is also one result of a decline over time in degree of job commitment. People preparing to leave an organization experience both a decline in rewards and an increase in the quality of alternatives and the cost of staying. They begin to find more and more reasons why leaving makes sense, and more and more reasons why sticking around does not. Reasons why people leave have been explored by a number of researchers. The highest-ranked reasons generally are growth opportunity, salary and financial benefits, job satisfaction, and work conditions. My own research confirms this finding. "Growth and opportunity" is the reason you hear most if you survey people who have changed jobs. My guess is that this reason is a euphemism covering a multitude of both employer and employee sins. What does "growth and opportunity" mean? Does it mean that the person got a higher-level, better-paying position in another organization? Does it mean that he took a similar position in another organization that was growing faster, or where his immediate superior was more likely to move on? Or does "growth and opportunity" really mean that the individual disliked his ex-organization and its management?

To say that you are quitting for more growth and opportunity sounds good and causes neither you nor your former employer any embarrassment. It is hardly the stuff that makes for a good lawsuit. It is not, however, particularly helpful to the perplexed and would-be effective manager, puzzling about what the departed employee really meant.

Parasuraman (1982) studied 160 nonmanagers who quit. Their average age was 36.7 years. Turnover was related to felt stress, a desire to leave, and a lack of commitment to the organization. Turnover was not related to personal variables, nor was it related to absenteeism. Other studies have found that increased absenteeism is usually an early warning sign that turnover will occur. The individual is disengaging. If you like your job, you are less likely to quit, but even the relationship between job satisfaction and sticking around is not particularly strong (Mobley, 1977). You may like your job but not really like the work itself, and that increases the chances you will quit. Turnover is caused by frustration and disillusionment, which in turn are related to unrealistic expectations formed during the selection step of the employment cycle (Scott, Deadrick, and Tayler, 1983). Some researchers recommend painting warts and wrinkles on the picture of the job during the recruiting stage. This way, they say, prospective employees know exactly what they are getting into. Other researchers say full disclosure does not make any difference and that disillusion eventually casts a pall over any position and can lead to resignation.

Money matters in who quits; but here, too, the causal trail is faint and branched. The effects of pay on turnover are mediated primarily by pay satisfaction and intentions to quit. Surprisingly, pay expectation—the perceived probability of receiving more satisfying pay in another job—is not related to turnover (Motowidlo, 1983). People do not quit because they think they may make more money in another organization, but they may quit if they are dissatisfied with their current pay and if other factors have given them a predisposition to resign. Communicating a company's pay practices is important and helps control turnover. Lack of understanding and negative perceptions of a company's pay practices are related to turnover (Birkenbach and Van der Merwe, 1979).

Having employees who are in the right line of work helps control turnover. People who follow the advice of vocational counselors stay longer in their first jobs than do those who ignore such advice. A good match between the job and an individual's ability and interests is more important in predicting employment stability than any other facet of the person's personality. Many people quit simply because they do not like the work.

Predicting Who Will Quit

One of the values of understanding a phenomenon is being able to do something about it. Understanding why people quit is interesting. Predicting who will quit is useful.

The best single predictor of employee turnover is simply asking employees whether or not they intend to quit. Kraus (1980) surveyed 911 sales representatives working for a large manufacturing company, asking whether they intended to stay with the organization. Eighteen months after their attitudes were surveyed, turnover for sales representatives who earlier had stated their intention to remain with the organization was only 9 percent. Turnover for those who were less committed was 30 percent. Examination of the data showed that intention to remain was most closely tied to liking the work itself and to good feelings about the company as a place to work. Feelings about immediate supervisors were less important.

Managers attempting to predict turnover should listen to their employees. Negative comments about the company, its pay practices, or the work itself are indicators of future turnover. Complaints about you as a boss, if people like the work and feel satisfied with the company, do not necessarily indicate future turnover.

You can spot potential turnovers by a dropoff of interest in their work. A good predictor of turnover is lack of commitment. Potter (1980) found this to be the case when he studied the employment history of over 200 management trainees in a large retail company over a fifteen-month period. Trainees who left the company voluntarily during the initial fifteen-month employment period had begun to show a definite decline in commitment prior to quitting. The earlier the decline in commitment, the earlier the person left the company.

These studies all point back to the importance of the selection step in the employment cycle. They tell us not to hire people merely because they need jobs and can perform the work we have. We should hire them only if they enjoy the type of work we need done. In bad economic times, managers may not be troubled by turnover among those who are misfitted for their positions because of their lack of interest, but when times are good such individuals will leave for work they find more enjoyable.

While turnover is related to loss of interest in a job, it is not directly related to ability. Arguments about ability and turnover cut both ways. Some authors argue that it is the most able individuals who leave an organization, but many managers have seen that it is also the less able who voluntarily leave an organization, realizing they would be more successful and happier elsewhere. Every employee is a potential quitter. Every category of performer includes potential quitters. The distinguished performer may be recruited away by another organization. The average performer may leave, correctly concluding that his chances for promotion are only modest. The incompetent employee may voluntarily look for work he can perform more effectively.

Another indicator of potential turnover can be found in

the résumé or employment application of the employee. A person who has changed jobs every two to three years in the past is likely to change jobs again. A track record of frequent job change indicates an individual who tends to run out of energy and enthusiasm, either through boredom or the realization that promotion is unlikely. Job hoppers decide, perhaps subconsciously, that they have a better chance of being promoted with a new employer than with the current one.

If recruiting or keeping a stable work force is one of your goals, you should consider recruiting older workers. A five-year study of 1,000 male and female employees between the ages of twenty-one and seventy showed that career stability increases with age for both men and women (Gottfredson, 1978). Do people become more stable with age for intrinsic reasons, or are they simply reflecting the realities of the more limited options available to them? McAuley (1977) found that most people between the ages of forty and retirement believe that they are victims of age discrimination, especially if they are holding white-collar jobs in large cities. This suggests that older workers make fewer job changes, not because they are happy with their jobs but because they think that age discrimination will reduce their chances of obtaining different employment. The manager seeking stable employees may also want to consider hiring more women. Professional females who are highly career-oriented are less likely to quit their jobs than males are to quit theirs (Bartol and Manhardt, 1979).

According to O'Reilly and Caldwell (1981), turnover is lower among employees who choose your job over at least one other. The moral of their research is "Don't hire people who have only one job offer (yours), and don't give a job to someone who can't get a job somewhere else." The feeling that one chose one's job voluntarily makes it easier to tolerate the inevitable stress and disappointment that come in time with any job. During the selection process, it is a good practice to give all candidates a realistic picture of the job. You will have just as many people accept the job when a balanced picture is presented. Those who do accept will have more realistic job expectations and fewer thoughts of quitting. They will have a slightly higher job survival rate than those who are painted a more rosy, less realistic picture. You should provide realistic information, not only about the job but also about the organization.

In addition to looking at an employee's track record to see if there is a history of job change, the manager should also monitor attendance as another early-warning sign. There is a continuation of withdrawal from absenteeism to turnover. Absenteeism is a form of withdrawal behavior, and has in common with turnover disengagement from the organization and a negative impact on productivity. In reviewing the literature on absenteeism, Bhatia and Valecha (1981) concluded that absenteeism is associated with personal factors, including family size, travel distance to work, and anxiety. People who are worried, who have lengthy transportation to contend with, and who have to arrange for childcare are more likely to be no-shows. Some absenteeism is also, according to this review, associated with factors under the manager's control. These factors include job satisfaction, negative perceptions of working conditions, highly repetitive jobs, and low-status jobs.

Whatever its causes, absenteeism is expensive. Goddard (1982) estimates that absenteeism results in 400 million lost work days each year, at a cost of $2.64 billion. For a company with 2,000 employees, even four absences per employee per year cost between $500,000 and $1.5 million. Any steps management can take to reduce absenteeism will improve productivity.

Retirement

In our idyllic scenario of the effective manager making people productive, the competent employee remains until retirement. The closer workers get to retirement, the less attractive it is to them (Ekerdt and others, 1976). The preference to delay retirement is not an outright rejection of retirement per se, nor is it an absolute preference for work. People delay retirement because working has more status than nonworking and because retiring is stressful.

That retirement is stressful is attested to by the percentage of people who die within two to four years of leaving work. A study of 2,100 workers in the tire industry between the ages of fifty-six and sixty-four (Haynes, McMichael, and Tyroler, 1977) found that death rates in this group decreased before retirement (people were hanging on) and increased in the three to four years after retirement (because of the resulting stress and depression).

Impending retirement is a psychologically significant event for older workers. In recent studies, it has been shown that the lower the status of the worker, the more likely the worker was to die within three years of retirement. The higher the status of the worker, the more likely the worker was to die five years after retirement. The higher the status of your job, the longer you are likely to live after retirement. These findings of early death after retirement are consistent with other findings that show older people experiencing an elevated death rate after removal from familiar surroundings. An alternative to formal retirement is to do less stressful work. Meltzer (1981) found high job satisfaction and a low rate of retirement among elderly lawyers, who controlled the stress of both work and retirement by controlling the number and nature of their clients.

Promotion

Promotion is turnover with a happy ending: Promoted people are more productive. Keller and Holland (1981) compared employees who had been promoted, or assigned different jobs, with a similar group that had stayed put. Those who had been promoted showed greater increases in performance, innovation, and job satisfaction. The correlation between productivity and promotion can be attributed to a number of factors. There is novelty in the new job, and novelty itself is energizing. There is pride in being promoted, and there is fear of failure. These emotions push the promotee to strive hard for success.

Increases in productivity that result from promotion point to the wisdom of promoting from within. The best of all policies is for a company to stress promotion from within, a policy that creates a domino effect. It promotes several people at the same time, each of whom moves up a level. The main disadvantage of promotion from within is that it can and does tend to create parochialism. Nevertheless, it is a policy much to be preferred over recruiting from outside. To improve productivity, promote many and promote often.

When I was a manager, I obtained the most satisfactory results when I initially selected high-potential people without much experience and then followed a policy of promotion from within. As a group, these individuals were more productive than the seasoned people I occasionally recruited from other firms. Promotion from within is always a more productive management technique than recruitment from outside. In an ideal world, there would be no executive recruiters, only college recruiters.

Employees who want to be promoted, of course, need to demonstrate competence in their current jobs in order to be considered candidates for higher-level jobs; this is conventional but valid wisdom. It also helps to have a mentor who can pull you along. The employee pushing for promotion should be careful about what she communicates. There is a negative relationship between being promoted and communicating work-related problems to superiors (Read, 1962), a conflict that has been called the dilemma of leadership. The best strategy for those seeking promotion is to communicate good news only and work quietly to solve problems, so that the good news of a successful solution can be brought to the superior's attention.

If you want to get promoted, it is a good idea also to keep your personal problems to yourself. If you are having emotional or psychological problems, don't let your prospective or current employer know about them. It lowers your chances of getting a job (Farina and Felner, 1973), and if you are anything but positive about all aspects of your personal and professional life, you imperil your potential for promotion. Misery in a company does not have much company. Remember Nash's Law: "Never say nothing negative to nobody about nothing."

Firings

If promotions are stories with happy endings, then firings are the tear-jerkers. Getting fired or firing someone is clear evidence of failure to be or make someone productive. It is traumatic for both management and employees. Ordinarily it is expensive and, with the increasing intrusion of the government and lawyers into the termination phase of the employment cycle, each termination raises the specter of economic catastrophe for the organization. In no other phase of the employment cycle is the potential cost to management so high.

Getting fired is like dying (Finley and Lee, 1981). People who are fired go through the same emotional phases as people who are told they have terminal diseases. In the initial phase, they experience shock, disbelief, anger, and relief. (Yes, relief!) Later, they experience bargaining, depression, and acceptance. The first reaction of the fired employee is a momentary feeling of utter surprise. This is true even when the person has suspected it was going to happen for a long time. Surprise and disbelief are quickly followed by anger and relief, although not always in that order. Every person who is fired at some point feels anger, and it is this anger that can become so dangerous if it takes a litigious turn.

Besides being on sound legal ground when firing someone, the effective manager will want to remember a few *dos* and *don'ts* when firing someone. Managers are advised to fire people early in the week, not on Friday. The rationale is that if the person has the weekend to stew over being fired, the inevitable anger they feel will be intensified. (This advice occurs frequently in the literature, but I fail to understand why people will be less angry on weekdays than they will be on weekends.) Secondly, fire someone in his own office. Here, the rationale is to minimize the misbalance of power. Third, make the employee's immediate supervisor the bearer of the bad news. Do not delegate the dirty work to some other party who is not in the chain of command—the personnel manager, for example. When firing someone, the effective manager will communicate three things: that the employee is fired; the conditions of the firing—that is, the date on which the person is no longer considered an employee of the company, the financial terms of the separation, and so on; and instructions on what do do next. These can include such administrative matters as when to vacate the office, when to turn in keys, and so on.

Those are the *dos* of firing; here are the *don'ts*. Don't give extensive reasons for why you are firing the person. Don't talk about past performance. Don't prolong the discussion; keep it under fifteen minutes. The point here is that you want to prevent the meeting, whose primary purpose is to tell the employee *that* he is terminated, from disintegrating into a justification as to *why* he has been terminated. Once the decision has been made to fire someone, do it quickly, quietly, and without malice. After you have made your decision, a discussion of the reasons why the person is fired is not going to get him unfired. It is irrelevant and, in the event of a lawsuit, is even dangerous.

The stress of being fired ranks high on the list of life's unpleasant experiences—below, but not far below, devastating experiences like death of a spouse or divorce. Getting a new job can be a positive experience for the fired individual, but for the immediate time after termination, emotional feelings are all negative. The stress of unemployment is felt by everyone, but among white-collar workers, unemployment stress is most pronounced for married men in their thirties and for Ph.D.s (Kaufman, 1982). The former's family is threatened by his loss of employment, and he is at an age when he is supposed to be moving rapidly up the organization, rather than back down it. The Ph.D. is considered overqualified for almost any job by almost any employer and wonders what good all those years of education did. (People are suspicious of Ph.D.s, which is why so many are forced to become school teachers and consultants.) The nonfinancial disadvantages of unemployment are felt most intensely by individuals from higher social classes (Van Wezel, 1975). The financial disadvantages are felt most keenly by those at lower social levels.

Because getting fired is so odious, and because wrongful termination suits are so expensive, more employers are developing programs to assist fired employees to find new jobs. This assistance may be as simple and informal as suggesting books on the subject (Taylor, 1975), or it may mean using a new technique in the termination phase of the employment cycle. This technique is called *outplacement,* a structured process to help terminated employees make the transition from employment in one organization to employment in another.

Outplacement

Outplacement is the orderly termination of individuals who have been displaced for a variety of reasons, including lack of fit between the job and the individual (Branham, 1983). The practice includes assistance in developing or refurbishing skills required to gain new employment. The benefits of outplacement are said to include cost reduction, risk minimization, morale improvement, corporate-image development, promotional opportunities for other people, and improved productivity. Individuals who are being outplaced need to learn the relative efficacy of various job-search methods and how to improve their employability (Kaufman, 1982). Proof of the benefits of outplacement as a management tool is in the statistics concerning executives who have been through the process. According to Kaufman, 78 percent of outplaced executives obtain new employment, 12 percent become consultants, and 10 percent start their own businesses. Almost all who receive outplacement help improve their level of compensation, with the average increase in income reported to be 20 percent. Ironically, this is roughly the increase they would have had if they had been promoted internally or had terminated voluntarily after being recruited into new organizations.

Summary

Turnover is the antithesis of productivity. Except when an employee has been promoted or retired, turnover means that management has failed to make people productive. The individual who leaves a company voluntarily is saying that another organization affords her a work environment that better meets her needs. When the employee leaves involuntarily, management is saying it made a mistake in selection, training, goal setting and performance appraisal, compensation, or current job assignment. It failed somewhere in the employment cycle. In most companies, annual turnover averages between 20 and 25 percent. Most men will turn over eight jobs in their careers, and most women will turn over six. The negative impact on organizational productivity is enormous. Management needs to understand turnover so as to control it.

People quit their jobs for a variety of reasons. The four most frequently mentioned reasons are opportunity for growth, salary and financial benefits, job satisfaction, and working conditions. People quit when their jobs no longer satisfy them and when economic conditions are safe enough that they are willing to risk leaving. The major modifier of turnover is the economic climate, with turnover dropping during recessions that feature high unemployment.

To control turnover, learn to predict it. A good predictor of turnover is an individual's directly or indirectly stated intention to leave the organization. Intentions to stay or to leave can be interpreted from employees' behavior—conversation, enthusiasm for work, absenteeism, and general attitude toward the organization. These signals give effective managers the opportunity to utilize various managerial devices to re-engage employees' commitment.

In its worst form, turnover is termination—firing the employee. To ease the transition out of one organization and into another, companies, particularly for executives, are using a new technique: outplacement. Executives who go through outplacement improve their income by an average of 20 percent, and most find positions with other organizations. The remainder go into business for themselves.

To prevent turnover, pick the right people. Make sure people's abilities and interests fit their jobs, communicate thoroughly what they can expect from their jobs and from the organization, and be sure they have a choice between your organization and some other organization during the search process. Then, practice the other techniques, covered in previous chapters, that have been shown effective in making people productive. By doing so, managers will have a reasonably good chance of retaining satisfied people, who are the subject of the next chapter.

13

Increasing
Job Satisfaction

The last chapter was about turnover, about failing to make people productive. This chapter is about job satisfaction and its relationship to productivity. Job satisfaction is one of the most heavily researched topics in the psychology of work, yet satisfaction is no guarantee of productivity.

There are some work satisfiers and dissatisfiers that are considered universal. Some satisfiers are obvious, such as high pay and security, but others are surprises. Because work varies in importance from individual to individual, job satisfaction varies in its impact on an individual's satisfaction with life. People for whom work is a central life interest have the opportunity to experience high levels of job satisfaction if they are doing work that uses their skills. Work satisfaction changes with age and with the employment cycle. Certain organizational characteristics influence job satisfaction, and the effective manager will want to be aware of these.

Job satisfaction is not the same as job performance, and it is important to distinguish between the two (Lawler, 1970). Job satisfaction is an indicator of an employee's motivation to

come to work, but it influences job performance only indirectly. Nevertheless, the volume of research on job satisfaction
would certainly suggest that satisfaction is important. Weintraub (1981) argues, on the basis of research, that job satisfaction and work performance in fact are not related at all. If job
satisfaction is not important to productivity and performance,
then why study it? To enrich the quality of life in the workplace? Out of pure scientific curiosity? Should managers concern themselves about whether their employees are happy or
unhappy with their jobs?

According to one survey, a Gallup poll, Americans are increasingly unhappy about work (Glenn and Weaver, 1982). The
decline is more a result of changes in workers' attitudes than of
changes in working conditions or in the nature of work. Other
surveys, covering shorter time periods (1972-1978), have
found that American workers feel about the same job satisfaction (Weaver, 1980). In these more recent surveys, the people
who are most satisfied with their work are older, highly educated individuals in good jobs that pay well.

Thus, the data are mixed. The long-term trend toward
less job satisfaction, if it is real, is attributed to a decline in the
work ethic and a decay in religious faith (Balchin, 1970). Replacing these two value systems is the idea that people should
work because the work itself is satisfying. Work should be enjoyable, and the ultimate aim of the working person should be
to perform only those tasks that give satisfaction.

What causes job satisfaction? Job satisfaction results from
the interaction of several variables and cannot be primarily attributed to only one or two main causes (Vasudeva and Rajbia,
1976).

The factors that affect work satisfaction are many and
changing. One example is time already spent on the job. Job satisfaction declines once new employees pass through a honeymoon period and then go through a transformation in their relationship with the organization—from that of outsiders to that
of experienced insiders. The transformation involves a decline
in expectations about intrinsic satisfiers, to a lower and more
realistic level. Expectations about extrinsic satisfiers tend to re-

main the same. Joining an organization is like falling in love: Temporary blindness afflicts new employees as well as persons newly in love.

A major factor in work satisfaction is the intrinsic nature of the work itself. An individual who genuinely likes the content of the job will be more satisfied with it. How can you find out what kind of job the individual likes? Here are seven questions to ask prospective employees that are related to job satisfaction (Rawls and Nelson, 1975).

1. *Do you prefer line jobs or staff jobs?* If you put a line personality in a staff position, she will succeed but be frustrated. Put a staff person in a line job, and he is sure to fail.

2. *Do you prefer a large organization or a small organization?* People who like small organizations enjoy the intimacy. Working in a small group is like being a member of a family, but large companies, with their more formal structures, offer a greater variety of activities and opportunities. Larger companies are more prestigious, and for some people this is important. Some individuals enjoy the internal anonymity but external name recognition of a large company. For others, large companies are depersonalizing. As organizations grow from small and entrepreneurial to large and bureaucratic, they change in the ways in which they satisfy people.

3. *Do you like old companies or new companies?* Old companies offer history, tradition, and a sense of stability. New companies offer flexibility, informality, and the excitement of rapid growth and change.

4. *Do you enjoy frequent, moderate, or infrequent travel?* People with a need to be physically active are happiest in jobs where they have the opportunity to go out of doors or to move around from place to place. They like jobs where they are required to travel at least two or three times a month. People who dislike travel should not be in sales or field auditor positions, nor should they become consultants.

5. *Do you prefer meeting new people or working with the same group of people?* Individuals with good initial social skills who have a tendency to wear thin are different from individuals with more modest social skills who wear well.

6. *Do you like working in groups, or do you like working one-on-one?* An individual who enjoys playing Lone Ranger will be unhappy as just another rider in the cavalry.

7. *Do you like being able to immediately refer problems to someone above you, or do you prefer being left alone?* Some people resent being told what to do and are most productive when they can set their own priorities and decide for themselves both what to do and how to do it. This need for autonomy is highest in entrepreneurs. Others are happier when they have a clear idea of what is expected of them and can check with a supervisor about any questions that arise. Individuals with strong needs for autonomy or strong needs for support will not be happy if the freedom to act in their jobs varies significantly from their preferences.

One study of what people want most in a job found that the greatest satisfaction resulted from jobs that had high rewards, low costs, few alternatives, and a large personal investment (Rusbult and Farrell, 1983). If it takes considerable effort to obtain a position (through education, experience, or achievement), if you can make a lot of money at it, if you do not have to work very hard to make the money, and if you cannot think of any other job where you could do as well, then you should be absolutely wild with satisfaction about your job. Other research has found this same preference for the easy-money, easy-living kind of position. Bhushan (1976) found that industrial workers want jobs with high pay, high security, promotional opportunity, few hours of work, and friendly supervisors. If you can afford to provide your workers with that kind of job, they should be very happy. They may not, however, be any more productive.

Universal Satisfiers and Dissatisfiers

As you might expect, research into job satisfaction has led to a search for common or universal satisfiers and dissatisfiers. The results of two major studies are typical of this type of quest. Jurgensen (1978) studied job preferences in 57,000 employees of the Minnesota Gas Company. Preferences were measured over a thirty-year period. Jurgensen found that there was not much difference in job preferences by age, sex, marital status, number of dependents, education, or occupation. Jurgensen's satisfiers are shown in Table 7. Jurgensen noted that over

Table 7. Ten Universal Job Preferences and Satisfiers.[a]

Men	Women
1. Security	1. Type of work
2. Advancement	2. Company
3. Type of work	3. Security
4. Company	4. Coworkers
5. Pay	5. Advancement
6. Coworkers	6. Supervision
7. Supervision	7. Pay
8. Benefits	8. Working conditions
9. Hours	9. Hours
10. Working conditions	10. Benefits

[a]In order of importance

Source: Jurgensen (1978).

the ten-year period there had been an increase in the importance of benefits, pay, and type of work, and a decrease in the importance of advancement and security. Another study, this time of the top ten job dissatisfiers, was conducted by Bauer (1980). Bauer's dissatisfiers are shown in Table 8. Notice that

Table 8. Ten Universal Job Dissatisfiers.[a]

1. Unclear responsibilities
2. Never seeing the finished product
3. Red tape
4. Two-faced supervisors
5. Poor working conditions
6. Poor communications
7. Getting transferred
8. Getting a new boss
9. Being in the wrong job
10. Boredom

[a]In order of importance

Source: Bauer (1980).

the two lists do not overlap much; dissatisfiers are not just the flip side of satisfiers.

Managers should take heart that most of the dissatisfiers are within the control of managers. Bauer's ranking first of unclear responsibilities substantiates the research I presented earlier, which shows why it is important that managers provide structure. Structure is achieved through job descriptions and goal setting. Structure is also provided through the creation and distribution of organizational charts.

There are no really good excuses for failing to publish organizational charts, yet I have clients who refuse to issue them. In one company, the president has obscured which of his executives are accountable for various parts of the organization and has created dual reporting relationships. In another instance, the top executives have decided as a group not to issue such charts because of the overstaffing that exists in their departments. Their average span of management is one manager for every three employees. The top executives are convinced that if the president—the tightfisted entrepreneur who founded the company—ever saw tables of organization, he would have a stroke. In yet another organization, the reason given for not having organizational charts available is that the rate of turnover in the company is so high that embarrassed management stopped publishing the charts. Even when they published them twice a year, the charts quickly were filled with crossed-out names. Another client of mine can be described only as paranoid. Here, the reason no charts are published is to thwart rapacious headhunters who might be lurking behind the potted plants. There really are paranoid companies. I have at least two clients, both in perfectly respectable businesses, who refuse to have the company name on the door. One of them also refuses to give the company name when answering the phone: You are supposed to know who you are calling.

The second item on Bauer's list of dissatisfiers—never seeing the finished product—is a tougher problem to fix, but managers can do something about it, too. If the company manufactures something, then have samples of the finished product placed prominently throughout the organization. If the product is something an employee can use, then the organization should have a company store. One of the most popular employee benefits at Levi Strauss is a catalogue store, where employees can order, at a discount, the clothes and accessories sold by the company. If the product is not something an employee would buy, and if it is not convenient to scatter samples of it around and about (if the company makes ten-wheel trucks, for example), then efforts still should be made to find opportunities to troop the product past the employees periodically or to troop the employees past the product. If the product is a service and not a piece of manufactured goods, then tell employees about the consequences of their service. Secretaries like to know the outcome of proposals they have typed. Receptionists and switchboard operators enjoy hearing that the irate customer they handled so well is happy again. Let the bank teller know that the shabby old man she referred to the new-accounts officer opened a certificate of deposit for $100,000.

The next dissatisfier, after never seeing the end result, is red tape. That red tape dissatisfies is understandable, but seasoned managers carefully investigate complaints about red tape before leaping in with their scissors flashing. Often there is a good reason for a rule or a procedure that irritates employees. Most procedures are in place because the organization has learned the hard way that they are needed. Still, it is true that some red tape—often the brightest and stickiest kind—is unnecessary and can be removed.

Employees are dissatisfied with duplicity in their supervisors. Managers who say one thing in an employee's presence and another in her absence are motivated either by fear or by malice. A common pattern is for the manager to show consideration behavior in front of the employee and then task behavior in her absence. Face to face, the considerate manager acts understanding, sympathetic, conciliatory, appreciative, forgiving, and friendly, or he makes promises. Then, with the employee out of sight and earshot, the task-oriented manager is demanding and critical or indicates no intention of keeping his promises. Managers who act this way do so because they are afraid of conflict or because they think that being devious is being clever. Employees overwhelmingly prefer a manager who is forthright. The employee may not like the manager's position and may disagree strongly, but she knows where she stands.

Although working conditions are a dissatisfier, you should investigate complaints about working conditions in the same way that you investigate complaints about red tape—cautiously. Occasionally, working-condition complaints are justified and can be corrected. Some offices are in fact cold; the factory may in fact be noisy. More often, though, working-condition complaints are frivolous. For every two people who think a room is too cold, there is one person who thinks the temperature is just right and another who would like it a little cooler. Complaints about working conditions can be symptoms of other, more serious problems. Like a pain or a fever, a complaint may be a sign that something else is wrong; again, it may be something as simple as a pain that a couple of aspirin could fix.

Like catching cold, complaints about poor communications are inevitable. At one time or another, every employee in every organization believes that communications are poor. Assume you can never overcommunicate. You can, of course, through too many meetings and memos, but this is rare. People like to know what is going on, because being in the know is fun. Information is power and status. The people who know the most soonest have the highest status and the most power. If all your information is late and second-hand, you obviously are not very important.

Getting transferred is dissatisfying, a finding that should surprise no one. Security is a satisfier. People settle into their jobs, their routines, and their communities and do not like being uprooted. People respond poorly to transfers that they see as arbitrary, as nonnegotiable, or as substitutions for getting fired. Even transfers that are legitimate promotions may be resented. Here is a paradox: While advancement ranks high on the list of desired job attributes second for men and fifth for women—getting transferred ranks seventh as a dissatisfier. The ideal situation is when a promotion is awarded in place. The employee does not have to move anywhere except to a different chair. This happens more often in larger, centralized companies than in smaller, decentralized ones. The best case is the large, centralized enterprise, where the career ladders are tall and in the same city. People can go up many rungs without having to physically relocate. The worst case—many short ladders scattered all over the landscape—is that of decentralized, geographically dispersed organizations. An example is a company with many regional offices or manufacturing facilities.

Getting a new boss is also a dissatisfier that management can do something about. When replacing a boss, I have tried the technique of letting employees participate in the selection process. The employees choose from three or four candidates, any of whom, they are told, are acceptable for the position. Satisfaction with subsequent supervision improved when I did this. The employees felt responsible for the success of their boss. The new boss felt that she was the preferred candidate over other applicants, and I did not feel that I had imposed the new supervisor on the group.

The remaining two dissatisfiers are also partially within management's control. Being in the wrong job can be ameliorated by better initial selection or by transferring the unhappy employee into a better-fitting job. Boredom is a problem that is easily fixed if the problem is not having enough to do. If the problem is having to do what needs to be done, then the situation calls for job enrichment, for providing some temporary variety and excitement, or for transfer to a new job. Any job done long enough becomes boring, and any employee, not just those in service positions, can burn out.

Work as a Central Life Interest

Work satisfies people differently, not only because they value different types of work but also because they value work differently. People for whom work constitutes the primary sense of self-identity are more sensitive to work satisfiers and dissatisfiers. Life satisfaction influences job satisfaction; but, generally speaking, job satisfaction influences life satisfaction more (Chacko, 1983). If you are happy with your job, you will be happy with your life, but if you are happy with your life, you will not necessarily be happy with your job.

People for whom work is a central life issue are more able and more likely to experience high job satisfaction than those who do not see work as a central life interest (Dubin and Champoux, 1977). Unfortunately, even for most American middle managers, work is not a central life interest (Dubin and Goldman, 1972). Work is definitely not a central life interest for production workers. Work is most likely to be a central life interest for upper-level managers and for professionals. Which is the chicken and which is the egg? Do managers reach the top because work is their main interest in life, or do the responsibilities and rewards of top management make work become their central interest? What are people like who have work as their main interest?

Dubin and Champoux (1975) distributed a central life interest questionnaire to 568 male and female blue-collar workers at a telephone company. Workers who perceived work as their central life interest described themselves as having a high level of decisiveness, initiative, and supervisory ability. Workers whose central life interests were outside their jobs had lower scores on decisiveness, need for occupational achievement, and initiative. Two years later (1977), the same authors reported that workers with the most job satisfaction were those who viewed work as the central aspect of their lives. Those with nonwork-oriented central life interests had the lowest job satisfaction.

It would be flattering for you as a manager to believe that your company could provide the kind of environment and work challenge that would make work a central life interest for everyone. Forget it. There are some people who simply see work as a means to an end. If work is not very important to an employee, then there is little that management can do about it except try to let the employee do the work that best matches his skills.

Work That Uses Workers' Skills

The strongest predictor of job satisfaction is whether the job makes use of your skills. Skill utilization accounts for 42 percent of the variance in job satisfaction (O'Brien and Pembroke, 1982). Do you recognize a familiar old refrain? Are they playing our song—"Match the Right Person to the Job"? Occupational dissatisfaction results from lack of congruence between one's work and one's interests and personality (Campbell and Klein, 1975). Job satisfaction depends more than anything else on the job's ability to fulfill the job-content needs of the worker. Job satisfaction is contingent on perceiving that the job uses your skills (Humphreys, 1981). Working in a job that matches your education and training is satisfying but less so than working in a job that matches your perception of your skills.

Perceptions of the skills of coworkers also influence satisfaction. Both men and women prefer working with competent males rather than with competent females. Blacks prefer working with blacks, and females prefer working with females (Haefner, 1977). Of course, management can no longer accommodate these preferences. To do so is illegal.

Time and Age

Besides being related to the factors just noted, job satisfaction is also related to age, both chronological age and tenure in the job. Job satisfaction is a curvilinear function of time. It is high earlier and later and low in the middle. People experience the highest job satisfaction during the honeymoon period with an organization. Then job satisfaction erodes, reaching a low point eighteen to thirty-six months after employment. With time, job satisfaction increases again (Smith, Scott, and Hulin, 1977). The relationship between time and job satisfaction is U-shaped (Ronen, 1978).

We find a positive relationship between age and job satisfaction, with the relationship being asymptotic. This means that with age, satisfaction keeps rising to a theoretical limit (Gibson and Klein, 1970). People are most dissatisfied with their jobs and most likely to quit when they are below the age of thirty. They are more satisfied with their jobs and less likely to quit from their mid-forties until retirement. With advancing age, people either find work they like to do or become tolerant and satisfied with the work they have to do (Schwab and Heneman, 1977; Smith, Scott, and Hulin, 1977).

Young workers in low-status jobs are least satisfied with their work (Altimus and Tersine, 1973). Among blue-collar workers, dissatisfaction with work is chronic, even as they age (Phillips, Barrett, and Rush, 1978). Blue-collar blues notwithstanding, why are older workers generally more satisfied with their jobs? Wright and Hamilton (1978) offer three possible explanations. First, younger workers have a nonmaterial set of values that generates more discontent than older workers. Second, the standards of satisfaction of the old have been eroded by experience, and they have learned to be satisfied with less. Third, older workers have better jobs. The authors note that the bulk of research evidence tends to support the last hypothesis, but they believe a latitudinal study is necessary to reach a final conclusion.

Is there something about growing old that results in an increase in job satisfaction, or are the values of one's peers different when one is older? Is the increase with age in job satisfaction due to age itself or to cohort membership? O'Brien and Dowling (1981) tried to answer the question but could not untangle the relationship. They concluded that the phenomenon of increased job satisfaction with increasing age was the result of a decreasing discrepancy between desired and perceived job attributes: As you grow older, you lower your expectations and are satisfied with less. Other researchers (Janson and Martin, 1982) have also thrown up their hands and decided that neither a cohort explanation (differences in education and values) nor a life-cycle explanation (older workers have better jobs) makes sense. The basic finding holds, although a satisfactory explanation is still lacking. Older workers are more satisfied with their jobs and are less likely to quit.

There are older people who do change jobs, particularly those who change careers in midlife. What are they like? Weiner and Vaitenas (1977) compared people who had midcareer job changes with a group of stable controls. People who change careers are lower in ascendancy, dominance, responsibility, endurance, orderliness, and discipline. That is not too encouraging. Maybe they are happier. Do middle-aged job changers move into jobs more congruent with their personalities? After all, if people go to the trouble of changing jobs, you would hope they would find jobs more to their liking. And you would expect them to be more satisfied with their new jobs than they were with their old ones. Thomas and Robbins (1979) tested these assumptions experimentally. Middle-aged males who changed jobs did not find jobs more congruent with their interests and skills, and they were not more satisfied with their new jobs. Stick or switch, it doesn't make any difference. You take your misery with you.

Education and Gender

Better-educated workers are more satisfied with their jobs, but the correlation between job satisfaction and education is small. Job satisfaction is greatest when the individual first receives a college degree (Quinn and Baldi de Mandilovitch, 1980). For job satisfaction, we find that education matters but that gender does not. Weaver (1978) looked at three independent national samples and found no significant sex differences in level of job satisfaction. The effect of gender on job satisfaction is minimal. When sex differences do occur in job satisfaction, they may be the result of reward differences attributable to different occupational levels.

So far we have seen that the single most important variable in job satisfaction is a good match between the individual and the job. People are happiest in work that uses their perceived skills. The older individuals become, the more satisfied they are with their jobs. Education does not matter much, and gender matters not at all.

Job Status

Job status matters. Managers experience more job satisfaction than nonmanagers (Vroom, 1964). People higher up in an organizational structure experience more job satisfaction than those lower down in the organization. People in professional jobs experience more satisfaction than people in nonprofessional jobs (Pyke and Weisenberg, 1976). People with complicated jobs are happier than those with less complex jobs (Alderfer, 1967). People with middle-class jobs are more satisfied with their work than people with working-class jobs. The research is consistent. Those at the top of the job-status heap feel better about their work than those at the bottom of the heap. The happiest individuals should be the heads of large professional organizations. Still, all research has its exceptional findings, and job happiness can come even to those in low-status jobs. Walsh (1982) compared the job satisfaction of garbage collectors with the job satisfaction of college professors. The garbage collectors were just as satisfied with their jobs as the college professors.

Company Characteristics

The attributes of an organization affect job satisfaction. Of eleven climate measures studied by Batlis (1980), organizational clarity has the highest correlation with job satisfaction, which means that it is important for managers to provide structure. Satisfaction is higher when managers are clear about their own roles as well as those of employees (Keller, 1975) and when they show consideration (Osborn and Hunt, 1975). To make employees satisfied, manufacture a product rather than providing a service (Friedlauder and Pickle, 1970)—and give them windows (Finnegan and Solomon, 1981).

Summary

Job satisfaction is different from job performance. Satisfaction is related only indirectly to performance. Productivity may not really be affected much even if employees are happy, since there is not much evidence that happy employees perform better. Still, the effective manager will want to keep people satisfied, if only to avoid turnover.

Satisfaction is one of the most heavily researched topics in the psychology of work. Job satisfaction generally seems to be on the decline because of changes in workers' attitudes. The work ethic is no longer so strong as it was once, and fewer people have work as their central life interest. No job will satisfy two individuals in exactly the same way, since individuals bring with them differing propensities for experiencing job satisfaction. People want jobs that provide interesting work in stable environments with good pay and chances for advancement. People dislike jobs that mismatch their interests and skills. If employees' primary interest is work, they will derive much satisfaction from work. If their primary interest lies outside work, there is little you can do about it except to have jobs match employees' interests and skills. Except for professionals, entrepreneurs, and top managers, work is no longer a central life interest for most Americans.

The best single predictor of job satisfaction is having work that allows you to utilize your skills and that matches your interests. People are more satisfied when they are working with other people who are competent. Older employees are more satisfied with their jobs than younger employees are with theirs. The relationship between job satisfaction and job tenure is U-shaped—high at the beginning, low after eighteen to thirty-six months, and higher again after that. The people who are most dissatisfied with their jobs are blue-collar workers under thirty. The people who are most satisfied with their jobs are high-ranking, well-educated executives in professional organizations. Gender does not make any difference in job satisfaction.

Besides understanding the constituents of job satisfaction, managers can help by making good person-job matches and by providing job and organizational clarity. To satisfy employees, managers should be forthright, communicate frequently, avoid unnecessary changes, and recognize good performance when it occurs.

14

Summary
of Guidelines
for Making People
Productive

In this, the final chapter, I will summarize the major concepts on making people productive through the employment cycle. What managers need most is an integration of existing research, translated into practical guidelines that they can use in their own organizations. America has a productivity problem. It threatens our national standing as an economic world power, and it threatens our individual standards of living. While we still rank as one of the most productive nations in the world, we are last among major industrialized countries in our rate of growth in productivity. We are slipping rapidly in our growth in productivity and need to do something to stop the erosion. Making people productive, an important challenge facing U.S. organizations, has been the dominant theme of this book.

A simple measure of productivity is output per person hour. Although technology and capital do affect productivity, substantial opportunities for improved organizational effectiveness can be found in better utilization of America's human resources.

While poor productivity has been blamed on everything

and everyone, a favorite scapegoat is the blue-collar worker, but the facts fail to support the accusation. We can say that the number of blue-collar workers has declined, and so has the quality of their labor. Still, we cannot hold them primarily to blame for the decline in productivity.

The United States has shifted from a manufacturing to a service economy, increasing the number of white-collar jobs. White-collar workers work at only half speed, and there may be too many managers. While improvement in productivity will come through better management of the white-collar work force, that alone is also not the answer. Advances in technology definitely will help. Robotics, computers, and so on can and will improve productivity, but the manager's best chance for direct and immediate productivity improvement still lies in making employees more productive throughout the employment cycle.

Industrial and organizational psychology can help companies improve productivity. Up to 87 percent of the interventions by industrial and organizational psychologists have resulted in improvements in at least one concrete measure of productivity. The programs that work best are compensation, goal setting, and training.

Psychological Theories and Productivity

A number of psychological theories have concerned themselves with the prediction of performance. These theories have asked: Who are the best performers, under what circumstances, and provided with what kind of leadership? What produces job satisfaction, and does it matter? Can improved performance be taught? Does training work?

We looked at a number of encompassing theories: Maslow's needs hierarchy; Herzberg's motivation-hygiene theory; McGregor's Theory X and Theory Y; expectancy theory; equity theory; leadership theory; and behavior modification. The most useful theories are goal-setting theory, expectancy theory, and equity theory. People are motivated by fairness. The effects on behavior of both under-reward inequity and over-reward inequity are fairly clear. Under-rewarding increases quantity of output. Over-rewarding may increase quality of output.

Goal-setting theory also is credible. Goal specificity, goal difficulty, and participation in goal setting are positively related to performance. To improve productivity, there is one simple rule all managers should follow: "<u>SET SPECIFIC HARD GOALS</u>." Managers need to set both group and individual goals and to revise them periodically, because the effects of goal setting dissipate over time. As in many areas of personnel work, the technique is less important than the act. An elaborate program is not necessary for productivity, but specific hard goals are.

Expectancy theory also is an aid to the participating manager. People behave in ways consistent with their expectations. If desirable outcomes are made available to employees, and if they can believe that their behavior will lead to the acquiring of those outcomes, performance will improve. People get what they expect. There is real magic in positive thinking and visual imagery. In the workplace, as in other aspects of life, we are the beneficiaries or the victims of our own self-fulfilling prophecies. The Pygmalion effect exists and is a valuable motivator. People perform at the levels that we expect of them and that they expect of themselves. A powerful combination is strong expectancy and a difficult goal to be achieved.

In summing up the utility of psychological theories, we can say that certain motivational theories—achievement motivation, equity, goal setting, and expectancy—are useful in predicting performance, but each is limited to its own domain and applies only to certain individuals under certain circumstances. There is no general psychological theory of productivity, and there is little reason to believe we will have one soon.

Selection

The first step in the employment cycle is selection. The challenge to managers is to select the people who will be productive in the future. To do so, managers must understand the aptitudes and abilities correlated with those who are successful.

In the selection process, it is best to insist on congruence between people's interests and job responsibilities, find evidence of intelligence, and determine the strength of individual motivations to achieve.

Three techniques are commonly used to make selection decisions. Two of them, psychological tests and biographical information, are valid; but the most frequently used selection method, the interview, is of questionable validity. The conscientious manager conducting an interview will take time to analyze the applicant's past record of achievement and will resist the temptation to formulate a quick and superficial first impression. The same manager will acquire the additional skills of evaluating ability and motivation or will avail himself of psychological appraisal techniques shown to be effective in predicting success.

Matching Jobs and People

Managers need to know about individual differences and job families and how they relate to productivity. They need to understand the contribution that the employee makes to the input/output productivity equation, as well as the types of traits known to be efficacious for employees generally and in specific job families. The successful person produces something, demonstrating mastery of situations faced. Individual productivity is both a relative concept and a comparison to a standard. Some productivity predictors can be gleaned from a résumé. Background and prior work experience are important. Past achievement is more important than job-specific experience, which in turn is more important than years of experience. Personal attributes predict performance. These include appearance, marital status, ego, and work as a central life interest. Hire good-looking, mature, sole wage earners for whom their work is their life. Internal attributors will bring you success; external attributors will bring you nothing but grief. Hire people who blame themselves for failure. A high level of energy is a universal trait of productive people. In the long run, sustained interest and continuous application of energy win over differ-

ences in talent. Hire high-energy workaholics obsessed with the
need to succeed. Different job families—research and development, engineering, manufacturing, personnel, finance, general
management, and sales—have their own personalities. Sales has
received the most attention, because if you don't sell your
product, you don't have a business. Different jobs have different productivity profiles, and the first step in the employment
cycle should be a careful matching of the job and the employee.

Training

Training is a powerful tool in making people productive.
Above 80 percent of the time, training programs work. What
should you train for? You should train for information and job-
specific content, or you should train for role modeling. To train
for problem-solving skills is probably ineffective. You can train
for human relations skills, but the effects are not lasting, and
the relationship between good human relations skills and productivity is tenuous. You can and should also train for certain
other types of functional skills—for example, skills in sales. This
is best done through simulations and behavior modeling. Some
training programs attempt to make people better managers. This
is effective at the first level of supervision, where you can teach
the rudiments of personnel management. It is more difficult at
the middle and upper management levels because of problems in
defining leadership and describing what a leader does.

An encouraging body of research emerging from the
training literature concerns the efficacy of self-development,
especially guided visual imagery. In this modality, the individual
rehearses in his or her mind the behaviors and outcomes that are
desired. When certain rules of imagery and suggestion are followed, the evidence is that some of the effects are about as good
as those obtained through formal trainer/trainee interactions.

Motivators

Expectancy theory tells us that expectations are motivating. People behave in the ways they themselves and their supervisors expect them to behave. Successful, productive people

represent self-fulfilling prophecies of high levels of achievement. Belief in self-efficacy can be developed through repeated affirmation and guided imagery. Self-expectancy has more predictive power for productivity than ability does.

People are also motivated at work by the fantasies or needs that dominate their thoughts. Three common motivational needs are affiliation, power, and achievement. The need to achieve is the most significant for productivity. The achievement motive is significantly higher in economically successful individuals, companies, and countries. While the need for achievement is formed by childrearing practices, in working adults the trait can be developed through special training. The need to achieve is especially high in entrepreneurs, and companies wanting to encourage entrepreneurs may wish to offer achievement motivation training.

Effective Managers

Understanding what makes managers effective requires, first, that we define what we mean by *manager* and, second, that we agree on what managers do. A practical and useful definition of *manager* is "anyone who is directly responsible for getting work done through others." Managers are more alike than different, despite functional speciality, level in the organizational structure, or cultural context. The primary factor that makes someone a manager is that he or she must plan, organize, and control the work of other people. Exhaustive lists of the critical incidents in a manager's job run to over 3,000 incidents, but the essence of these lists is that the effective manager successfully produces work through guiding other people.

There is a huge literature on what makes managers successful, but its important conclusions are few. Successful managers are brighter than their followers, have stronger personalities, and are more driven to lead and be successful. Elite managers—individuals who have reached the top of the organization—have intense, narrow interests and a strong drive to achieve. High-achieving managers decide early in their careers what they want to do and then pursue their goal maniacally. They sweep others along toward this goal, refusing to be stopped by criticism, lack of support, or temporary failure. The highly successful manager is often no more able than less successful colleagues but is always more motivated and has a higher set of self-expectations.

Managers have different styles, and at least four have been identified. The most successful is a consultative style, followed by the one that emphasizes salesmanship. One style that does not work well is the authoritarian style of management. An effective manager structures the work to be done by identifying goals, distributing tasks, setting deadlines, and reviewing results. The effective manager also shows consideration for people's opinions, feelings, and general well-being.

After years of research, and thousands and thousands of articles about what makes a good manager, a fairly simple picture remains. A good manager is a cut above the other employees in brains, personality, and ambition. The productive manager structures the work and shows concern for the welfare of the people who must do the work. That is the essence of an effective manager.

Effective Management Techniques

What techniques of management have proved effective? Setting goals definitely improves productivity. To be effective, a goal need only be specific, difficult, and communicated. It is not crucial whether goals are assigned, developed on one's own, or established in a participatory setting. There are individual differences in how people respond to goals. Well-educated people and top managers merely need to be told what the goals are. Less-educated people and lower-level employees have more need for explanation and periodic feedback. Goal setting is a continuous process requiring variety to avoid plateauing and burnout among employees. Of all the productivity techniques available to management, nothing has been found to be as consistently useful as setting tough goals.

Research results are mixed about the efficacy of participatory management practices. Most of the time, participation in decision making and goal setting does improve employee acceptance and satisfaction, but participation does not improve work quality and seems to have only a limited ability to improve work quantity. As a consideration technique of management, an important value of participation is its ability to improve employee satisfaction. Work simplification, a variant of techniques first introduced by Frederick Taylor around the turn of the century, emphasizes structure and task. There is now a revival of interest in this technique. Work simplification seeks to eliminate and simplify work, improving productivity by reducing labor input. Another task-oriented technique is time management. Since productivity is directly related to time, more effective use of time is a worthwhile technique that managers can apply, both to themselves and to their employees.

Techniques emphasizing consideration for employees are based on two assumptions: that a cared-for employee is a satisfied employee, and that a satisfied employee is a productive employee. We are still gathering empirical evidence to prove these assumptions. In the meantime, employee assistance programs are common in large companies and increasing in other companies.

In general, research indicates that management techniques emphasizing structure improve productivity, while techniques emphasizing consideration improve satisfaction. One technique for effectively combining consideration and structure is behavior modification. A small but generally positive body of literature suggests that behavior modification works, but its widespread adoption as a management technique is unlikely.

Goal Setting and Performance Appraisal

Goal setting and performance appraisal is an effective technique for making people productive, because it combines the structure functions with the consideration functions of effective management. Setting goals and appraising performance is a difficult task. It is unpleasant because of the inherent potential for conflict, but perhaps no other single factor is as directly related to organizational effectiveness as establishing and communicating the goals of the organization, parceling them out to individuals, and keeping track of who is doing his share.

Individuals vary in their needs to achieve and in their responsiveness to goal setting and performance appraisal. It is hard to know exactly how difficult to make goals, but tough goals result in greater productivity than easy goals do. Whether or not employees participate in the goal-setting process depends on the preferences of employees as well as on those of managers.

Measuring performance is never easy and often exasperating. No perfect appraisal system exists, although we continue to search for one. Such quests are quixotic. Any appraisal system has problems with reliability, validity, and the value systems of appraisers and appraisees alike. All managers can do is be aware of the more obvious pitfalls and take steps to avoid them.

While most managers appraise performance only because they are told to do so, the objective of performance appraisal should be to modify behavior. Behavior modification requires managers to provide employees with feedback about performance. Behavior will not change unless feedback is provided and the desired behavior is reinforced. The best way to change behavior is to provide information about desired behavior and the way in which current behavior deviates from it. Managers cannot be too careful or too tactful in communicating negative information.

Companies that have no performance appraisal programs or have trait-oriented programs should establish goal setting-based performance appraisal programs. They can expect to encounter numerous problems in setting up and maintaining these programs, yet there is little alternative. Goal setting and performance appraisal are indispensable to making people productive.

Compensation

Compensation, especially incentive compensation, is one of the more powerful of all management techniques for improving productivity. The first scientists of management, people like

Frederick Taylor, advocated the use of various compensation techniques, such as incentives to make people productive. After World War II, with the influence of the human potential movement on management psychologists, theories of compensation as a motivator fell into disrepute. With the rise of humanistic psychology in the workplace, U.S. productivity declined. Humanists said people did not work for money. With the rising alarm over U.S. productivity problems, by 1980 compensation was once again recognized as a useful method for stimulating worker output.

Effective managers use compensation to stimulate productivity. Consistent with their role of providing structure, effective managers define job content through position descriptions and establish a hierarchy of job values through job evaluations or job rankings. Research has shown that the exact techniques used to do this are not important; most reputable techniques work equally well. Because employees are most concerned with how their pay relates to that of others, managers will see to it that salary surveys are made so that the company can communicate its competitive posture.

There are some known correlates of pay that the manager will find useful. The most important of these is that people produce more when they believe that pay is contingent on individual performance. Most organizations try to tie pay to performance through the use of differential salary increases on an annual basis. This is called merit pay. While popular, merit pay is not especially effective.

Incentive pay is psychologically more sound and pragmatically more economical than merit pay. Incentive pay improves productivity at all organizational levels. While much remains to be learned about how incentives work, productivity increases of 20 percent are common with incentives. Output is also more stable with incentives, and pay satisfaction increases.

Compensation programs must be communicated, and employees' satisfaction tends to increase under conditions of open pay disclosure. Full disclosure, however, is inadvisable, and communications programs are best limited to general descriptions of program objectives and specific details about the individual employee's compensation opportunity.

Turnover

Turnover is the antithesis of productivity. Turnover means that management has failed to make people productive. The individual who leaves a company voluntarily is saying that another organization affords her a work environment that better meets her needs. When the employee leaves involuntarily, management is saying it made a mistake in selection, training, goal setting and performance appraisal, compensation, or current job assignment; it failed somewhere in the employment cycle. In most companies, turnover averages between 20 and 25 percent annually. Turnover's negative impact on organizational productivity is enormous in money and morale. Management needs to understand turnover so as to control it.

People quit their jobs for a variety of reasons. The four mentioned most frequently are opportunity for growth; salary and financial benefits; job satisfaction; and working conditions. In simplistic terms, people quit because their jobs no longer satisfy them and when economic conditions permit them to risk leaving. The major modifier of turnover is the economic climate. Turnover drops during recessions that have high unemployment.

To control turnover, managers have to learn what causes it and then learn how to predict it. A good predictor of turnover is an individual's directly or indirectly stated intention to remain with or leave the organization. Such intentions are seldom expressed directly but can be interpreted from employees' conversation, enthusiasm for work, absenteeism, and general attitudes toward the organization. These signals give effective managers an opportunity to utilize various managerial devices to re-engage employees' commitment.

Turnover, in its worst form, is termination—firing the employee. To ease the transition out of one organization and into another, companies are using a new technique, outplacement, particularly for executives. Outplacement appears to be helpful. Executives who go through an outplacement experience improve their income by an average of 20 percent, and three quarters find positions with other organizations. The remainder go into business for themselves.

To prevent turnover, pick the right people. Make sure people's abilities and interests fit their jobs, communicate thoroughly what people can expect from their jobs and from the organization, and be sure individuals have opportunities for growth. Then practice effective management techniques. By doing so, managers will have a reasonably good chance of retaining satisfied people.

Satisfaction

Job satisfaction is different from job performance. Satisfaction is only indirectly related to performance. Surprisingly, there is not much explicit evidence that happy employees perform better. Still, the effective manager will want to keep people satisfied, if only to avoid turnover.

Job satisfaction seems generally to be on the decline in America because of changes in workers' attitudes. The work ethic is no longer so strong, and fewer people have work as their central life interest. No job will satisfy two individuals in exactly the same way, since individuals have different propensities for experiencing job satisfaction. Everyone wants a job that provides interesting work in a stable environment, with good pay and a chance for advancement. People dislike jobs that do not match their interests and skills. If an employee's primary interest is work, she will derive more satisfaction from her work. Except for professionals and top managers, work is no longer a central life interest for most Americans.

The best single predictor of work satisfaction is for an employee to be in a job that allows him to utilize his skills and that matches his interests. People are more satisfied when they are working with other people who are competent, including competent managers. Managers can help by making good person-job matches and providing job and organizational clarity. Satisfying managers also are honest, communicate frequently, avoid unnecessary transfers, and recognize good performance when it occurs.

Making people productive is a complex and endless challenge. Opportunities for improvement occur throughout the

employment cycle. By applying the findings of research in psychology, employees and managers alike can contribute to increasing the productivity of their organizations and the quality
of their own lives.

References

Acuff, H. A. "Quality Control Is Employee Selection." *Personnel Journal,* 1981, *60* (7), 562-565.

Adams, J. S. "The Structure and Dynamics of Behavior in Organizational Boundary Roles." In M. D. Dunnette (ed.), *Handbook of Industrial and Organizational Psychology.* Skokie, Ill.: Rand McNally, 1976.

Alderfer, C. P. "An Organizational Syndrome." *Administrative Science Quarterly,* 1967, *12,* 440-460.

Allen, M. P., and Panian, S. K. "Power, Performance, and Succession in the Large Corporation." *Administrative Science Quarterly,* 1982, *27* (4), 538-547.

Alluisi, E. A., and Meigs, D. K. "Potentials for Productivity Enhancement from Psychological Research and Development." *American Psychologist,* 1983, *38* (4), 487-493.

Altimus, C. A., and Tersine, R. J. "Chronological Age and Job Satisfaction: The Young Blue Collar Worker." *Academy of Management Journal,* 1973, *16,* 53-66.

Anderson, D. C., and others. "Behavior Management in the Public Accommodations Industry: A Three-Project Demonstration." *Journal of Organizational Behavior Management,* 1982, *4* (1-2), 33-66.

Andrews, K. R. "Is Management Training Effective?" *The Harvard Business Review,* 1957, *35,* 63-72.

Argyris, C. "Some Limitations of the Case Method: Experiences in a Management Development Program." *Academy of Management Review,* 1980, *5,* 291-298.

Atkinson, J. W., and Feather, N. T. (eds.). *A Theory of Achievement Motivation.* New York: Wiley, 1966.

Attarian, P. J. "Early Recollections: Predictors of Vocational Choice." *Journal of Individual Psychology,* 1978, *34* (1), 56–62.

Bain, D. *The Productivity Prescription.* New York: McGraw-Hill, 1982.

Balchin, N. "Satisfaction in Work." *Occupational Psychology,* 1970, *44,* 165–173.

Banks, C. F., and Gleck, W. H. "Good Taste in Organizational Behavior: 57 Varieties." *Contemporary Psychology,* 1984, *29* (1), 63.

Barling, J., and Beattie, R. "Self-Efficacy Beliefs and Sales Performance." *Journal of Organizational Behavior Management,* 1983, *5* (1), 41–51.

Bartol, K. M., and Manhardt, P. J. "Sex Differences in Job Outcome Preferences: Trend Among Newly Hired College Graduates." *Journal of Applied Psychology,* 1979, *64* (5), 477–482.

Bass, B. M. "Further Evidence of the Dynamic Character of Criteria." *Personnel Psychology,* 1962, *15,* 93–97.

Bass, B. M. "Quality Standards for Ready-to-Use Training and Development Programs." *Journal of Applied Behavioral Science,* 1977, *13* (4), 518–532.

Bass, B. M., and others. *Assessment of Managers: An International Comparison.* New York: Free Press, 1979.

Basset, G. A., and Meyer, H. H. "Performance Appraisal Based on Self-Review." *Personnel Psychology,* 1968, *21,* 421–430.

Batlis, N. C. "The Effect of Organizational Climate on Job Satisfaction, Anxiety, and Propensity to Leave." *Journal of Psychology,* 1980, *104* (2), 233–240.

Bauer, M. "Do You Hate Your Job? There May Be Top Ten Reasons Why." *Extra,* November 1980, pp. 11–15.

Bayne, R. "Can Selection Interviewing Be Improved?" *Journal of Occupational Psychology,* 1977, *50* (3), 161–167.

Beehr, T. A., and Gilmore, D. C. "Applicant Attractiveness as a Perceived Job-Relevant in Selection of Management Trainees." *Academy of Management Journal,* 1982, *25* (3), 607–617.

Belcher, D. W., and Atchison, T. J. "Compensation for Work." In R. Dubin (ed.), *Handbook of Work, Organization, and Society.* Skokie, Ill.: Rand McNally, 1976.

Bellows, R. M. *Executive Skills: Their Dynamics and Development.* Englewood Cliffs, N.J.: Prentice-Hall, 1962.

Bennett, P. D., and Harrell, G. D. "Role of Confidence and Understanding in Predicting Buyers' Attitudes and Purchase Intentions." *Journal of Consumer Research,* 1975, *2,* 110-117.

Bennis, W. G. "Chairman Mac in Perspective." *The Harvard Business Review,* 1972, *50,* 140-149.

Bennis, W. G. "Qualities of Elite Leaders." Speech to the Hay Group. Washington, D.C., 1981.

Berger, P. K., and Ivancevich, J. M. "Birth Order and Managerial Achievement." *Academy of Management Journal,* 1973, *16,* 515-519.

Bhatia, S. K. "Trends in Performance Appraisal." *Indian Journal of Industrial Relations,* 1981, *17* (1), 111-119.

Bhatia, S. K., and Valecha, G. K. "A Review of the Research Findings on Absenteeism." *Indian Journal of Industrial Relations,* 1981, *17* (2), 229-285.

Bhushan, L. I. "A Study of Attitudes Toward Incentives in Two Industrial Units." *Indian Journal of Behavior,* 1976, *1* (1), 1-8.

Biesheuvel, S. "Personnel Selection." *Annual Review of Psychology,* 1965, *16* (1), 16.

Birkenbach, X. C., and Van der Merwe, R. "Black Employees' Perceptions of Organizational Pay Practices: The Development and Application of an Instrument." *Psychologia Africana,* 1979, *18,* 46-64.

Blake, R. R., and Mouton, J. S. *The Managerial Grid.* Houston: Gulf, 1964.

Blake, R. R., and Mouton, J. S. *Productivity: The Human Side.* New York: American Management Association, 1981.

Blake, R. R., and Mouton, J. S. "A Comparative Analysis of Situationalism and Management by Principle." *Organizational Dynamics,* 1982, *10* (4), 20-43.

Boeyens, M. J., and de Jager, J. J. "Management Style and Research Leader Efficiency." *Psychologia Africana,* 1982, *21,* 103-117.

Borenstein, P. I. "When Training Is Not Enough." *Training and Development Journal,* 1983, *37* (4), 92-94.

Bowles, S., Gordon, D., and Weisskopf, T. E. *Beyond the Wasteland: A Democratic Alternative to Economic Decline.* New York: Anchor Press/Doubleday, 1983.

Branham, F. L. "How to Evaluate Executive Outplacement Services." *Personnel Journal,* 1983, *62* (4), 323-326.

Brenner, D. C., and Tomkiewicz, J. "Relationship Between Aggression and Managerial Effectiveness." *Psychological Reports,* 1980, *47* (1), 271-274.

Bridgewater, C. A. "The Risks of Pressuring Employees." *Psychology Today,* 1983, *17* (4), 19.

Brooks, E. "What Successful Executives Do." *Personnel,* 1955, *32* (3), 210-225.

Brousseau, K. R. "Toward a Dynamic Model of Job-Person Relationships: Findings, Research Questions, and Implications for Work System Design." *Academy of Management Review,* 1983, *8* (1), 33-45.

Bryan, J. F., and Locke, E. A. "Goal Setting as a Means of Increasing Motivation." *Journal of Applied Psychology,* 1967, *51,* 274-277.

Buchholz, R. A. "An Empirical Study of Contemporary Beliefs About Work in American Society." *Journal of Applied Psychology,* 1978, *63* (2), 219-227.

Burke, R. J. "Characteristics of Effective Appraisal Interviews: 1) Open Communications and Acceptance of Subordinate Disagreements." *Training and Development Journal,* 1970, *24,* 9-12.

Burke, R. J., Deszca, G. and Weitzel, W. "Subordinate Expectations and Satisfaction with the Performance Appraisal Interview." *Journal of Psychology,* 1982, *111* (1), 41-49.

Bursk, E. C., and Blodgett, T. B. (eds.). *Developing Executive Leaders.* Cambridge: Harvard University Press, 1971.

Busch, P., and Wilson, D. T. "An Experimental Analysis of a Salesman's Expert and Referrent Basis of Social Power in the Buyer-Seller Dyad." *Journal of Marketing Research,* 1976, *13,* 3-11.

Byzzotta, V. R., and Lefton, R. E. "What Makes a Sales Winner?" *Training and Development Journal,* 1981, *35* (11), 70-77.

Cammann, C. F. T., and Lawler, E. E. III. "Employer Reaction to Pay Incentive Plan." *Journal of Applied Psychology,* 1973, *58,* 163-172.

Campbell, D. P., and Klein, K. L. "Job Satisfaction and Vocational Interest." *Vocational Guidance Quarterly,* 1975, *24,* 125-131.

Campbell, J. "Personnel Training and Development." *Annual Review of Psychology,* 1971, *22,* 565-602.

Campbell, J. P., Daft, R. L., and Hulin, C. L. *What to Study: Generating and Developing Research Questions. Studying Organizations: Innovations in Methodology.* Vol. 6. Beverly Hills, Calif.: Sage, 1982.

Campbell, J. P., Dunnette, M. D., Lawler, E. E., and Weich, K. E. *Managerial Behavior, Performance, and Effectiveness.* New York: McGraw-Hill, 1970.

Carey, J., and others. "A Test of Positive Re-enforcement of Customers." *Journal of Marketing,* 1976, *40,* 98-100.

Carlson, S. *Executive Behavior: A Study of the Work Load and the Working Methods of Managing Directors.* Stockholm: Strombergs, 1951.

Carroll, S. J., and Schneier, C. E. *Performance Appraisal and Review Systems.* Glenview, Ill.: Scott Foresman, 1982.

Cascio, W., and Bernardin, J. "Implications of Performance Appraisal Litigation for Personnel Decisions." *Personnel Psychology,* 1981, *34* (2), 211-226.

Cash, T. F., Gillen, B., and Burns, D. S. "Sexism and Beautyism in Personnel Consultant Decision Making." *Journal of Applied Psychology,* 1977, *62* (3), 301-310.

Chacko, T. I. "Job and Life Satisfaction: A Casual Analysis of Their Relationship." *Academy of Management Journal,* 1983, *26* (1), 163-169.

Cherry, N. "Persistent Job Changing: Is It a Problem?" *Journal of Occupational Psychology,* 1976, *49* (4), 203-221.

Clemens, B., and others. "Engineers' Interest Patterns: Then and Now." *Educational and Psychological Measurement,* 1970, *30,* 675-685.

Cleveland, J. N., and Landy, F. J. "The Influence of Rater and Ratee Age on Two Performance Judgments." *Personnel Psychology,* 1981, *34* (1), 19-29.

Cleveland, S. E. "Reflections on the Rise and Fall of Psycho-Diagnosis." *Professional Psychology,* 1976, *7,* 309-318.

Clowers, M. R., and Fraser, R. T. "Employment Interview Literature: A Perspective for the Counselor." *Vocational Guidance Quarterly,* 1977, *26* (1), 13-26.

Cooper, H. "Statistical Synthesis of Research Literature." *Contemporary Psychology,* 1983, *28* (11), 835-836.

Crawford, K. D., Thomas, E. D., and Fink, J. J. "Pygmalion at Sea: Improving the Work Effectiveness of Low Performers." *Journal of Applied Behavioral Science,* 1980, *16* (4), 482-505.

Crowley, A. D. "Predicting Occupational Entry: Measured Versus Expressed Interests." *Journal of Occupational Psychology,* 1983, *56* (1), 57-61.

Crystal, G. Address to American Compensation Association, Western Regional Conference, San Diego, Calif., June 1984.

Darley, J. G. "A Journal Is Born." *Journal of Applied Psychology,* 1969, *52,* 1-9.

Dawson, C. M. "Will Career Plateauing Become a Bigger Problem?" *Personnel Journal,* 1983, *62* (1), 78-81.

Deci, E. *Intrinsic Motivation.* New York: Plenum, 1975.

DeNisi, A. D., and Shaw, J. B. "Investigation of the Uses of Self-Reports of Abilities." *Journal of Applied Psychology,* 1977, *62,* 641-644.

Dennison, E. *Machine Design,* November 23, 1979, p. 2.

Deterline, W. A. "Speaking from Experience: The 'Magic Gadget' and the 'Every Man a Shrink' Phenomenon." *Training and Development Journal,* 1978, *32* (6), 44-46.

De Vries, D. L., and others. *Performance Appraisal on the Line.* New York: Wiley, 1981.

Dickson, J. W. "Top Managers' Beliefs and Rationales for Participation." *Human Relations,* 1982, *35* (3), 203-217.

Dipboye, R. L. "In Quest of the Job/Person Matrix." *Contemporary Psychology,* 1983, *28* (10), 749.

Dipboye, R. L., and de Pontbriand, R. "Correlates of Employee

Relations to Performance Appraisals and Appraisal Systems." *Journal of Applied Psychology,* 1981, *66* (2), 248-251.

Dipboye, R. L., and others. "Relative Importance of Applicant Sex, Attractiveness, and Scholastic Standing in Evaluation of Job Applicant Resumes." *Journal of Applied Psychology,* 1975, *60,* 39-43.

Divingston, J. S. "New Trends in Applied Management Development." *Training and Development Journal,* 1983, *37* (1), 15-24.

Dodson, C. R., and Haskew, B. S. "Why Public Workers Stay." *Public Personnel Management,* 1976, *5,* 132-138.

Dossett, D. L., and Greenberg, C. L. "Goal Setting and Performance Evaluation: An Attributional Analysis." *Academy of Management Journal,* 1981, *24* (4), 767-779.

Dossett, D. L., and Hulvershorn, P. "Increasing Technical Training Efficiency: Peer Training via Computer-Assisted Instruction." *Journal of Applied Psychology,* 1984, *144,* 20-24.

Drucker, P. F. *Management Tasks, Responsibilities, and Practices.* New York: Harper & Row, 1974.

Drucker, P. F. *Managing in Turbulent Times.* New York: Harper & Row, 1980.

Drucker, P. F. "Why America's Got So Many Jobs." *The Wall Street Journal,* January 24, 1984, CX(16), p. 28.

Dubin, R., and Champoux, J. E. "Workers' Central Life Interests and Personality Characteristics." *Journal of Vocational Behavior,* 1975, *6,* 165-174.

Dubin, R., and Champoux, J. E. "Central Life Interests and Job Satisfaction." *Organizational Behavior and Human Performance,* 1977, *18* (2), 366-377.

Dubin, R., and Goldman, D. R. "Central Life Interests of American Middle Managers and Specialists." *Journal of Vocational Behavior,* 1972, *2,* 133-141.

Dubin, R., and others. "Central Life Interests and Organizational Commitment of Blue Collar and Clerical Workers." *Administrative Science Quarterly,* 1975, *20,* 411-421.

Dubruszek, Z. "The Personality of Managers." *Polish Psychological Bulletin,* 1975, *6,* 207-216.

Dudek, E. E. "Personnel Selection." *Annual Review of Psychology,* 1963, *14* (1), 14.

Dunnette, M. D., and Fleishman, E. A. (eds.). *Human Capability Assessment.* Hillsdale, N.J.: Erlbaum, 1982.

Dunnette, M. D., and Kirchner, W. K. "Validation of Psychological Tests in Industry." *Personnel Administration,* 1958, *21,* 20-27.

Durand, D. E. "Relation of Achievement and Power Motives to Performance Among Black Businessmen." *Psychological Reproach,* 1975, *37,* 11-14.

Dyer, L., Schwab, D. P., and Theriault, R. D. "Managerial Perceptions Regarding Salary Increase Criteria." *Personnel Psychology,* 1976, *29* (2), 233-242.

Eden, D., and Ravid, G. "Pygmalion Versus Self-Expectancy: Effects of Instructor- and Self-Expectancy on Trainee Performance." *Organizational Behavior and Human Performance,* 1982, *30* (3), 351-364.

Eden, D., and Shani, A. B. "Pygmalion Goes to Boot Camp: Expectancy, Leadership, and Trainee Performance." *Journal of Applied Psychology,* 1982, *67,* 194-199.

Ekerdt, D. J., and others. "Longitudinal Change in Preferred Age of Retirement." *Journal of Occupational Psychology,* 1976, *49,* 161-169.

Eysenck, H. J. "Personality Patterns and Various Groups of Businessmen." *Occupational Psychology,* 1967, *4,* 249-250.

Fallis, R. F. "The Determination, Weighting, and Cross-Validation of Criterion Dimensions of Salesmen's Performance." *Dissertation Abstract,* 1967, *27,* 2523-2524.

Farina, A., and Felner, R. D. "Employment Interviewer Reactions to Former Mental Patients." *Journal of Abnormal Psychology,* 1973, *32,* 268-272.

Fear, R. A. *The Evaluation Interview.* New York: McGraw-Hill, 1984.

Feather, N. T. (ed.). *Expectations and Actions: Expectancy Value Models in Psychology.* Hillsdale, N.J.: Erlbaum, 1982.

Feldman, D. C., and Arnold, H. J. "Position Choice: Comparing the Importance of Organizational and Job Factors." *Journal of Applied Psychology,* 1978, *63* (6), 706-710.

Ferguson, L. W. "Ability, Interest, and Aptitude." *Journal of Applied Psychology,* 1960, *4,* 126-131.

Fiedler, F. E. *A Theory of Leadership Effectiveness.* New York: McGraw-Hill, 1967.

Fineman, S. "The Influence of Perceived Job Climate upon Relationship of Managerial Achievement Motivation and Performance." *Journal of Occupational Psychology,* 1975, *48,* 113–124.

Finley, M. H., and Lee, A. T. "The Terminated Executive: It's Like Dying." *Personnel and Guidance Journal,* 1981, *59* (6), 382–384.

Finley, R. E., and Ziobro, H. R. (eds.). *The Manufacturing Man and His Job.* New York: American Managers Association, 1966.

Finnegan, M. C., and Solomon, L. Z. "Work Attitudes in Windowed and Windowless Environments." *Journal of Social Psychology,* 1981, *115* (2), 291–292.

Flanagan, J. C. "The Critical Incident Technique." *Psychological Bulletin,* 1954, *51,* 327–358.

Flanagan, J. C., and Krug, R. E. "Testing in Management Selection: State of the Art." *Personnel Administration,* 1964, *27,* 33–39.

Fleishman, E. A. "Twenty Years of Consideration and Structure." In E. A. Fleishman and J. G. Hunt (eds.), *Current Developments in the Study of Leadership.* Carbondale: Southern Illinois University Press, 1973.

Ford, J. K., and Wroten, S. P. "A Content Validity Ratio Approach to Determine Training Needs." Paper presented at annual meeting of the American Psychological Association, Washington, D.C., 1982.

Freeman, G. L., and Taylor, E. K. *How to Pick Leaders: A Scientific Approach to Executive Selection.* New York: Funk & Wagnalls, 1950.

Friedlauder, F., and Pickle, H. B. "Employee and Societal Satisfactions Provided Organizations and Different Industries." *Personnel Journal,* 1970, *49,* 577–582.

Fryans, L. (ed.). *Achievement Motivation: Recent Trends in Theory and Research.* New York: Plenum, 1982.

Futrell, C. M. "Effects of Pay Disclosure on Satisfaction for Sales Managers: A Longitudinal Study." *Academy of Management Journal,* 1978, *21* (1), 140–144.

Futrell, C. M., and Jenkins, O. C. "Pay Secrecy Versus Pay Disclosure for Salesmen: A Longitudinal Study." *Journal of Marketing Research,* 1978, *15* (2), 214–219.

Garland, H. "The Effects of Piece-Rate Underpayment and

Overpayment on Job Performance: A Test of Equity Theory with a New Induction Procedure." *Journal of Applied Social Psychology,* 1973, *3,* 325-334.

Garvey, W. F., and Griffith, B. C. "Scientific Communication: Its Role in the Conduct of Research and Creation of Knowledge." *American Psychologist,* 1971, *26,* 349-361.

Gaudet, F. J., and Carli, A. R. "Why Executives Fail." *Personnel Psychology,* 1957, *X,* 7-21.

Georgopoulos, B. S., Mahoney, G. M., and Jones, N. W. "A Path-Goal Approach to Productivity." *Journal of Applied Psychology,* 1957, *41,* 345-353.

Gergen, K. J., Morse, S. J., and Bode, K. A. "Overpaid or Overworked? Cognitive and Behavioral Reactions to Inequitable Rewards." *Journal of Applied Social Psychology,* 1974, *4,* 259-274.

Ghiselli, E. E. "Traits Differentiating Management Personnel." *Personnel Psychology,* 1959, *12,* 535-544.

Ghiselli, E. E. "Dr. Ghiselli Comments on Dr. Tupes' Note." *Personnel Psychology,* 1964, *17,* 61-63.

Ghiselli, E. E. *The Authority of Occupational Aptitude Tests.* New York: Wiley, 1966.

Ghiselli, E. E. "Some Motivational Factors in the Success of Managers." *Personnel Psychology,* 1968, *21,* 431-440.

Gibson, J. L., and Klein, S. M. "Employee Attitudes as a Function of Age and Length of Service: A Reconception." *Academy of Management Journal,* 1970, *13,* 411-420.

Gilbert, A. C., and Downey, R. G. "Validity of Peer Ratings Obtained During Ranger Training." *U.S. Army Research Institute for the Behavioral and Social Sciences,* 1978, *344,* 18.

Gilbert, T. F. *Human Competence: Engineering Worthy Performance.* New York: McGraw-Hill, 1978.

Gilmore, J. V. *Productive Personality.* New York: Albion, 1974.

Glasgow, Z., Simkins, M. L., and Guerrieri, J. A. "Job Performance Appraisal System Training Program." *Technical Report,* 1981, *30,* 56-80.

Glenn, N. D., and Weaver, C. N. "Enjoyment of Work by Full-Time Workers in the U.S., 1955 and 1980." *Public Opinion Quarterly,* 1982, *46* (4), 459-470.

Glogow, E. "What Makes a Good Leader? Perspectives of Administrators of the American Association of Homes for the Aging." *Educational Gerontology*, 1979, *4* (1), 77–84.

Goddard, R. W. "I Won't Be In Today." *Management World*, November 1982, pp. 9–13.

Goldstein, I. L. "The Application Blank: How Honest Are the Resources?" *Journal of Applied Psychology*, 1971, *55*, 491–492.

Goldstein, I. L. "Training in Work Organizations." *Annual Review of Psychology*, 1980, *31*, 229–272.

Gomez-Mejia, L. R., Page, R. C., and Tornow, W. W. "A Comparison of the Practical Utility of Traditional, Statistical, and Hybrid Job Evaluation Approaches." *Academy of Management Journal*, 1982, *25* (4), 790–809.

Good, L., and others. "Attitude, Similarity and Attraction to a Company." *Psychology*, 1974, *11*, 52–55.

Gordon, M. E., and Fitzgibbons, W. J. "Empirical Test of the Validity of Seniority as a Factor in Staffing Decisions." *Journal of Applied Psychology*, 1982, *67* (3), 311–319.

Gottfredson, L. S. "The Construct Validity of Holland's Occupational Classification in Terms of Prestige, Census, Department of Labor and Other Classification Systems." *Center for Social Organization of Schools Report, Johns Hopkins University*, 1978, *260*, 1–70.

Gottfredson, L. S., and Becker, H. J. "A Challenge to Vocational Psychology: How Important Are Aspirations in Determining Male Career Development?" *Journal of Vocational Behavior*, 1981, *18* (2), 121–137.

Gould, S., and Werbel, J. D. "Work Involvement: A Comparison of Dual Wage Earner and Single Earner Families." *Journal of Applied Psychology*, 1983, *68* (2), 313–319.

Graen, G. "Instrumentality Theory of Work Motivation: Some Experimental Results and Suggested Modifications." *Journal of Applied Psychology Monograph*, 1969, *53* (2), 21–29.

Grant, D. L. "Issues in Personnel Selection." *Professional Psychology*, 1980, *11* (3), 369–384.

Greenberg, H., and Mayer, D. "A New Approach to the Scientific Selection of Successful Salesmen." *Journal of Psychology*, 1964, *57*, 113–123.

Greenberg, J., and Ornstein, S. "High Status Job Title Compensation of Underpayment: A Test of Equity Theory." *Journal of Applied Psychology*, 1983, *68* (2), 285-297.

Greene, C. N. "The Reciprocal Nature of Influence Between Leader and Subordinate." *Journal of Applied Psychology*, 1975, *60*, 187-193.

Greller, M. M. "Subordinate Participation and Reactions to the Appraisal Interview." *Journal of Applied Psychology*, 1975, *60*, 544-549.

Grunwald, W., and Bernthal, W. F. "Controversy in German Management: The Harzburg Model Experience." *Academy of Management Review*, 1983, *8* (2), 233-241.

Gutteridge, T. G., Gallson, S., and Zimmerman, P. "An Annotated Research Bibliography: Career Planning and Development—Perspectives of the Individual and the Organization, 1975+ Update." *Catalog of Selected Documents in Psychology*, 1981, *11*, 90.

Gutteridge, T. G., and Otte, F. L. "Organizational Career Development: What's Going On Out There?" *Training and Development Journal*, 1983, *37* (2), 22-26.

Hackman, J. R., Lawler, E. E. III, and Porter, L. W. *Perspectives on Behavior in Organizations*. (2nd ed.) New York: McGraw-Hill, 1983.

Haefner, J. E. "Sources of Discrimination Among Employees: A Survey Investigation." *Journal of Applied Psychology*, 1977, *62* (3), 265-270.

Hagman, J. D. "Effects of Training Task Repetition on Retention and Transfer of Maintenance Skill." *ARI Resource Rep.*, 1980, p. 1271.

Haire, M., Ghiselli, E. E., and Porter, L. W. *Managerial Thinking: An International Study.* New York: Wiley, 1982.

Haizer, J. H. "Manager Action." *Personnel Psychology*, 1972, *25*, 511-521.

Hall, D., and Lerner, P. "Career Development in Work Organizations: Research and Practice." *Professional Psychology*, 1980, *11* (3), 428-435.

Hamner, W. C. "Reinforcement Theory and Contingency Management in Organizational Settings." In H. L. Tosi and W. C. Hamner (eds.), *Organizational Behavior and Management: A Contingency Approach.* Chicago: St. Clair, 1974.

Hamner, W. C., and Hamner, E. P. "Behavior Modification on the

Bottom Line." *Organizational Dynamics,* 1976, *4* (4), 3-21.

Harrell, T. W. *Managers' Performance and Personality.* Cincinnati: South-Western Publishing Company, 1961.

Harrell, T. W., and Harrell, M. "Relation of Second-Year MBA Grades to Business Earnings." *Personnel Psychology,* 1974, *27,* 487-491.

Haynes, S. G., McMichael, A. J., and Tyroler, H. A. "The Relationship with Normal Involuntary Retirement to Early Mortality Among U.S. Rubber Workers." *Social Science and Medicine,* 1977, *11,* 105-114.

Heath, D. H. "Adolescent and Adult Predictors of Vocational Adaptation." *Journal of Vocational Behavior,* 1976, *9,* 1-19.

Heisler, W. J. "The Performance Correlate of Personal Control Beliefs in an Organizational Context." *Journal of Applied Psychology,* 1974, *59,* 504-506.

Heneman, H. G. "Comparisons of Self and Superior Ratings of Managerial Performance." *Journal of Applied Psychology,* 1974, *59,* 638-642.

Henry, W. E. "Identifying the Potentially Successful Executive." *American Management Association Personnel Series,* 1949, *127,* 14-19.

Herzberg, F. *Work and the Nature of Man.* Cleveland: World, 1966.

Hines, G. H. "Money and Motivation." *Department of Business Studies, Massey University, Occasional Papers,* 1975, *4,* 15.

Hinrichs, J. R. "Psychology of Men at Work." *Annual Review of Psychology,* 1970, *21* (1), 421-441.

Hinton, B. L. "The Experimental Extension of Equity Theory to Interpersonal and Group Interaction Situations." *Organizational Behavior and Human Performance,* 1972, *8,* 434-449.

Hitt, M. A., and Morgan, C. P. "Organizational Climate as a Predictor of Organizational Practices." *Psychological Reports,* 1977, *40* (3, Pt. 2), 1191-1199.

Hmid, P. N., and Stringfield, P. A. "Like Status Sells: A Field Test of Belief Congruence." *New Zealand Psychologist,* 1973, *2,* 63-69.

Holzbach, R. L. "Rater Bias in Performance Ratings: Superior, Self- and Peer Ratings." *Journal of Applied Psychology,* 1979, *63* (3), 579-588.

Hook, R. C. "Executive Development: A Different Approach." *Training Director's Journal,* 1963, *17,* 29-31.

Hopkins, T. "Trends in Testing as a Screening Device." *Personnel Management—Policies and Practices,* June 20, 1983, *XXXI* (1).

Hultman, K. E. "Increasing Your Leverage with Line Managers." *Training and Development Journal,* 1981, *35* (9), 99-105.

Humphreys, P. "The Effect of Importance upon the Relation Between Perceived Job Attributes and Job Satisfaction." *Australian Journal of Psychology,* 1981, *33* (2), 121-133.

Hunt, J. W. "The Costs of Corporate Dependence: Managers Caught in the Middle." *Managerial Psychology,* 1981, *2* (2), 13-32.

Ivancevich, J. M. "A Longitudinal Assessment of Management by Objectives." *Administrative Science Quarterly,* 1972, *17,* 126-138.

Ivancevich, J. M. "The Effects of Goal Setting on Performance and Job Satisfaction." *Journal of Applied Psychology,* 1976, *61,* 605-612.

Ivancevich, J. M. "Different Goal Setting Treatments and Their Effects on Performance and Job Satisfaction." *Academy of Management Journal,* 1977, *20,* 406-419.

Ivancevich, J. M., and McMahon, J. T. "Education as a Moderator of Goal Setting Effectiveness." *Journal of Vocational Behavior,* 1977, *11* (1), 83-94.

Janson, P., and Martin, J. K. "Job Satisfaction and Age: A Test of Two Views." *Social Forces,* 1982, *60* (4), 1089-1102.

Jennings, E. E. *The Executive in Crisis.* East Lansing: Division of Research, Bureau of Business and Economic Research, Graduate School of Business Administration, Michigan State University, 1965.

Jennings, E. E. *Routes to the Executive Suite.* New York: McGraw-Hill, 1976.

Johnson, D. P. "Social Organization of an Industrial Work Group: Emergence and Adaptation to Environmental Change." *Sociological Quarterly,* 1974, *15,* 109-126.

Johnson, E. W. *Raising Children to Achieve: A Guide for Motivating Success in School and Life.* New York: Walker, 1984.

Jones, L. K. "Holland's Typology and the New Guide for Occupational Exploration: Bridging the Gap." *Vocational Guidance Quarterly,* 1980, *29* (1), 70-76.

Jones, W. S. "The Manager's Role in Developmental Planning." *Training and Development Journal,* 1976, *30,* 3-9.

Jurgensen, C. E. "Job Preferences (What Makes a Job Good or Bad)." *Journal of Applied Psychology,* 1978, *63* (3), 267-276.

Kahn, R. L. "Organizational Development: Some Problems in Proposals." *Journal of Applied Behavioral Science,* 1974, *10,* 485-502.

Kanter, R. M. "Dilemmas of Managing Participation." *Organizational Dynamics,* 1982, *11* (1), 5-27.

Katzell, R. A., and Guzzo, R. A. "Psychological Approaches to Productivity Improvement." *American Psychologist,* 1983, *38* (4), 468-472.

Kaufman, H. G. *Professionals in Search of Work: Coping with the Stress of Job Loss and Underemployment.* New York: Wiley, 1982.

Kay, A. "Where Being Nice to Workers Didn't Work." *Business Week,* January 20, 1973, pp. 98-100.

Kearney, W. J., and Marten, D. "Sensitivity Training: An Established Management Development Tool?" *Academy of Management Journal,* 1974, *17,* 755-760.

Keeley, M. "Subjective Performance Evolution and Person-Role Conflict Under Conditions of Uncertainty." *Academy of Management Journal,* 1977, *20* (2), 301-314.

Keenan, A., and Wedderburn, A. A. "Putting the Boot on the Other Foot: Candidates' Descriptions of Interviews." *Journal of Occupational Psychology,* 1980, *53* (1), 81-89.

Keller, R. T. "World Conflict and Ambiguity Correlates with Job Satisfaction and Value." *Personnel Psychology,* 1975, *28,* 57-64.

Keller, R. T., and Holland, W. E. "Job Change: A Naturally Occurring Field Experiment." *Human Relations,* 1981, *34* (12), 1053-1067.

Kelly, P. J. *The Making of a Salesman.* New York: Abelard-Schuman, 1965.

Kerr, S., Von Glinow, M. A., and Schriesheim, J. "Issues in the Study of Professionals in Organizations: The Case of Scientists and Engineers." *Organizational Behavior and Human Performance,* 1977, *18* (2), 329-345.

Khoury, R. M. "Are Professionals 'Smarter' Than Non-Professionals?" *Psychological Reports,* 1980, *46* (3, Pt. 2), 1263-1266.

Kim, J. S., and Hamner, W. C. "Effect of Performance Feedback and Goal Setting on Productivity and Satisfaction in an Organizational Setting." *Journal of Applied Psychology,* 1976, *61,* 48-57.

Kipnis, D., Schmidt, S., Price, K., and Stitt, C. "Why Do I Like Thee: Is it Your Performance or My Orders?" *Journal of Applied Psychology,* 1981, *66* (3), 324-328.

Kirchner, W. K., and Reisberg, D. J. "Differences Between Better and Less Effective Supervisors in Appraisal of Subordinates." *Personnel Psychology,* 1962, *15,* 295-302.

Kirkland, E. C. *Dream and Thought in the Business Community, 1860-1900.* Ithaca, N.Y.: Cornell University Press, 1956.

Kirkpatrick, D. L. "Determining Training Needs: Four Simple and Effective Approaches." *Training and Development Journal,* 1977, *31* (2), 22-25.

Klopfer, W. G., and Taulbee, B. S. "Projective Tests." *Annual Review of Psychology,* 1976, *27,* 543-567.

Kohn, V., and Parker, T. C. "The Value of Expectations in Management Development." *Training and Development Journal,* 1972, *26,* 26-30.

Koretz, G. "Service Industries Aren't to Blame for Lower Productivity." *Business Week,* June 13, 1983, *2794,* 21.

Korman, A. K. "Self-Esteem, Social Influence, and Task Performance: Some Tests of Theory." In *Proceedings of the 76th Annual Convention of the American Psychological Association,* 1966, pp. 567-568.

Korman, A. K., Glickman, A. S., Frey, R. L. "More Is Not Better: Two Failures of Incentive Theory." *Journal of Applied Psychology,* 1981, *66* (2), 255-259.

Kraus, W. A. *Collaboration in Organizations: Alternatives of Hierarchy.* New York: Human Sciences Press, 1980.

Krausz, M., and Izraeli, D. "Differences in Stage of Occupational Field and Subfield Choice Among Students of Three Engineering Subfields." *Journal of Occupational Psychology,* 1980, *53* (3), 177-180.

Kuder, F. "Career Matching." *Personnel Psychology,* 1977, *30* (1), 1-4.

Lamb, W., and Turner, D. *Management Behavior.* London: G. Dreckworth, 1969.

Lamont, L. M., and Lundstrom, W. J. "Identifying Successful Industrial Salesmen by Personality and Personal Characteristics." *Journal of Marketing Research,* 1977, *14* (4), 517-529.

Landy, F. J., Barnes, J. L., and Murphy, K. R. "Correlates of Perceived Fairness and Accuracy of Performance Evaluation." *Journal of Applied Psychology,* 1978, *63* (6), 751-754.

Larson, E. "Why Are Some Managers Top Performers? A Researcher Picks Out 16 Characteristics." *The Wall Street Journal,* January 21, 1983, p. 25.

Larson, L. L., Hunt, J. G., and Osborn, R. N. "The Great Hi-Hi Leader Behavior Myth: A Lesson From Occam's Razor." *Academy of Management Journal,* 1976, *19,* 628-641.

Latham, G. P., and Marshall, H. A. "The Effects of Self-Set, Participatively Set and Assigned Goals on the Performance of Government Employees." *Personnel Psychology,* 1982, *35* (2), 399-404.

Latham, G. P., Mitchell, T. R., and Dossett, D. L. "Importance of Participative Goal Setting and Anticipated Rewards on Goal Difficulty and Job Performance." *Journal of Applied Psychology,* 1978, *63,* 163-171.

Latham, G. P., and Saari, M. "The Importance of Union Acceptance for Productivity Improvement Through Goal Setting." *Personnel Psychology,* 1982, *35* (4), 781-787.

Latham, G. P., Steele, T. P., and Saari, L. M. "The Effects of Participation and Goal Difficulty on Performance." *Personnel Psychology,* 1982, *35* (3), 677-686.

Latham, G. P., and Wexley, K. N. *Increasing Productivity Through Performance Appraisal.* Reading, Mass.: Addison-Wesley, 1981.

Lau, A. W., and Pavett, C. M. "The Nature of Managerial Work: A Comparison of Public and Private-Sector Managers." *Group and Organizational Studies,* 1980, *5* (4), 453-466.

Lawler, E. E. III. "Job Attitudes and Employee Motivation: Theory, Research, and Practice." *Personnel Psychology,* 1970, *23,* 223-237.

Lawler, E. E. III. *Pay and Organization Development.* Reading, Mass.: Addison-Wesley, 1981.

Lawshe, C. H. "A Quantitative Approach to Content Validity." *Personnel Psychology,* 1975, *28,* 563-575.

Lehrer, R. N. (ed.). *White Collar Productivity.* New York: McGraw-Hill, 1983.

Levinson, H. *Psychological Man.* Cambridge, Mass.: Levinson Institute, 1976.

Lewandowski, D. G., and Saccuzco, D. P. "The Decline of Psychological Testing." *Professional Psychology,* 1976, *7,* 177-184.

Lipsett, L., Rodgers, F. P., and Kentner, H. M. *Personnel Selection and Recruitment.* Newton, Mass.: Allyn & Bacon, 1964.

Locke, E. A. "Relationship of Success and Expectation to Affect on Goal-Setting Tasks." *Journal of Personnel Social Psychology,* 1967, *7,* 125-134.

Locke, E. A., Bryan, J. F., and Kendall, L. M. "Goals and Intentions As Mediators of the Effects of Monetary Incentives on Behavior." *Journal of Applied Psychology,* 1968, *52,* 104-121.

Long, R. J. "The Effects and Formal Employee Participation in Ownership and Decision Making on Perceived and Desired Patterns of Organizational Influence: A Longitudinal Study." *Human Relations,* 1981, *34* (10), 847-876.

Lopez, F. M., Jr. "Evaluating Executive Decision Making: The In-Basket Technique." *American Management Association Research Study,* 1966, p. 75.

Louis, M. R. "Managing Career Transition: A Missing Link in Career Development." *Organizational Dynamics,* 1982, *10* (4), 68-77.

Love, K. G. "Empirical Recommendations for the Use of Peer Rankings in the Evaluation of Police Officer Performance." *Public Personnel Management,* 1983, *12* (1), 25-32.

McAuley, W. J. "Perceived Age Discrimination in Hiring: Demograph and Economic Correlates." *Industrial Gerontology,* 1977, *4,* 21-28.

McCall, M. W., Jr., and Lombardo, M. M. "Looking Glass, Inc.: The First Three Years." Greensboro, N.C.: Century Creative Leadership Technical Report no. 13, 1979.

McClelland, D. C. *The Achieving Society.* New York: D. Van Nostrand, 1961.

McClelland, D. C. *Achievement Motive.* New York: Irvington, 1982.

McClelland, D. C. *Human Motivation.* Glenview, Ill.: Scott Foresman, 1985.

McClelland, D. C., and Boyatzis, R. E. "Leadership Motive Pattern and Long-Term Success in Management." *Journal of Applied Psychology,* 1982, *67* (6), 737-743.

McGregor, D. *The Professional Manager.* New York: McGraw-Hill, 1967.

MacKinnon, D. W. "Selecting Students with Creative Potential." In P. Heist (ed.), *The Creative College Student: An Unmet Challenge.* San Francisco: Jossey-Bass, 1968.

McMahon, D. "Selection and Follow-Up of Engineering Apprentices." *Occupational Psychology,* 1962, *36,* 53-58.

Maggison, L. C. "Management Selection, Development, and Motivation in the United States." *Management International,* 1963, *2,* 97-106.

Mahoney, T. "Compensation Preferences of Managers." *Industrial Relations,* 1964, *3,* 135-144.

Mahoney, T. A., and others. "Identification and Prediction of Managerial Effectiveness." *Personnel Administration,* 1963, *26,* 12-22.

Maier, N. R. F. *Principles of Human Relations: Applications to Management.* New York: Wiley, 1952.

Malone, E. L. "The Non-Linear Systems Experiment in Participative Management." *Journal of Business,* 1975, *48,* 52-64.

Mancuso, J. S. J. (ed.). *Occupational Clinical Psychology.* New York: Praeger, 1983.

Maslow, A. H. *Eupsychian Management.* Homewood, Ill.: Irwin, 1965.

Massey, R. H., Mullins, C. J., and Earles, J. A. "Performance Appraisal Ratings: The Content Issue." *USAF HRL Technical Report,* December 1978, pp. 69-78.

Matsui, T., Okada, A., and Kakuyama, T. "Influence of Achievement Need on Goal Setting, Performance, and Feedback Effectiveness." *Journal of Applied Psychology*, 1982, *67*, 645-648.

Matsui, T., Okada, A., and Mizuguchi, R. "Expectancy Theory Prediction of the Goal Theory Postulate: The Harder the Goals, the Higher the Performance." *Journal of Applied Psychology*, 1981, *66* (1), 54-58.

Meier, E. L., and Kerr, E. A. "Capabilities of Middle-Aged and Older Workers: A Survey of the Literature." *Industrial Gerontology*, 1976, *3*, 147-156.

Meltzer, M. W. "The Reduction of Occupational Stress Among Elderly Lawyers: The Creation of a Functional Niche." *International Journal of Aging and Human Development*, 1981, *13* (3), 209-219.

Mettlin, C. "Occupational Careers and the Prevention of Coronary-Prone Behavior." *Social Science and Medicine*, 1976, p. 10.

Meyer, H. H. "The Pay-for-Performance Dilemma." *Organizational Dynamics*, 1975, *3* (3), 39-50.

Meyer, H. H. "Whither Leadership and Supervision?" *Professional Psychology*, 1982, *13* (6), 930-941.

Miles, W. G., and Briggs, W. D. "Common, Recurring and Avoidable Errors in Management Development." *Training and Development Journal*, 1979, *33* (2), 32-35.

Miner, J. B. *Studies in Management Education*. New York: Springer, 1965.

Miner, J. B. "Levels of Motivation to Manage Among Personnel and Industrial Relations Managers." *Journal of Applied Psychology*, 1976, *61*, 419-427.

Miner, J. B. *Theories of Organizational Behavior*. Hinsdale, Ill.: Dryden, 1980.

Miner, J. B., and Crane, D. P. "Motivation to Manage and the Manifestations of a Managerial Orientation in Career Planning." *Academy of Management Journal*, 1981, *2*, 626-633.

Miner, M. G., and Miner, J. B. *Policy Issues in Contemporary Personnel and Industrial Relations*. New York: Macmillan, 1977.

Misumi, J., and Fujita, M. "Effects of PM Organizational Development in Supermarket Organization." *Japanese Journal of Experimental Social Psychology*, 1982, *21* (2), 93-111.

Mitchell, T. R. *People in Organizations: An Introduction to Organizational Behavior.* (2nd ed.) New York: Wiley, 1982.

Mitchell, T. R., and Wood, R. E. "Supervisors' Responses to Subordinates' Poor Performance: A Test of an Attributional Model." *Organizational Behavior and Human Performance,* 1980, *25* (1), 123–138.

Moberly, A. L., and Buffa, E. S. *Executive Understudies: A Survey of the Selection and Training of Understudies by Manufacturing Executives in Wisconsin.* Madison: School of Commerce, University of Wisconsin, 1948.

Mobley, W. H. "Intermediate Linkages in the Relationship Between Job Satisfaction and Employee Turnover." *Journal of Applied Psychology,* 1977, *62* (2), 237–240.

Mobley, W. H. *Employee Turnover: Causes, Consequences, and Control.* Reading, Mass.: Addison-Wesley, 1982.

Montgomery, G. W. G. "Predicting Success in Engineering." *Occupational Psychology,* 1962, *36,* 59–68.

Moore, M. L., and Dutton, P. "Training Needs Analysis: Review and Critique." *Academy of Management Review,* 1978, *3,* 532–545.

More, D. M., and Suchner, R. W. "Occupational Status, Prestige, and Stereotypes." *Sociology of Work and Occupations,* 1976, *3,* 169–186.

Morgan, J. I., and Skovholt, T. M. "Using Inner Experience: Fantasy and Daydreams in Career Counseling." *Journal of Counseling Psychology,* 1977, *24* (5), 391–397.

Morgan, J. N., and others. *Productive Americans: A Study of How Individuals Contribute to Economic Progress.* Ann Arbor: Institute for Social Research, University of Michigan, 1966.

Morrison, R. F., Owens, W. A., Glennon, J. R., and Albright, L. E. "Factored Life History Antecedents of Industrial Research Performance." *Journal of Applied Psychology,* 1962, *46,* 281–284.

Motoaki, H., and others. "Analysis of Personality Traits of Car Salesmen." *Japanese Journal of Psychology,* 1972, *43,* 113–124.

Motowidlo, S. J. "Relationship Between Self-Rated Performance and Pay Satisfaction Among Sales Representatives." *Journal of Applied Psychology,* 1982, *67* (2), 209–213.

Motowidlo, S. J. "Predicting Sales Turnover from Pay Satisfaction and Expectation." *Journal of Applied Psychology,* 1983, *68* (3), 484–489.

Muchinsky, P. "Why Do I Leave Thee? Let Me Count the Ways." *Contemporary Psychology,* 1983, *28* (3), 223.

Mukherjee, B. N. "Achievement Values and Scientific Productivity." *Journal of Applied Psychology,* 1968, *52,* 145–147.

Murray, H. A., and others. *Assessment of Men.* New York: Rinehart, 1948.

Nash, A. N. "Development of an SVIB Key for Selecting Managers." *Journal of Applied Psychology,* 1966, *50,* 250–254.

Nash, M. "Reading for Self Development: A Strategy for Businessmen." *Manage,* April 1972, pp. 7–12.

Nash, M. *Managing Organizational Performance.* San Francisco: Jossey-Bass, 1983.

Nash, M., and Zimring, F. "Prediction of Reaction to Placebo." *Journal of Abnormal Psychology,* 1969, *74,* 568–573.

Neider, L. L. "Training Effectiveness: Changing Attitudes." *Training and Development Journal,* 1981, *35* (12), 24–28.

Newcomber, M. *The Big Business Executive.* New York: Columbia University Press, 1955.

"Nobel Establishment." *Scientific Research,* 1967, *11,* 48–50.

Nystrom, P. C. "Managers and the Hi-Hi Leader Myth." *Academy of Management Journal,* 1978, *21* (2), 325–331.

O'Brien, G. E., and Dowling, P. "Age and Job Satisfaction." *Australian Psychologist,* 1981, *16* (1), 49–61.

O'Brien, G. E., and Pembroke, M. "Crowding, Density and the Job Satisfaction of Clerical Employees." *Australian Journal of Psychology,* 1982, *34* (2), 151–164.

Oda, M. "An Analysis of Relation Between Personality Traits and Job Performance in Sales Occupations." *Japanese Journal of Psychology,* 1982, *53* (5), 274–280.

Olson, V. *White Collar Waste: Gain the Productivity Edge.* Englewood Cliffs, N.J.: Prentice-Hall, 1983.

O'Reilly, C. A., and Caldwell, D. F. "The Commitment and Job Tenure of New Employees: Some Evidence of Post-Decisional Justification." *Administrative Science Quarterly,* 1981, *26* (4), 597–616.

Osborn, R. N., and Hunt, J. G. "Relations Between Leadership, Size and Subordinate Satisfaction in a Voluntary Organization." *Journal of Applied Psychology,* 1975, *60,* 730–735.

Osman, A. C. "Personality Comparisons of Men and Women Students." *Accountant,* 1973, *169,* 696-697.

O'Toole, J. *Making America Work: Productivity and Responsibility.* New York: Continuum, 1981.

O'Toole, J. "Work and Love (But Mostly Work)." *Journal of Psychiatric Treatment and Evaluation,* 1982, *4* (3), 227-237.

Otto, L. B., and Alwyn, D. F. "Athletics, Aspirations, and Obtainments." *Sociology of Education,* 1977, *50,* 102-113.

Parasuraman, S. "Predicting Turnover Intentions and Turnover Behavior: A Multivariate Analysis." *Journal of Vocational Behavior,* 1982, *21* (1), 111-121.

Patchen, M. "Supervisory Methods and Group Performance Norms." *Administrative Science Quarterly,* 1962, *7,* 275-294.

Peterson, D. "Clear Pictures of a Dreary Landscape." *Contemporary Psychology,* 1983, *20* (10), 785.

Phelan, J. G. "Projective Techniques in the Selection of Management Personnel." *Journal of Projective Techniques,* 1962, *26,* 102-104.

Philips, J. "Measuring the Return on Training and Development." *Personnel Management Policies and Practices,* 1983, *XXXI* (1), v-viii.

Phillips, J. S., Barrett, G. V., and Rush, M. C. "Job Structure and Age Satisfaction." *Aging and Work,* 1978, *1* (2), 109-119.

Phillips, S. D. "The Development of Career Choices: The Relationship Between Patterns of Commitment and Career Outcomes in Adulthood." *Journal of Vocational Behavior,* 1982, *20,* (2), 141-152.

Phillips-Jones, L. "Establishing a Formalized Mentoring Program." *Training and Development Journal,* 1983, *37* (2), 38-42.

Pinder, C. C. "Concerning the Application of Human Motivation Theories in Organizational Settings." *Academy of Management Review,* 1977, *2,* 384-397.

Pinder, C. C., and Pinto, P. R. "Demographic Correlates of Managerial Style." *Personnel Psychology,* 1974, *27,* 257-270.

Piotrowski, Z. *The Perceptanalytic Executive Scale.* New York: Grune & Stratton, 1963.

Piotrowski, Z. *Perceptanalysis.* Philadelphia: Ex Libris, 1965.

Popper, A. "The Revival of Productivity." *Business Week,* February 13, 1984, pp. 92-99.

Porter, L. W., and Lawler, E. E. III. *Managerial Attitudes of Performance.* Homewood, Ill.: Irwin, 1968a.

Porter, L. W., and Lawler, E. E. III. "What Attitudes Tell About Maturation." *Harvard Business Review,* 1968b, *46,* 118-126.

Potter, B. *Turning Around: The Behavioral Approach to Managing People.* New York: Amacom, 1980.

Pritchard, R. D. "Enhancing Productivity Through Feedback and Goal Setting." *U.S. Technical Report,* 1981, *TR 81-7,* 54.

Pritchard, R. D., and Curts, M. I. "The Influence of Goal Setting and Financial Incentives on Task Performance." *Organizational Behavior and Human Performance,* 1973, *10,* 175-183.

Pritchard, R. D., Montagno, R. V., and Moore, J. R. "Enhancing Productivity Through Feedback and Job Design." *Technical Report,* 1978, *45,* 44-78.

Pyke, S. W., and Weisenberg, F. "Desired Job Characteristics for Male and Female." *Canadian Counsellor,* 1976, *10,* 185-191.

Quaintance, M. K. "The Impact of the Uniform Selection Guidelines on Public Merit Systems." *Public Personnel Management,* 1980, *9* (3), 125-133.

Quinn, R. P., and Baldi de Mandilovitch, M. S. "Education and Job Satisfaction, 1962-1977." *Vocational Guidance Quarterly,* 1980, *29* (2), 100-111.

Quinn, R. P., Taber, J. M., and Gordon, L. K. *The Decision to Discriminate: A Study of Executive Selection.* Ann Arbor: Institute for Social Research, University of Michigan, 1968.

Rao, T. V., and Misra, S. "Effectiveness of Varying Sales Styles on Consumer Orientations." *Vikalpa,* 1976, *1* (4), 19-26.

Rawls, J. R., and Nelson, O. T. "Characteristics Associated with Preferences for Certain Managerial Positions." *Psychological Reports,* 1975, *36,* 911-918.

Read, W. H. "Upward Communication in Industrial Hierarchies." *Human Relations,* 1962, *15,* 3-15.

Rehder, R. R. "Education and Training: Have the Japanese Beaten Us Again?" *Personnel Journal,* 1983, *62* (1), 42-47.

Reich, R. B. *The Next American Frontier.* New York: Times Books, 1983.

Rezke, I. "Social Prestige: The Concept and the Indicators." *Studia Sociologiczne,* 1978, *3* (70), 77-100.

Rhode, J. G., and Peterson, R. A. "Vocational Interest of Marketing Professionals." *Journal of Vocational Behavior,* 1972, *2,* 13-23.

Rim, Y., and Frez, M. "A Note About Tactics Used to Influence Superiors, Coworkers and Subordinates." *Journal of Occupational Psychology,* 1980, *53* (4), 319-321.

Rizzo, J. R. "Measuring Work Experiences." *Contemporary Psychology,* 1983, *28* (5), 361.

Robertson, I., and Downs, S. "Learning and the Prediction of Performance: Development of Trainability Testing in the United Kingdom." *Journal of Applied Psychology,* 1979, *64,* 42-50.

Roe, A. "Crucial Life Experiences in the Development of Scientists." In E. P. Torrance (ed.), *Talent and Education.* Minneapolis: University of Minnesota Press, 1960.

Ronen, S. "Job Satisfaction and the Neglected Variable of Job Security." *Human Relations,* 1978, *31* (4), 297-308.

Ronen, W. W. "Effects of Goal Setting and Supervision on Worker Behavior in Industrial Situations." *Journal of Applied Psychology,* 1978, *58,* 302-307.

Rosen, B., and Jerdee, T. H. "Effects of Decision Performance on Managerial Willingness to Use Participation." *Academy of Management Journal,* 1978, *21* (4), 722-725.

Rosen, B., Jerdee, T. H., and Lynn, R. O. "Effects of Performance Appraisal Format, Age, and Performance Level on Retirement Decisions." *Journal of Applied Psychology,* 1981, *66* (4), 515-519.

Rosen, B. C., and others. *Achievement in American Society.* Cambridge, Mass.: Schenkman, 1969.

Ross, J. E. *Managing Productivity.* Reston, Va.: Reston Publishing, 1977.

Ross, J. E. *Productivity, People and Profits.* Reston, Va.: Reston Publishing, 1981.

Ross, P. F., and Dunfield, N. M. "Selecting Salesmen for an Oil Company." *Personnel Psychology,* 1964, *17,* 75-84.

Rowe, A. R. "The 'Attraction Value' for a Scientific Career in Industry." *Psychology,* 1973, *10,* 44-49.

Ruch, W. A., and Hershauer, J. *Factors Affecting Worker Productivity.* Tucson: Arizona State University, 1974.

Rusbult, C. E., and Farrell, D. "A Longitudinal Test of the Investment Model: The Impact on Job Satisfaction, Job Commitment, and Turnover of Variations in Rewards, Costs, Alternatives, and Investments." *Journal of Applied Psychology,* 1983, *68* (3), 429–438.

Salinger, R. D., and Deming, B. S. "Practical Strategies for Evaluating Training." *Training and Development Journal,* 1982, *36,* (8), 20–29.

Sands, E. *How to Select Executive Personnel.* New York: Reinhold, 1963.

Schendel, J. D., and Hagman, J. D. "On Sustaining Procedural Skills over a Prolonged Retention Interval." *Journal of Applied Psychology,* 1982, *67,* 605–610.

Schmidt, F. L., and Hunter, J. E. "Individual Differences in Productivity: An Empirical Test of Estimates Derived from Studies of Selection Procedure Utility." *Journal of Applied Psychology,* 1983, *68* (3), 407–414.

Schmidt, F. L., Hunter, J. E., and Pearlman, K. "Assessing the Economic Impact of Personnel Programs on Workforce Productivity." *Personnel Psychology,* 1982, *35* (2), 333–347.

Schmidt, N., and Coyle, B. W. "Applicant Decisions in the Interview." *Journal of Applied Psychology,* 1976, *61,* 184–192.

Schwab, D. P., and Heneman, H. G. "Age and Satisfaction with Dimensions of Work." *Journal of Vocational Behavior,* 1977, *10* (2), 212–220.

Scissons, E. H. "An Ecological Study of the Reliability of Clinical Judgment in Executive Appraisal." *Journal of Vocational Behavior,* 1978, *12* (3), 343–350.

Scott, D., Deadrick, D., and Tayler, S. "The Evolution of Personnel Research." *Personnel Journal,* 1983, *20* (3), 624–629.

Scott, W. D., and others. *Personnel Management.* (6th ed.) New York: McGraw-Hill, 1961.

Seeborg, I. "The Influence of Employee Participation in Job Redesign." *Journal of Applied Behavioral Science,* 1978, *14* (1), 87–98.

Selover, R. B. "Identifying College Graduates with High Potential for Advancement." Unpublished Report, Prudential Insurance Company of America, 1962.

Senger, J. "Managers' Perceptions of Subordinates' Confidence Is a Function of Personal Value Orientations." *Academy of Management Journal,* 1971, *14,* 415-423.

"Senior Managers Speak Out on Human Resources." *Personnel Management Policies and Practices,* 1982, *XXX* (8), 917.

Shanteau, J., and Bristow, A. R. "What Did You Expect?" *Contemporary Psychology,* 1983, *28* (4), 295.

Shapiro, H. J. "Pay Incentives and Work Motivation Past and Present." *Psychological Reports,* 1978, *42* (1), 89-96.

Sheehan, D., and Lester, D. "Attitudes of Short Versus Tall Police Officers." *Perceptual and Motor Skills,* 1980, *51* (3, Pt. 1), 878.

Siegel, J. P., and Ghiselli, E. E. "Managerial Talent, Pay, and Age." *Journal of Vocational Behavior,* 1971, *1,* 129-135.

Sikula, A. F. "Values and Value Systems of Industrial Personnel Managers." *Public Personnel Management,* 1973, *2,* 305-309.

Simonds, R. H., and Orife, J. N. "Worker Behavior Versus Enrichment Theory." *Administrative Science Quarterly,* 1975, *20,* 606-612.

Sims, H. P., and Manz, C. C. "Modeling Influences on Employee Behavior." *Personnel Journal,* 1982, *61* (1), 58-65.

Singh, P., Mathew, T., and Das, G. S. "Organizational Culture and Its Impact on Managerial Remuneration." *Indian Journal of Industrial Relations,* 1977, *13* (1), 1-14.

Skovholt, T. M., and Morgan, J. I. "Career Development: An Outline of Issues for Men." *Personnel and Guidance Journal,* 1981, *60* (4), 231-237.

Smith, F. J., Scott, K. D., and Hulin, C. L. "Trends in Job-Related Attitudes of Managerial and Professional Employees." *Academy of Management Journal,* 1977, *20* (3), 454-460.

Snelgar, R. J. "The Comparability of Job Evaluation Methods in Supplying Approximately Similar Classifications in Rating One Job." *Personnel Psychology,* 1983, *36* (2), 371-380.

Snyder, R. A., and Williams, R. R. "Self Theory: An Integrative Theory of Work Motivation." *Journal of Occupational Psychology,* 1982, *55* (4), 257-267.

Sredalus, D. J., Marinelli, R. P., and Messing, J. K. *Career Devel-*

opment: Concepts and Procedures. Monterey, Calif.: Brooks/ Cole, 1982.

Srinivas, K. M., and Long, R. J. "Organizational Climate and Effectiveness of MBO." *Interpersonal Development,* 1975-1976, *6* (1), 8-24.

Srivastava, A. K., and Krishna, A. "The Effect of Job-Anxiety on Job Performance." *Indian Journal of Social Work,* 1980, *41* (3), 255-260.

Stagner, R. "Past and Future of Industrial/Organizational Psychology." *Professional Psychology,* 1982, *13* (6), 892-903.

Stanton, E. S. *Successful Recruiting and Selection: With EEO-Affirmative Action Guidelines.* New York: American Management Association, 1980.

Stanton, E. S. "A Critical Reevaluation of Motivation, Management and Productivity." *Personnel Journal,* 1983, *62* (3), 208-214.

Staw, B. M. "Motivation in Organizations: Toward Synthesis and Redirection." In B. M. Staw and G. R. Salancik (eds.), *New Directions in Organizational Behavior.* Chicago: St. Clair, 1977.

Stein, R. T. "Accuracy of Process Consultants and Untrained Observers in Perceiving Emergent Leadership." *Journal of Applied Psychology,* 1977, *62,* 755-759.

Sterrett, J. H. "The Job Interview: Body Language and Perceptions of Potential Effectiveness." *Journal of Applied Psychology,* 1978, *63* (3), 338-390.

Stewart, R. *Managers and Their Jobs.* London: Macmillan, 1967.

Stryker, P. *The Men from the Boys.* New York: Harper & Row, 1960.

Super, D. E. "Self-Concepts in Career Development: Theory and Findings After Thirty Years." Paper presented at International Congress of Applied Psychologists, Edinburgh, Scotland, 1982.

Sydiaha, D. "Bales' Interaction Process Analysis of Personnel Selection Interviews." *Journal of Applied Psychology,* 1961, *45,* 393-401.

Talbert, T. L., and others. "A Study of the Police Officer Height Requirements." *Public Personnel Management,* 1974, *3,* 103-110.

Taylor, C. W., Smith, W. R., Ghisselin, B., and Ellison, R. *Explorations in the Measurement and Prediction of Contributions of One Sample of Scientists.* Publication no. ASD-TR-61-96. Lackland Air Force Base, Texas: Personnel Lab, 1961.

Taylor, E. K., and Nevis, E. C. "Personnel Selection." *Annual Review of Psychology,* 1961, *12,* 389-412.

Taylor, F. *How to Succeed in the Business of Finding a Job.* Chicago: Nelson-Hall, 1975.

Taylor, F. W. *The Principles of Scientific Management.* New York: Harper & Row, 1911.

Taylor, R. L., and Zayacki, R. A. "Collaborative Goal Setting in Performance Appraisal: A Field Experiment." *Public Personnel Management,* 1978, *7* (3), 162-170.

Tenopyr, M. L. "The Realities of Employment Testing." *American Psychologist,* 1981, *36* (10), 1120-1127.

Tenopyr, M. L., and Oeltjen, P. D. "Personnel Selection and Classification." *Annual Review of Psychology,* 1982, *33* (1), 581-618.

Terborg, J. R. "The Motivational Components of Goal Setting." *Journal of Applied Psychology,* 1976, *61,* 613-621.

Terman, L. M., and Oden, M. H. *The Gifted Group at Mid-Life: Thirty-Five Years' Follow-Up of the Superior Child.* Stanford, Calif.: Stanford University Press, 1959.

Tessler, R., and Sushelsky, L. "Effects of Eye Contact and Social Status on the Perception of a Job Applicant in an Employment Interviewing Situation." *Journal of Vocational Behavior,* 1978, *13* (3), 338-347.

Thomas, L. E., and Robbins, P. I. "Personality and Work Environment Congruence of Mid-Life Career Changers." *Journal of Occupational Psychology,* 1979, *52* (3), 177-183.

Thompson, F. J. "The Performance Appraisal of Public Managers: Inspiration, Consensual Tests and the Margins." *Public Personnel Management,* 1982, *11* (4), 306-313.

Toffler, A. *The Third Wave.* New York: William Morrow, 1980.

Toscano, D. J. "Toward a Typology of Employee Ownership." *Human Relations,* 1983, *36* (7), 581-601.

Treadwell, D., and Redburn, T. "Workplace: Site of Latest Revolution." *Los Angeles Times,* April 24, 1983, p. 1.

Tucker, D. H., and Rowe, P. M. "Consulting the Application

Form Prior to the Interview: An Essential Step in the Selection Process." *Journal of Applied Psychology,* 1977, *62* (3), 283-287.

Tullar, W. L., Mullins, T. W., and Caldwell, S. A. "Effects of Interview Length and Applicant Quality on Interview Decision Time." *Journal of Applied Psychology,* 1979, *64* (6), 669-674.

Turnbull, A. A. "Selling and the Salesman: Prediction of Success and Personality Change." *Psychological Reports,* 1976, *38,* 1175-1180.

Umstot, D. D., Bell, C. H., and Mitchell, T. R. "Effects of Job Enrichment and Task Goals on Satisfaction and Productivity: Implications for Job Design." *Journal of Applied Psychology,* 1976, *61,* 379-394.

Uris, A. *Developing Your Executive Skills.* New York: McGraw-Hill, 1955.

Uris, A. *The Efficient Executive.* New York: McGraw-Hill, 1957.

Vaitenan, R., and Weiner, Y. "Developmental, Emotional, and Interest Factors in Voluntary Mid-Career Change." *Journal of Vocational Behavior,* 1977, *11* (3), 291-304.

Van der Bruggen, A. L., and den Hertog, J. F. "Labor Management with Regard to Classification Levels." *Mens en Onderneming,* 1976, *30* (6), 334-353.

Van Wezel, P. "The Experience of Being Unemployed." *Gedrag: Tijdschrift voor Psychologie,* 1975, *32,* 63-79.

Varga, K. "Need Achievement, Need Power, and Effectiveness of Research and Development." *Human Relations,* 1975, *28,* 571-590.

Vasudeva, P., and Rajbia, T. "Correlates of Job Satisfaction Amongst Industrial Workers." *Indian Journal of Social Work,* 1976, *37* (3), 275-279.

Vecchio, R. P. "The Contingent-Noncontingent Compensation Controversy: An Attempt at Resolution." *Human Relations,* 1982, *35* (6), 449-462.

Veroff, J., and others. "The Use of Thematic Apperception to Assess Motivation in a Nation-wide Interview Study." *Psychology Monograph,* 1960, p. 74.

Vroom, V. H. *Work and Motivation.* New York: Wiley, 1964.

Vroom, V. H. *Motivation in Management.* New York: American Foundation for Management Research, 1965.

Vroom, V. H., and Pahl, B. "Relationships Between Age and Risk-Taking Among Managers." *Journal of Applied Psychology,* 1971, *55,* 399-405.

Wade, T., and Baker, T. B. "Opinions and Use of Psychological Tests: A Survey of Clinical Psychologists." *American Psychologist,* 1977, *32,* 874-882.

Waetjen, W. B., Schuerger, J. M., and Schwartz, E. B. "Male and Female Managers: Self-Concept, Success, and Failure." *Journal of Psychology,* 1979, *103* (1), 87-94.

Wald, R. M., and Doty, R. A. "The Top Executive—A First-Hand Profile." *Harvard Business Review,* 1954, *32* (4), 45-54.

Wallace, W. L., and Gallagher, M. W. "Activities and Behaviors of Production Supervisors." Technical research report no. 946. Washington, D.C.: Department of the Army, April 30, 1952.

Walsh, E. J. "Prestige, Work Satisfaction, and Alienation: Comparisons Among Garbagemen, Professors, and Other Work Groups." *Work and Occupations,* 1982, *9* (4), 475-496.

Weaver, C. N. "Sex Differences in the Determinants of Job Satisfaction." *Academy of Management Journal,* 1978, *21* (2), 265-274.

Weaver, C. N. "Job Satisfaction in the United States in the 1970s." *Journal of Applied Psychology,* 1980, *65* (3), 364-367.

Webster, E. P. (ed.). *Decision-Making in the Employment Interview.* Montreal: Ego, 1964.

Wehrenberg, S. B. "How to Decide on the Best Training Approach." *Personnel Journal,* 1983, *62* (2), 117-118.

Weiner, Y., and Vaitenas, R. "Personality Correlates of Voluntary Mid-Career Change in Enterprising Occupations." *Journal of Applied Psychology,* 1977, *62* (6), 706-712.

Weintraub, Z. "The Relationship Between Job Satisfaction and Work Performance." *Revista de Psihologie,* 1981, *27* (1), 59-67.

Weller, D. R., and Blaiwes, A. S. "Leadership Dimension of Navy Recruit Company Commanders and Recruit Morale and Performance." *Psychological Reports,* 1976, *39,* 767-770.

Weller, L., and others. "Birth Order, Sex, and Occupational Interest." *General and Vocational Behavior,* 1976, *8,* 45-50.

Wexley, K. N., and Latham, G. P. *Developing and Training Human Resources in Organizations.* Glenview, Ill.: Scott Foresman, 1981.

White, D. D. "Factors Affecting Employee Attitude Towards the Insulation of a New Management System." *Academy of Management Journal,* 1973, *16,* 636-646.

Whitehead, H. *How to Become a Top Executive.* New York: T. Nelson, 1959.

Wikoff, M., Anderson, D. C., and Crowell, C. R. "Behavior Management in a Factory Setting: Increasing Work Efficiency." *Journal of Organizational Behavior Management,* 1982, *4* (1-2), 97-127.

Williams, R. E. "A Description of Some Executive Abilities by Means of Critical Incident Techniques." Unpublished doctoral dissertation, Columbia University, 1956.

Williams, R., Walker, J., and Fletcher, C. "International Review of Staff Appraisal Practices: Current Trends and Issues." *Public Personnel Management,* 1977, *6* (1), 5-12.

Wittmer, J., and others. *Journal of Employment Counseling,* 1974, *11,* 16-21.

Work in America Institute. *Putting the Work Ethic to Work.* New York: Public Agenda Foundation, 1984.

Worthington, R. E. "Use of the Personal History Form as a Clinical Instrument." Unpublished doctoral dissertation, University of Chicago, 1951.

Wright, J. D., and Hamilton, R. F. "Work Satisfaction and Age: Some Evidence for the Job Change Hypothesis." *Social Forces,* 1978, *56* (4), 1140-1158.

Yoder, T. *Personnel Management and Industrial Relations.* (5th ed.) Englewood Cliffs, N.J.: Prentice-Hall, 1962.

Yukl, G. A., and Latham, G. P. "Interrelationships Among Employee Participation, Individual Differences, Goal Difficulty, Goal Acceptance, Goal Instrumentality and Performance." *Personnel Psychology,* 1978, *31* (2), 305-323.

Yukl, G. A., Latham, G. P., and Pursell, E. D. "The Effectiveness of Performance Incentives Under Continuous and Variable Ratio Schedules of Reinforcement." *Personnel Psychology,* 1976, *29,* 221–231.

Zoittowski, D. G. "Predictive Validity of the Kuder's Preference Record, Form B, Over a 25-Year Span." *Measurement and Evaluation and Guidance,* 1974, 7, 122–129.

Index

H

I

DATE DUE